THE NEOLIBERAL REPUBLIC

CORPUS

The Humanities in Politics and Law

JURIS

Series editor: Elizabeth S. Anker, Cornell University

CORPUS JURIS: THE HUMANITIES IN POLITICS AND LAW PUBLISHES BOOKS AT THE INTERSECTIONS BETWEEN LAW, POLITICS, AND THE HUMANITIES—INCLUDING HISTORY, LITERARY CRITICISM, ANTHROPOLOGY, PHILOSOPHY, RELIGIOUS STUDIES, AND POLITICAL THEORY. BOOKS IN THIS SERIES TACKLE NEW OR UNDERANALYZED ISSUES IN POLITICS AND LAW AND DEVELOP INNOVATIVE METHODS TO UNDERTAKE THOSE INQUIRIES. THE GOAL OF THE SERIES IS TO MULTIPLY THE INTERDISCIPLINARY JUNCTURES AND CONVERSATIONS THAT SHAPE THE STUDY OF LAW.

THE NEOLIBERAL REPUBLIC

Corporate Lawyers, Statecraft, and the Making of Public-Private France

Antoine Vauchez and Pierre France
translated by Meg Morley
foreword by Samuel Moyn

CORNELL UNIVERSITY PRESS   ITHACA AND LONDON

Originally published as: *Sphère publique, intérêts privés: Enquête sur un grand brouillage* © 2017 Presses de Sciences Po. English-language translation, © 2020 Cornell University

First published 2020 by Cornell University Press

Library of Congress Cataloging-in-Publication Data
Names: France, Pierre, 1987– author. | Vauchez, Antoine, author.
Title: The neoliberal republic : corporate lawyers, statecraft, and the making of public-private France / Antoine Vauchez and Pierre France ; translated by Meg Morley ; foreword by Samuel Moyn.
Other titles: Sphère publique, intérêts privés. English
Description: Ithaca [New York] : Cornell University Press, 2020. | Series: Corpus juris : the humanities in politics and law | Translation of: Sphère publique, intérêts privés : enquête sur un grand brouillage, published by Presses de la Fondation Nationale des Sciences Politiques, 2017. | Includes bibliographical references and index.
Identifiers: LCCN 2020026688 (print) | LCCN 2020026689 (ebook) | ISBN 9781501752544 (hardcover) | ISBN 9781501752551 (paperback) | ISBN 9781501752568 (epub) | ISBN 9781501752575 (pdf)
Subjects: LCSH: Political corruption—France. | Conflict of interests—Political aspects—France. | Politicians—France—Attitudes. | Public administration—Moral and ethical aspects—France. | Political ethics—France. | Law—Political aspects—France. | Public interest—France. | Corporate lawyers—Malpractice—France. | France—Politics and government—Moral and ethical aspects.
Classification: LCC JN2738.C6 F7313 2020 (print) | LCC JN2738.C6 (ebook) | DDC 364.1/3230944—dc23
LC record available at https://lccn.loc.gov/2020026688
LC ebook record available at https://lccn.loc.gov/2020026689

CONTENTS

This book adds to the emerging story of the rise of neoliberalism around the world, showing how corporate lawyers in France ushered in rapid privatization after the end of the Cold War and transformed the famously strong state in that country. The process that Pierre France and Antoine Vauchez reveal is not simply that of the state becoming less and less of a counterweight to markets (and, instead, more geared toward their establishment and protection) nor of its assets and activities being transferred to private actors. That happened elsewhere. Rather, they detail how, in France, the regulatory task of the state was itself privatized, and that corporate lawyers were the pivotal actors in this astonishing development, inventing an unprecedented "public-private state."

The authors deserve immense credit for so successfully blending novel and startling facts, especially with regard to the revolving door between public and private service, with an astute sense of the overall trajectory of neoliberalism in one country—while at the same time incorporating a broader analysis of that phenomenon and offering insights into how its opponents can still resist it. The literacy with the theory of the modern state in various locales on display in these pages makes this book far more than a case study of one place or even one time.

After their eye-opening account of the rise of the corporate lawyer from the grave of the public-minded advocate in the country's republican tradition, France and Vauchez compellingly demonstrate that lawyers representing "private" interests were able to bring their expertise to bear in substituting for the state's former regulatory power a new governmental form that blurred the divide between public and private. In this argument, the authors hew to an emerging orthodoxy that whatever neoliberalism is, it is not "market fundamentalism," defined as a rollback of the state; rather, it is a transformation of the state in the image of business interests and as their tool. "Lobbying is an extension of legal counsel," one source reports. Experts move back and forth between the offices of state and the corporate bar, the authors show in their bravura survey of officials. Amazingly, one-time bureaucratic hubs have been displaced by breakaway new outposts of public authority where business interests are regulated in a mode that comes close to self-regulation in the guise of state oversight. In the place of the state once epitomized by Talleyrand, a corporate lawyer sits—literally in the same room where Talleyrand died, as France and Vauchez saw firsthand.

Ultimately, this book hints at a new kind of reality in the history of the state form—and not merely one in which the corporate lawyers abet its transformations. No longer can Alexis de Tocqueville's mythology of the constant tendency toward administrative centralization from the Old Regime to the French Revolution to post–World War II dirigisme prevail. But the potential reality elsewhere—of the displacement of the state—also fails to match the new facts of France's regulatory scheme. Rather, as the authors helpfully suggest, the neoliberal state in France is not primarily defined by privatization of enterprise, though it has certainly occurred there and accelerated since the millennium. Instead, a "public-private state" has begun to crystallize.

Part of the transformation concerns career paths. Where once the "state nobility" as a destination of personal achievement might have appealed to the best and the brightest, now it is plausible to assert (as an informant does here) that one is "defending the public interest in the private sector." Such beliefs transcend individual or even collective rationalizations to be part of a credible and widely shared common sense. One of the richest sections in the book illustrates the dense new sociability that sustains what is, in the end, a delusional mistake that no one within its boundaries can recognize as such. This error persists in spite of prior national assumptions that would have regarded such activities as sacrificing the general interest and will to particular agendas and concerns. Beyond personal trajectories, the scope of this change is reflected in the vocation of institutions. As France and Vauchez detail, the *Conseil d'État*—the country's supreme administrative court since the days of Napoleon—has maintained its traditional charge of ensuring national legal unity, while redefining the terms of its mandate to reflect the new porosity between the public and private realms. The work that the *Conseil d'État* and other legal institutions of the state are conducting, supposedly for the benefit of the French people, is not only reconstructing the public economic interest as market promotion but doing so through a constellation of nominally public authorities. This is not a tale of a restricted or underfunded state but one empowered to rule by personnel moving so regularly between public and private capacities as to blur the line between them.

After reviewing the abstention of other authorities that could deter these results, France and Vauchez conclude by appealing to American political theorist Michael Walzer's notion of "the art of separation." Walzer's insight is that much of the endurance and legitimacy of political institutions concern not what rules they are following but whether they are able to maintain their own spheres of authority without molestation from outsiders. This book shows that just the reverse is occurring in France, in a kind of unholy deconstruction of the public/private distinction for which feminist theorists have called in a very different context. Where the erosion of that separation, feminists insisted, allowed for collective approaches to forms of domination hitherto viewed as "private" and therefore unassailable, this book highlights that the authority of the public needs to *be* public in the first place in order to have authority over other actors.

No doubt, much of the account in this book is exceptional—perhaps not least, the public-mindedness of a neoliberalism that rules unashamedly elsewhere through private empowerment. Even as a case study, this book offers an astonishing scenario of the revolt of the elites—lawyers in particular—in our time. But there are general themes that resonate in these pages, too. The book dramatizes one more episode in the loss and perversion of the public good. No one seriously interested in the history of neoliberalism and the role of the legal profession in its entrenchment can afford to miss France and Vauchez's measured but hard-hitting investigation. Among the many pressing questions this indispensable book raises are how broadly applicable its conclusions are and whether its authors' recommendations for changing the trajectory of this less than salutary story can play out in France—and everywhere neoliberalism is creating destructive new state forms.

Samuel Moyn

ACKNOWLEDGMENTS

The transatlantic mobility of this book, initially published in Paris in 2017 under the title *Sphère publique, intérêts privés: Enquête sur un grand brouillage* (Presses de Sciences Po, Paris), and which now starts an anglophone life in Ithaca, could come as a surprise. As it engages in a thick description of France's field of power in the current neoliberal context, this opus was not necessarily an obvious candidate for translation to an American audience. It took many opportunities and a lot of enthusiasm for this transnational circulation to happen. It all started in Paris, in my little office under the roof of the old Sorbonne, when Pierre France, a PhD candidate in political science at the Université Paris 1-Sorbonne, agreed to help me conduct an in-depth exploration of the world, visions, and trajectories of French politicians and top-level bureaucrats who had moved en masse into the corporate bar over the past two decades. As our collaboration developed, Pierre played an instrumental role in the making of the book through continuous dialogic exchanges that proved critical in shaping its storyline. While he has mostly contributed to the writing of the second chapter, the whole book bears the trace of our many fruitful discussions.

But the transatlantic part of the book's journey only started later on. Camille Robcis, a member of the editorial board of the Corpus Juris: The Humanities in Law and Politics series, first envisioned a possible passage. Elizabeth Anker, the editor of this book series, took an immediate interest in welcoming the book. Her early and contagious conviction that it was telling a story of broader scope and significance helped me all the way through the editing process (as did a number of friendly dinners enjoyed in Paris over that period together with Stéphanie and Mitch). Yet the book also needed a connector to make less exotic the many French idiosyncracies that are unavoidable when it comes to discussing notions of the public and the state. Samuel Moyn was kind enough to accept the challenge. Given his scholarship at the crossroads of history, politics, and law; his strong engagement with the politics of neoliberalism; and his own long-standing relationship with France, I could not think of a better person for authoring the foreword to this book, which I am confident will enhance its relevance beyond audiences merely interested in the case of France. I wish to thank him here. As the journey moved to its more concrete steps, the financial and institutional support of Labex Tepsis, an international research platform in the social sciences of politics housed by the *Ecole des hautes études en sciences sociales* (EHESS), proved essential in making the translation possible. As for my previous books, Meg Morley agreed to do most of the translating work and I owe a special debt of gratitude to her. Yet the journey into the United States called for more than just a linguistic translation: it also needed some reformatting on a deeper level. I wish to thank Diane Berrett Brown, the managing editor of the series at Cornell University Press, and all the editorial team, who have been patient enough to help me through the many steps of the editing process.

There is finally one key element that has made this whole process possible, and it is time for me to confess it: I have my own "American in Paris," Stéphanie Hennette, whose long-standing and very special relationship with the United States has turned my own transatlantic move into a personal and loving journey, an adventure that has progressively extended to our sons Anatole and Basile. To them I gratefully dedicate this book.

THE NEOLIBERAL REPUBLIC

INTRODUCTION

June 2017: as Emmanuel Macron rises to power, the outgoing socialist prime minister Bernard Cazeneuve meets with the incoming one, Edouard Philippe, for the usual ceremony of transfer of power. Despite their different political affiliations, both share one striking feature: while the latter, a typical figure of French technocracy trained in elite state schools and member of the *Conseil d'État*,[1] is nominated after spending close to a decade as a business lawyer at the Debevoise & Plimpton law firm and later as a lobbyist in chief for France's large nuclear fuel company (Areva), the former is about to join August & Debouzy, an influential corporate law firm in Paris, as its expert in compliance. Similar transfers at the very top executive positions of the state are also worth noting. Out of the eight last chiefs of staff of the *Élysée* (the office of the president), while all of them were members of the state's *grands corps*, no less than five have been corporate lawyers.

It now seems that each day brings its load of news items relating to such cross-overs from top governmental positions to the Paris bar, and the list only seems to grow ever longer. In 2018, the daily newspaper *Le Monde* revealed that the opening political statement (the so-called *Exposé des motifs*) of a new legislative bill on transportation had been outsourced to the Paris branch of Dentons law firm by the government. Such a move into the privatization of legislative work is striking. All the more so because the firm's representative in this transaction was a former member of the *Conseil d'État* (and thus, of the top administrative elite) turned corporate lawyer. It is therefore fair to say that something is happening in France at the boundary between the state and markets, at the geometric locus where the "public" meets the "private" sphere. An ever-greater number of signals seems

---

1. As we engage in this exploration of France's field of power, we are bound to come across a whole set of idiosyncratic notions from the French political and bureaucratic lexicon. Rather than providing a word-by-word translation or identifying at all costs functional equivalents for these many idiosyncratic institutions and professions, we have listed them in a glossary (see appendix 2) that provides the definitional and contextual elements needed to make sense of these often "untranslatable" terms.

to indicate a blurring of the lines, verging on a confusion of roles that arguably imperils the public spirit of both politics and government.

To be sure, the boundary between the public and the private is not any social dividing line. It is fundamentally different from other sectoral and professional boundaries: it conveys a whole set of representations and expectations pertaining to the autonomy of state-actors (whether politicians, bureaucrats, judges, or regulators) as they engage in their government activities; it also sets out procedures of deliberation and decision-making that are different on either side of the line, thus effectively determining the social space in which citizenship and equal treatment will hold sway. It may certainly be tempting to consider that such sensitivity to the public-private divide is idiosyncratically French as France has long epitomized the "strong state"[2] par excellence, spearheaded by a ruling elite of lifetime civil servants with a strong hold over the definition of the *intérêt général*. And yet, while there are indeed profoundly different traditions regarding the ties between state elites and public interest, all democracies ground an essential part of their legitimacy in the maintaining of a somewhat robust distinction between public and private spheres.[3] It is hard to deny that the dividing line does carry an essential symbolic and political charge. It suffices to recall the unanimous moral outrage that erupts when affairs of corruption or graft are revealed; or the political condemnation that surrounds the many scandals caused by evidence of capture of public decision-making by large firms and the lobbying industry in matters as diverse as food safety, health norms, or environment protection. In short, this boundary is a fully political object. Any modification or muddling of this dividing line signifies much more than just a change in legal regime or in decision-making procedures; at stake are both the very autonomy of the spheres within which the public interest is defined and the conditions of possibility of a democratic citizenship. In other words, we stand here at the very boundaries of democracy.

Of course, the public-private boundary line was never drawn by a single and clear stroke of the pen; rather, it has lived through many vicissitudes over

---

2. See Bertrand Badie and Pierre Birnbaum, *The Sociology of the State*, trans. Arthur Goldhammer (Chicago: Chicago University Press, 1983).

3. Even in the United States, a state whose autonomy has long been considered to be weak (cf. Grant McConnell, *Private Power and American Democracy* [New York: Alfred Knopf, 1966]), recent historiography has pointed at the deeper and longer history of public law, well before the New Deal and the rise of regulatory agencies. Bill Novak in particular has identified its intellectual and political roots in the height of Progressive activism with a strong and lasting concern for the relationship between business and the American democracy: William Novak, "The Public Utility Idea and the Origins of Modern Business Regulation," in *Corporations and American Democracy*, ed. Naomi R. Lamoreaux and William J. Novak (Cambridge, MA: Harvard University Press, 2017), 139–76.

time.[4] Even in France, the public sphere never had the Gothic architecture envisioned by legal doctrine or political theory. The overlap, under the auspices of the state, of an ad hoc regime for public law, specific missions of *service public*, and an elite group of civil servants, has never been perfect. Even in its golden age (somewhere between the mid-1950s and the mid-1970s,[5] when it could be observed that the French state had acquired its "independence with regard to its personnel and its interests" and seemed alone to embody the public interest),[6] it already relied on a powerful system of collusive ties between segments of the state and segments of business.[7] However, back in the 1970s, the frequent mobility of top-level bureaucrats into large private corporations (most often firms operating in sectors of strategic importance, such as defense, or otherwise dependent on public procurement) was not usually interpreted as a weakening of the state. Rather, it was read as a sign of its preeminence as it allowed the state (through its *grands corps*) to act as coordinator in chief of France's mixed economy.[8]

But everything has changed, or nearly so. The hold that the state used to exercise over the French economy, notably through a substantial public sector in industry and banking, has become a thing of the past. Successive waves of privatization have dealt their blows, amputating sixty-five corporate entities from the state in August 1986, twenty-one more in July 1993, up until the very recent bill of April 2019 engaging the privatization of public entities—ones that even countries like the United States had never thought of privatizing—such as airports. This continuous movement was certainly amplified when the Single European Market was rolled out, as it triggered the liberalization of several strategic sectors including telecommunications, energy, and transport.[9] As EU competition law

---

4. France has indeed a long history of private management of public services and concession contracts. See Laurent de Carratier Dubois, "Le Conseil d'État, l'économie et le service public," *Revue d'histoire moderne et contemporaine* 52, no. 3 (2005): 51–74. Similarly, see deep-seated forms of joint regulation and mutual dependence between the state and the business sector: Claire Lemercier, *Un si discret pouvoir: Aux origines de la chambre de commerce de Paris (1803–1853)* (Paris: La Découverte, 2003).

5. Ezra Suleiman, *Politics, Power, and Bureaucracy in France: The Administrative Elite* (Princeton, NJ: Princeton University Press, 1974).

6. Pierre Birnbaum, *Les sommets de l'État: Essai sur l'élite du pouvoir en France* (Paris: Seuil, 1994; first published 1977 by Seuil).

7. On "the symbiosis and indissoluble link" between elite schools such as the *École nationale d'administration* (ENA), state *grands corps*, and top positions in the business sector, see Yves Mény, *La corruption de la République* (Paris: Fayard, 1991).

8. The notion of "mixed economy" was widely used until the mid-1980s to define the French economic system as featured by elements of market economies with interventionist policies, strong regulatory oversight and a large sector of state-owned companies in charge of the provision of public services in the fields of transport, energy, and telecommunications, but also banking, etc.

9. Daniel Kelemen, *Eurolegalism: The Transformation of Law and Regulation in the European Union* (Cambridge, MA: Harvard University Press, 2011).

required a strict equality between public and private actors in the economy, it directly caused reforms that drastically curtailed the state's capacity to organize public holdings as an alternative to private property. As a result of this significant shrinkage of the perimeter of the state, opportunities for high-level civil servants to move into state-owned companies (an until-then classic if temporary career move in top administrative positions) were brutally cut off. This, arguably, has contributed to redirecting some of their professional trajectories toward the private sector and, indeed, often toward major private companies that were formerly in the public sector.[10] Progressively, as the neoliberal turn consolidated in various policy domains,[11] the social and professional foundations for the interventionist state were dismantled.

While the territory of the public and the private has continually evolved before our eyes, the map that we collectively possess to get our bearings has remained more or less the same. The keywords of the public sector are still in use—"general interest," "public utility," "state prerogatives," "administrative law." Institutions that have a special role in preserving this state lexicon, starting with the *Conseil d'État*, continue to manipulate these categories with the care and caution once accorded to antique relics. But the reassuring continuity of vocabulary masks an unprecedented muddling of the cardinal points of the compass.[12] As the landscape has been transformed by the numerous upheavals of terrain that came with the neoliberal transformation of the state in the course of the past three decades, the binary diagram drawn up at the end of the 1970s (public/private) has lost a great deal of its descriptive power. The classic lexicon of the *summa divisio* separating the public and private sectors, although it is still routinely used to describe the workings of the state, does not account for the new blurring of missions, modes of action, and types of agents at work on either side of the dividing line. In fact, it conceals this blurring. As if it were burdened by the excessive load of political, economic, intellectual, and even moral significance

---

10. François-Xavier Dudouet and Éric Grémont, "Les grands patrons et l'État en France (1981–2007)," *Sociétés contemporaines* 68, no. 4 (2007): 105–31.

11. While it must be acknowledged that the lexicon of neoliberalism has been used and overused over the past years, to a point that it often becomes more confusing than really heuristic, it remains a powerful analytical tool to analyze the turn of state policies ever since the late 1970s. Hereafter, neoliberalism is defined as a specific family of economic policies and modes of governance geared toward the promotion and diffusion of procompetitive market stances in bureaucracies, professions, and among citizens. For a useful critique of the overstretching of the term, see James Ferguson, "The Uses of Neoliberalism," *Antipode* 41, no. 1 (2009): 166–84.

12. On neoliberalism and the "vanishing value and lexicon for public things and common good," see Wendy Brown, *Undoing the Demos: Neoliberalism's Stealth Revolution* (Cambridge, MA: MIT Press, 2015), 176.

that has been vested in this vocabulary, this lexicon muddles our view. As the overlap between state institutions, interventionist policies, and public service falls apart, the public/private binary now seems more of an obstacle when it comes to deciphering what is happening at the border between the state and markets.

Scholars are not without resources, however. Much work has been done to chronicle the neoliberal remaking of the state, in particular through inquiries into the progressive penetration of *new public management* within the bounds of the state. In sectors such as hospitals,[13] schools, taxation,[14] public utilities,[15] the superiority of business methods was extolled.[16] A whole literature has documented the managerial pathway taken by successive governments ever since the end of the 1990s—its elite as well as its preferred policy instruments: the ramping-up of power accorded to independent regulatory agencies in lieu of government offices, across-the-board promotion of public-private partnerships, increasing recourse to private consultants, subjection of public entities to the rules of the competitive market economy, and so forth; these are the fundamental components of the multiform (yet partial) process of neoliberalization of the state that has been underway for two decades.[17] But in focusing the analysis on the managerial reform of the public sector, scholars have too often turned away from the transformation, in many ways symmetrical, that has affected private sector entities—in particular consulting firms that were called upon to take part in this neoliberal reconstruction of the state. As one looks at the internal sectoral changes in government administration, the novel system of public-private transactions that progressively took shape at the confines of the state remains a blind spot.

---

13. Frédéric Pierru, "Les mandarins à l'assaut de l'usine à soins: Bureaucratisation néolibérale de l'hôpital et mobilisation de l'élite hospitalo-universitaire en France," in *La bureaucratisation néolibérale*, ed. Béatrice Hibou (Paris: La Découverte, 2013), 203–30.

14. Alexis Spire and Katia Weidenfeld, *L'impunité fiscale: Quand l'État brade sa souveraineté* (Paris: La Découverte, 2015).

15. Gery Deffontaines, "Les consultants dans les partenariats public-privé: Entre expertise au service du client public et intermédiation pour protéger le 'marché,'" *Politiques et management public* 29, no. 1 (2012): 113–33.

16. On the rise of *New Public Management* in France, see Philippe Bezes, "The Reform of the State: The French Bureaucracy in the Age of New Public Management," in *Developments in French Politics 4*, ed. Alistair Cole, Patrick Le Galès, and Jonah Levy (London: Palgrave Macmillan, 2008), 172–90; Julie Gervais, "The Rise of Managerialism as a Result of Bureaucratic Strategies and Power Games," in *Administrative Reforms and Democratic Governance*, ed. Jon Pierre and Jean-Michel Eymeri-Douzans (Abingdon: Routledge, 2011), 80–93.

17. Patrick Le Galès and Desmond King, "Introduction: A Reconfigured State? European Policy States in a Globalizing World," in *Reconfiguring European States in Crisis*, ed. Desmond King and Patrick Le Galès (Oxford: Oxford University Press, 2017), 1–42.

It is true that this borderline space is not easily scrutinized with the naked eye. Here again, our intellectual baggage reveals its limitations, as it is marked by a series of dichotomies—public/private, state/civil society—that continue to purvey the notion that the state is sole master in its domain, at most aided by some outside advisers.[18] In fact, a presumption of immunization has long prevailed, emphasizing the tenacious opposition of the state *grands corps* to the intrusion of consulting firms and to the "agencyfication" of markets' regulation. In this view, the French state and its power elite appear to have stood shoulder to shoulder in resisting the neoliberal reconfiguration process that has affected all European states for over two decades. And yet, as one looks at the actual economic and financial poles of the state today, all the evidence points conversely to a new pattern of public-private collusion that has grown up precisely along the porous fringes of the state and the fuzzy frontier of markets.[19]

The Public Fabric of Private Markets

To be able to grasp this transformation, there is a need for a different lens, one that looks for the state in places where scholars have not been used to finding it—in the field of law itself. There are of course several other points of entry into this border zone—be they the worlds of finance,[20] audit,[21] lobbying,[22] or political communication. But the law is uniquely suited for this much-needed investigation. By virtue of its historic ties to the state, at once the means of its action and one key principle of its legitimacy, the law offers an unrivaled observatory of the mutations of the forms and functions of the boundary between public and private. Because the law conforms to public policies like a second skin, it provides a view of state's regulation *across* sectors (banking and insurance, telecommunications, energy, health care, environment, defense, etc.) and policy instruments

---

18. Timothy Mitchell, "The Limits of the State: Beyond Statist Approaches and Their Critics," *American Political Science Review* 85, no. 1 (1991): 7–96.

19. See Sylvain Laurens, *Bureaucrats and Business Lobbyists in Brussels: Capitalism Brokers* (Abingdon: Routledge, 2017).

20. On crossovers between public and private sectors in banking, see Luc Rouban, "L'inspection générale des finances, 1958–2008: Pantouflage et renouveau des stratégies élitaires," *Sociologies pratiques* 21 (2010): 19–34.

21. Odile Henry and Frédéric Pierru, "Les consultants et la réforme des services publics," *Actes de la recherche en sciences sociales* 193, no. 3 (2012): 4–15.

22. Guillaume Courty and Hélène Michel, "Interest Groups and Lobbyists in the European Political Space," in *The Field of Eurocracy: Mapping EU Actors and Professionals*, ed. Didier Georgakakis and Jay Rowell (Basingstoke: Palgrave, 2013), 166–87.

(licensing regimes, public procurement, competition rules, regulation of financial and capital markets, etc.). From the point of view of the law, the state has not withdrawn from the economy. Quite the contrary. If there is an area in which the public sector is in full expansion, it is the regulation of markets, to the extent that the liberalized part of the state has redefined itself as a market-maker under the aegis of regulatory agencies.[23] In the neoliberalized state, there is a new form of public interventionism, placed under the sign of economic freedoms and undistorted competition. In part crafted in the European Union laboratory, this "pro-competitive re-regulation"[24] is aimed at facilitating the effective operation of markets and has triggered profound changes in policy instruments as well as in the very organization of the administrative apparatus.

In varying degrees,[25] many if not all Western states can be said to have embraced the model of the so-called "regulatory State"[26] whereby their main task no longer is to operate an alternative economic space in the name of *service public*, but rather to legally guarantee the free and undistorted operation of private markets. This operates in many ways: via licensing (to market products), prudential rules (designed to prevent market failure), and sophisticated systems of sanction of anticompetitive practices. Interestingly enough, this new type of state interventionism does have a counterpart in the private sector. Large companies very quickly understood that their market power lay not only in their economic and commercial innovations, but also in their capacity to wield influence in this public fabric of private markets. They soon engaged in continual interaction with regulators, top administrators, political leaders, and judges entrusted with the oversight of economic and fiscal affairs, at the national and the European level alike.[27]

And yet, while it is by now firmly established that the neoliberal turn and its promarket regulatory reforms is by no means a retreat of the state, we are still

23. Jonah Levy, *The State after Statism: New State Activities in the Age of Liberalization* (Cambridge, MA: Harvard University Press, 2006).

24. Steven Vogel, *Freer Markets, More Rules: Regulatory Reform in Advanced Industrial Countries* (Ithaca, NY: Cornell University Press, 1996).

25. Ibid.

26. Initially formulated by Giandomenico Majone, the notion of "regulatory state" is a useful heuristic device to trace the move away from the traditional redistributive welfare state based on expansive budgetary policies to a form of governance inspired by *New public management*, centered on market competition policies, independent regulatory agencies, and judicial enforcement: see Giandomenico Majone, "The Rise of the Regulatory State in Europe," *West European Politics* 17 (1994): 77–101. For an interesting discussion of the literature on this topic, see David Levi-Faur, "The Odyssey of the Regulatory State. Episode 1: The Rescue of the Welfare State," Jerusalem Papers in Regulation and Governance, working paper no. 39 (2011).

27. Colin Crouch, *The Strange Non-Death of Neoliberalism* (Malden, MA: Polity, 2011). See also Donatella Della Porta, Michael Keating, et al., "The Paradoxes of Democracy and the Rule of Law," in *Political Regulation, Governance, and Societal Transformations* (Cambridge University Press, 2018), 373–410.

short of understanding its political consequences. These however, are immense. Of particular importance are those that affect the public-private dividing line as well as the conditions in which the public interest is defined in our democracies. Far from clarifying the respective roles of states and markets, as the proponents of the neoliberal turn of public policies had touted as an incentive, the regulatory remaking of the state has created a zone of proximity and exchange between public and private actors that is without precedent. This gray zone that has emerged as the state plunged into the "icy water" of the liberal and competitive economy is the subject of this book. In the interstices of business, politics, and government, where the national echelon meets the European and the international, a field of public-private brokerage has indeed grown steadily over the past two decades, gaining in autonomy, scope, and political leverage. It is the purpose of this research to track the nascent and rapidly growing constellation of actors, organizations, and forms of knowledge that circulate across the public-private fault line, and to sharpen our understanding of its potential corrosive effects on the very definition of the public interest. France offers a topical empirical test case for such an endeavor. As sociologists of Western states have it: "in no other cases has the process of differentiation and institutionalization of the State been carried as far as in France."[28] And it is precisely this deep-seated sensitivity to the autonomy of the "public sphere" that makes France a particularly heuristic terrain when it comes to tracing the encounter between Western states and neoliberalism and revealing the transformative effects of the expanding public-private fault line.

Corporate Lawyers as Tracers of the Neoliberal Turn of the State

For such an exploration, one needs a guide able to lead through the byways and backwaters of this border space. Nothing will serve us better than the choice to follow those who are the hands-down champions in this new cross-border game: its experts—namely, corporate lawyers.[29] Classic works of American sociology, from those of Parsons to Wright Mills, have scrutinized lawyers as intermediaries "penetrating the boundary between public and private capacities and

---

28. Bertrand Badie and Pierre Birnbaum, *The Sociology of the State*, trans. Arthur Goldhammer (Chicago: Chicago University Press, 1983), 105.

29. Yves Dezalay and Bryant Garth who apprehend lawyers as a "pivotal profession" in national as well as transnational fields of power: "State Politics and Legal Markets," *Comparative Sociology* 10, no. 1 (2011): 38–66.

responsibilities"[30] or "professionals mediating between the economy, politics and military affairs."[31] While its role as cornerstone of the American power elite may have been somewhat overstated,[32] the Washington lawyer circulating between regulatory bodies and public affairs consulting firms, and from government cabinet positions to the halls of Congress offers an interesting reference point.[33] It forces us to look at lawyers not only for their technical expertise as defense litigants or legal counsels (roles that European legal professionals essentially did stick to until the early 1990s),[34] but also for their brokering role in-between a variety of fields (business, politics, government), as well as for the expertise of the state or statecraft that they help produce and disseminate.

Strangely enough, however, while there is an rich literature pointing at the rise of global law firms as providers of a vast array of services to their business clients (from litigation to legal counsel, arbitration, public affairs, and lobbying, etc.)[35], only a small number of inquiries have connected these transformations to the neoliberal turn of Western states[36]. And yet, ever since the 1990s, corporate lawyers in Europe have become key players not only in the business-consulting market, but also in public affairs, compliance, and regulatory expertise.[37] All the signs show that ever since the 1990s, the position of the legal profession in the playing field of power has been profoundly transformed[38].

---

30. Talcott Parsons, "A Sociologist Looks at the Legal Profession," in *Essays in Sociological Theory*, rev. ed. (New York: Free Press, 1964), 370–85.

31. Charles Wright Mills, *The Power Elite*, with a new afterword by Alan Wolfe (Oxford: Oxford University Press, 2000), 288–89.

32. See Robert Nelson and John Heinz, "Lawyers and the Structure of Influence in Washington," *Law and Society Review* 22, no. 2 (1988): 237–300.

33. Ronen Shamir, *Managing Legal Uncertainty: Elite Lawyers in the New Deal* (Durham, NC: Duke University Press, 1995); Patrick Schmidt, *Lawyers and Regulation: The Politics of the Administrative Process* (Cambridge: Cambridge University Press, 2005).

34. For a comparison among Western legal professions, see Mark Osiel, "Lawyers as Monopolists, Aristocrats, and Entrepreneurs," *Harvard Law Review* 103, no. 8 (1990): 2009–66.

35. See in particular Glenn Morgan und Sigrid Quack, "Institutional Legacies and Firm Dynamics: The Growth and Internationalization of British and German Law Firms," Organization Studies 26, no. 12 (2005): 1765-1785. And the rich overview of the literature presented: Mehdi Boussebaa, James Faulconbridge, "The work of global professional service firms," in Perspective on contemporary professional work. Challenges and experiences, ed. A. Wilkinson, D. Hislop, C. Coupland, (Edward Elgar: Cheltenham, 2016): 105-122.

36. A contrario, see Yves Dezalay and Bryant Garth, "Merchants of Law as Moral Entrepreneurs: Constructing International Justice out of the Competition for Transnational Business Disputes," *Law and Society Review* 29, no. 1 (1995): 27–64.

37. See Antoine Vauchez, *Brokering Europe: Euro-Lawyers and the Making of a Transnational Polity* (Cambridge: Cambridge University Press, 2015).

38. On the critical importance of the private-public legal nexus in the entrenchment of the rights of capital, and the role of lawyers in this context, see Katharina Pistor, *The Code of Capital: How the Law Creates Wealth and Inequality* (Princeton, NJ: Princeton University Press, 2019).

Lawyers are no longer simply specialists in legal defense and judicial chicanery. In the "full service" law firms where they henceforth pursue their trade, they define themselves as all-terrain experts offering a wide range of services, from legal and judicial counsel to political and governmental lobbying, drafting legislative amendments, or negotiating international arbitration agreements along the way. Today, researchers find business lawyers in the aisles of parliamentary assemblies as well as in the headquarters of major companies, in the hearing rooms of the economic and financial sections of the courts as well as in the corridors of the Directorate General for Competition in Brussels or in the lobby of regulatory agencies. The times where they essentially were to be found in the crowded halls of the courthouse are long gone. By tracking the dossiers that they handle, it quickly becomes clear that big corporate law firms established in Paris maintain a continual commerce along the fringes of the state. They may act *for* as well as *against* public entities (states, local governments, state-owned companies, etc.). Even as they intervene in defense of the latter, they act in a large variety of contexts: major financial and equity operations, investor-state arbitrations, public-private partnerships, state aid discussions at the European level. They may also present arguments *before* public institutions whether ministries, regulatory agencies, or courts, in Paris or in Brussels, in order to obtain favorable fiscal arrangements, market authorizations, or other government approvals. Yet, in all cases, they appear to be working in the shadow of the state, in close contact with its elites and departments.

While corporate lawyers now appear in many quarters of the state, state *grands corps* have symmetrically come to populate law firms. A great many people with former public experience in their title have joined corporate law firms over the years: key figures of the *Conseil d'État*, secretaries-general of either the presidential office at the *Élysée* or the prime minister's office at Matignon, junior as well as senior ministers of the economy or justice, heads of ministries' departments and poles in the fiscal law division, former chief cabinet advisers and market regulators. This flow toward the Paris business bar is intriguing. Not only because historians and sociologists have long established the demise of the *République des avocats* that was once in place during the Third Republic when the legal profession was the main breeding ground for the emerging Republican ruling elite. But also because today it is not so much lawyers who accede to politics and the government, as was the case in the late nineteenth century, but rather the contrary as former top civil servants and politicians seek to push through the revolving door into Paris law firms and take over their public affairs and public law departments.

Mapping the Field of Public-Private Intermediation

Lawyers and law firms may indeed be a privileged entry point in the transformation of the relationship between business, politics, and government (and the related blurring of the public-private divide) in the context of France's neoliberal turn of public policies.[39] Yet we need an analytical toolbox to make possible both an accurate description of the dynamics of this new public-private intermingling and a thorough assessment of its transformative effects. To this aim, the book draws from Pierre Bourdieu's field-theoretical approach as it allows us to build a spatial understanding of the new set of relations, transactions, and interdependences that cut across public and private sectors. In mobilizing this theoretical apparatus for the study of a weakly structured social space such as the emerging field of public-private intermediation, the book pursues a collective effort to remodel Pierre Bourdieu's analytical toolbox for the purpose of studying these *interstitial* fields that develop in-between more historically consolidated ones whether at the national or transnational level.[40] While they may be weak in their social and professional structure, their position at the crossroads of stronger fields such as politics, government, or business, makes them particularly critical as sites of coordination and homogenization of policy frames. Thereby, we hope to provide the analytical equipment to track not only the expanding creep in the public-private fault line but also its specific gravity (or field effect), hereafter defined as its capacity to transform the properties and coordinates of "any object (professions, policies, modes of governance) that traverses this space"[41] and capture professional strategies, government agendas, political imaginations.

There remains an empirical difficulty however, as the corporate bar is hard to penetrate. Journalists, political scientists, not to mention sociologists, are traditionally kept at arm's length. Not that lawyers shy away from giving interviews, quite the contrary. But discretion and secrecy are the cardinal virtues of their profession. A good deal of their professional excellence as mediators is indeed measured by their capacity to lead outsiders to forget that they are acting as such, and to protect their clients from outside scrutiny. The cult of anonymity and

39. Stephen Barley, "Building an Institutional Field to Corral a Government: A Case to Set an Agenda for Organization Studies," *Organization Studies* 31, no. 6 (2010): 777.

40. Stephanie Mudge and Antoine Vauchez, "Building Europe on a Weak Field: Law, Economics, Scholarly Avatars in Transnational Politics," *American Journal of Sociology* 118, no. 2 (2012): 449–92. See also Tom Medvetz, *Think Tanks in America* (Chicago: University of Chicago Press, 2012).

41. Pierre Bourdieu and Loïc Wacquant, *An Invitation to Reflexive Sociology* (Chicago: University of Chicago Press, 1992), 100 (emphasis added).

the shroud of professional secrecy are such that very few social scientists have been able to gain access to lawyers' dossiers and to follow their clients. It remains difficult to obtain direct knowledge of how they work. Scholars are often left standing at the doorstep of these law firms.[42] But sociologists occasionally strike it rich: the entrepreneurial turn of the legal profession in the 1990s has lifted a corner of the curtain of ignorance. As competition between law firms grows more intense, the prestigious deals, catches, and victorious coups of the players are increasingly aired on the firms' websites and in the columns of the specialized press. These media releases are biased of course, but they make public data and information that had traditionally been kept in the shadows because of the tradition of reserve and selfless neutrality espoused by the legal elite.[43]

In addition to twenty-five interviews with key actors (corporate lawyers and a variety of top civil servants and politicians who moved to the bar) and an in-depth exploration of the profession's rich professional gray literature, we have built a biographical database of the career paths of the more than two hundred politicians and high civil servants that have moved through many revolving doors over the past two decades (for details on the methodology, see appendix 1). The reason for such a strong focus on biographies and trajectories is not just that it brings living, acting people into what has up to now been a mostly disembodied narrative of reified collectives ("state," "agencies," "banks and firms") pursuing abstract goals and institutional interests. As we collect data on individual career moves and bring them into relation to each other, we are able to write a "relational collective biography" of the development of the *field* of public-private brokerage. And as we identify the breeding grounds, points of passage, and hubs for the conversion of different forms of social capital as well as the career paths and professional hierarchies among those who circulate across borders, it becomes possible to map out the various segments of politics, government, business that are swept away into this blurring dynamics.

This said, and at the risk of disappointing readers, this book does not intend in any way to supplant investigative journalists, and even less to take the place of judges. It does not seek to reveal the existence of hidden deals or secret agreements

---

42. Emmanuel Lazega's deep investigation into an American law firm is one notable exception, but his line of inquiry is different, as he studies the relational structure within the firm as an organization to pick out the internal dynamics and "micro-politics" that traverse it. Emmanuel Lazega, *The Collegial Phenomenon: The Social Mechanisms of Cooperation among Peers in a Corporate Law Partnership* (Oxford: Oxford University Press, 2001).

43. For a study of a similar phenomenon in the United States, see Michael Powell, "La nouvelle presse juridique et les métiers du droit," *Actes de la recherche en sciences sociales* 101–2 (1994): 63–76.

of a financial or political nature between the various protagonists along this border space. Nor is it aimed at stealing the thunder of the moralists who, in a context of recurring "affairs" and scandals, are bent on denouncing the "dangerous
liaisons" linking the political and governmental elite to the business world. The
ambition of this book lies elsewhere: our aim is to map out the *field* of public-
private brokerage populated by lawyers-lobbyists and former politicians or civil
servants turned lawyers and unearth its gravitational effects on both sides of the
public-private divide. In the end, it aims at analyzing the neoliberal remaking of
the state and assessing its transformative effects on *how* the public interest (and
ultimately, citizenship) is being defined in contemporary democracies.

Outline of the Book

The book is divided into four chapters that proceed as follows.

The first chapter is mostly historical and accounts for the new pattern of
public-private collusion that comes along the neoliberal turn of public policies
from the early 1990s onward. In particular, it traces the symmetrical transformations and mutual dependence of Paris law firms and France's "regulatory state"

The second chapter maps out this rapidly growing field of public-private
brokerage by assessing the scope and breadth of French revolving doors.

The third chapter moves on to analyze the transformative effects of this new
pattern of public-private collusion on prevailing conceptions and categories of
the public interest.

The last chapter engages with a normative assessment of the political risks
and diffuse democratic costs related to this blurring process, and considers its
cumulative effects from the standpoint of democratic theory. Revisiting Walzer's
account of the "art of separation"[44] for the sake of understanding the public-private
divide, the closing chapter points at the role of the public sphere's autonomy as
a critical condition for democratic citizenship. Because this gray area remains
largely shielded from most forms of political and professional oversight, it has
become a new democratic "black hole" in which professional intermediaries—
lawyers, consultants, and so forth—thrive and prosper.[45] When confronting this

---

44. Michael Walzer, "Liberalism and the Art of Separation," *Political Theory* 12, no. 3 (1984):
315–30.

45. Regarding these spaces, see Pierre Lascoumes and Dominique Lorrain, "Trous noirs du pouvoir: Les intermédiaires de l'action publique," *Sociologie du travail* 49 (2007): 1–9.

extraterritorial zone that has grown up at the core of our political systems, and the corrosive effects of its expansion, our democracies appear to be seriously underequipped. The blurring of the public-private divide not only weakens our capacity to produce a "public interest" that rests at bay from market asymmetries, but also our very ability to conceptually identify what such a "public interest" may be. This may be one of the biggest challenges ahead for neoliberalized democracies.

1

IN-BETWEEN THE PUBLIC AND THE PRIVATE / The New Lawyering Business

When our story begins, at the end of the 1980s, the French legal profession hardly overlaps with markets and government. The traditional professional ideals of the "classical bar"[1] (*barreau classique*) that had solidified in the context of the rise of French republican ideas were no stranger to these weak ties, as this deontology exalted disinterested detachment and distance from all the players, such as business agents, fiscal advisers, and proxies in the commercial courts, who were more directly involved with the business world and who managed the "dirty work" of securities portfolios, debt recovery, and bankruptcy proceedings, among others.[2] At this time, there was an embryonic bar specialized in advising corporations, but it was small in size, limited to dispute litigation, and often still coupled with generalist law practice for individual clients. In addition to this low degree of economic specialization among lawyers, multiple restrictions actually banned lawyers from taking a direct role in commercial companies whether as in-house legal counsel or as managing director or chair of the board of administrators. This intermittent relationship with market actors was mirrored by equally weak ties with the political and administrative elite of the Fifth Republic in France. While the legal profession had long been seen as the prime breeding ground for politicians, lawyers became rarer in politics as the "legicentrist" tradition of

---

1. Famously coined by French sociologist Lucien Karpik in his history of the French legal profession, the *barreau classique* refers to a specific model of professional excellence that solidified in the nineteenth century and remained mostly intact until the 1970s whereby lawyers (generalists, solo practitioners, socialized in courts practice) claimed to defend the public (against state arbitrariness) and promote political liberalism in great criminal cases and trials: Lucien Karpik, *French Lawyers: A Study in Collective Action, 1274–1994* (Oxford: Oxford University Press, 2000).

2. Lucien Karpik speaks of the "explicit rejection of the marketplace." Adding nuance to this view, it should be recalled that some well-known lawyers (who in some cases were also members of Parliament) handled the legal affairs of major companies, for instance Raymond Poincaré, but for the most part this merchant side of the profession remained in shadow.

the Third Republic waned[3] and the welfare state emerged, and the qualities of orator and legal competence lost much of their political value. At the end of the 1980s the *République des avocats* had declined to the point that less than 6 percent of parliamentary representatives came from the bar.[4] In addition, lawyers had very few occasions to represent political or administrative actors in their work. The historical monopoly enjoyed by a specialized branch, the so-called *avocats aux Conseils* prevented members of the Paris bar from handling public law cases before the *Conseil d'État*. While the state occasionally appeared in cases before the *ordinary* courts, and called upon lawyers to defend it in courts, these cases most often involved recurrent and low-paying litigation related to traffic accidents, indemnity for unlawful temporary detention, or other dysfunctions of the justice system. In short, at the end of the 1980s, the legal profession remained specialized in civil and criminal litigation with few and circumstantial points of intersection with market actors or the state.

And yet, in the mid-1990s, a surge of intense activity started to unsettle the legal profession at its economic, political, and administrative fringes. A series of major trials for economic and financial crimes emerged in the 1990s involving some French major oil (the Elf scandal) or bank (the Crédit Lyonnais scandal) companies, which suddenly threw lawyers into direct contact with a great many top-level economic, political, and administrative leaders. At the same time, the neoliberal turn of state policies, in particular privatizations and public subcontracting, brought a growing number of cases straddling the boundary between public law and private law, leading law firms to broaden the range of their knowhow, in order to accompany the state in its financial and stock market operations, and its new public-private partnerships. And as companies were becoming more aware that part of their market power was decided in the fast-growing regulatory state of French and EU agencies, business lawyers were called upon to go beyond the halls of justice and to frequent the bureaus of agencies and administrative departments in Paris and Brussels. It does indeed seem that French lawyers were renewing their ties with public affairs, but in a novel form that must now be analyzed. What is it that brought the legal profession back into close contact with the political and administrative worlds to the point that they are now enmeshed in a dense network of public-private transactions?

---

3. "Legicentrism" refers to the legal and political doctrine which had its heyday in the late nineteenth century and promoted the centrality of statute law and of parliamentary sovereignty: see Nicolas Roussellier, *La force de gouverner: Le pouvoir exécutif en France, XIXe–XXIe siècles* (Paris: Gallimard, 2015).

4. Gilles Le Beguec, *La République des avocats* (Paris: Armand Colin, 2003); Mattei Dogan, "The Mandarins among the French Elites," in *Elite Configurations at the Apex of Power*, ed. Mattei Dogan (Leiden: Brill, 2003).

To understand the formation of this new collusive system, one must first follow the parallel and in many ways symmetrical transformations of the top ranks
of the state and of the elite corps of the Paris business bar. At a time when the
notions of *new public management* were beginning to permeate public policy,
profoundly transforming state intervention in markets,[5] a few business law
firms reshaped themselves as veritable law enterprises that offered their clients
a new palette of services, from legal advice to political and government lobbying.[6] In the wake of this transformation new alliances and new relationships
were cemented between government institutions and market players. Hoping to
establish the legitimacy of the regulatory turn, the proponents of the *neoliberal*
revamping of state interventionism sought support from market professionals,
whether lawyers, bankers, or other private advisers. Symmetrically, the emergence within the Paris legal profession of a powerful *barreau d'affaires* (corporate
bar)[7] played out in the proximity that these new practitioners (*avocats d'affaires*)
were able to establish with public institutions, both national and European;
thereby they positioned themselves as brokers in a business world that was then
discovering the critical importance of the "regulatory state" (government offices,
regulatory agencies, courts' new financial and competition sections, the European Commission's Competition Directorate General, etc.) in the construction
of market positions. The rise of these *avocats d'affaires* allows us to map out the
development of a gray zone in-between a new segment of the public sector now
acclimated to entrepreneurial dynamics and in the habit of calling upon outside
consultants, and a pole of public affairs consultants that has been growing up
close along the flanks of the state.

The Corporate Bar's Public Affairs

The Paris bar has undergone a genuine cultural revolution in the past thirty
years. A significant cluster, both competitive and international in scope, has
emerged within the bar around what has come to be known as business law
(*droit des affaires*). This entrepreneurial aggiornamento of a large segment of the

---

5. Philippe Bezes, *Réinventer l'État: Les réformes de l'administration française, 1962–2008* (Paris:
Presses Universitaires de France, 2009).

6. See the classic work by Yves Dezalay, *Marchands de droit: La restructuration de l'ordre juridique
international par les multinationales du droit* (Paris: Fayard, 1992).

7. As the historical constellation of the *barreau classique* was fading away from the 1970s onward,
a *barreau d'affaires* (corporate bar) emerged characterized by specialized legal practices centered on
big business clientele (as opposed to personal clients) and developed in large practices with strong
entrepreneurial culture. Karpik, *French Lawyers*.

profession is closely tied to the formation of a European and global market in corporate legal consulting.[8] It has not, however, been constituted at a distance from public institutions, as is too often assumed. To the contrary, we argue that the invention of the *avocats d'affaires* happened in proximity to the state as these lawyers claimed a new role as an indispensable broker between companies and interest groups, on one side, and the ever more dense network of French and European political, legal, and administrative regulators on the other side.

The Invention of the Corporate Lawyer

It should be said that the odds were against the rise of such a professional figure in France; the syntagm *avocats d'affaires* was long considered an oxymoron, as the people involved in justice historically claimed a necessary distance from the business world. In the not so discreet social and professional hierarchy underlying legal specializations, corporate law was a little-valued activity, left to practitioners deemed to be the least equipped with a "juridical mind" and in most instances coming from the "lowest regions of the social space."[9] The representatives of the legal profession in France, heirs to a quasi-aristocratic conception of their role emphasizing disinterested detachment and noble vocation,[10] were careful to confine the legal specialists closest to mercantile activity (in-house legal counsel, business agents, notaries, etc.) to the periphery of the profession. The bar association also imposed an array of restrictions and safeguards to circumscribe the commercialization of the law—a ban on advertising, fee-based remuneration as opposed to percentages—and generally prevent lawyers from participating in business activity.

THE "GREAT LEGAL PROFESSION" PROJECT

In this context, the little group of practitioners who in the 1960s popularized the notion of *avocats d'affaires*, that is the most internationalized segments of the Paris bar and some highly visible representatives of the bar association such as its president René-William Thorp, were in many ways heretical figures.[11] The

---

8. See in particular: Glenn Morgan and Sigrid Quack, "Institutional Legacies and Firm Dynamics: The Growth and Internationalization of British and German Law Firms," *Organization Studies* 26, no. 12 (2005): 1765–85.

9. On this, see Anne Boigeol and Yves Dezalay, "De l'agent d'affaires au barreau: Les conseils juridiques et la construction d'un espace professionnel," *Genèses* 27 (1997): 49–68.

10. Osiel, "Lawyers as Monopolists, Aristocrats, and Entrepreneurs."

11. For one of the very first formal descriptions of this new professional figure, see Jean-Claude Goldsmith, *L'avocat d'affaires* (Paris: Béranger, 1964).

background circumstances are important. The advent of the Fifth Republic in France had dealt a fatal blow to the *République des avocats*. The networks of influence maintained by the profession in the field of government and politics had already deteriorated in the period between the two world wars as the "legicentrist" Republican tradition had become the target of many political and intellectual movements heavily criticizing the many failures of both *parliamentarism* and *legalism*. The *presidentialist* turn of the Fifth Republic was made possible by a convergence between the charismatic leadership of General de Gaulle who sought to restore the power of the executive, and the modernist state elite drawn from the *grands corps*, often trained in economics, who sought to rationalize government action. This was the coup de grace. Lawyers were the first victims of the rise of new pathways into politics that came with the 1958 Constitution, and in particular the continuous rise of various categories of civil servants in parliamentary representation, from 15 percent in 1946 to over 50 percent in 1981.[12] Yet the 1960s were also notable for another context—namely, the launch of Europe's Common Market.[13] The modernizers of the Paris bar mentioned above immediately seized upon the new context to call for the birth of a new type of law practitioner who would "no longer be exclusively a presenter of pleas, a stickler for procedure, a dealer in disputes and litigation," but would engage in "an ongoing collaboration as advisor on the problems and projects of the heads of companies."[14] The emergence of this type of lawyer with a new legal specialty, corporate law, that assembled the diverse strands of legal knowledge with relevance for modern companies (tax matters, commercial statutes, penal law, etc.) consummated the break with the archaic framework of a code of commerce and trades that was deemed to be fit for the bygone era of shopkeepers.

This new professional project was promoted by a small Parisian fraction of the profession with ties to major corporations and set to follow these companies on the European road that was just opening up. This was the case of the Gide firm, created in 1957 by three lawyers, Pierre Gide, Jean Loyrette, and Philippe Nouel. The firm was one of the first to take advantage of a 1954 decree that permitted lawyers to create groups of associated partners. Breaking with the solo practice tradition of the profession, Gide created one of the first entrepreneurial structures (*société civile professionnelle*, or professional partnership company)

---

12. Frédéric Sawicki, "Classer les hommes politiques," in *La profession politique, XIXe–XXe siècles*, ed. Michel Offerlé (Paris: Belin, 1999), 135–70.

13. Vauchez, *Brokering Europe*.

14. Fernand-Charles Jeantet, "Le rôle de l'avocat, conseil des sociétés," *La Vie judiciaire*, December 28–January 2, 1965, 1.

equipped to advise major corporate groups, in Paris and then in Brussels, where the firm opened an office as early as 1967.[15] Up until the late 1980s, Gide was the "national champion" and the only firm (with a couple of smaller ones such as Jeantet and Rambaud Martel, also present in Brussels very early on, or Bredin Prat) that could compete with large American and British law firms. Quite logically, it became a veritable "nursery" for future figureheads of the business bar (Jean Veil, Jean-Marie Burguburu, Didier Martin, Thierry Vassogne, Hubert Flichy, etc.) who took a dominant position in the legal and judicial affairs of major French companies.

The strategy followed by these "young Turks" of the business bar to conquer the market of corporate legal services gradually developed into the main reform agenda of the profession. Condensed into a Blue Book Report, this new professional project was actually endorsed in 1967 by the major professional union, the *Association nationale des avocats*. It called for "the elimination" of all historical competitors in the field of corporate law counsel from "in-house lawyers, legal or tax advisors, business agents, legal services of so-called fiduciary companies, trustees in commercial courts, business agents, goodwill and clientele brokers and real estate agents who prospect for clients and mediate between parties." Instead, the report called for the creation of a "great legal profession," "legal and judicial, liberal and monopolistic" that would be capable of fully assuming its role in the world of business.[16] Espoused by the most internationally savvy segments of the Paris bar, the strategic goal of gaining entry to the corporate law market was the prime objective of the reformers. This enterprise was successful, supported by the ministry of justice who had been pushing for years for rationalizing France's highly complex and fragmented system of legal professions shaped in the long history of professional turf.[17] Important laws were passed in 1971 and in 1990 that profoundly transformed the contours of the profession, merging first with *avoués* (an old legal profession which had the monopoly of representing personal clients before specific courts) and then more importantly with the *conseils juridiques* (which had developed into large firms specialized in legal and tax counseling). The expansion of the profession's perimeter resulted in an

---

15. "Ubiquistes avocats," *Le Monde*, November 25, 1986.

16. Alain Tinayre and Denis de Ricci, eds., *Au service de la justice: La profession juridique de demain* (Paris: Dalloz, 1967).

17. One of the singular features of these struggles at the fringe of the profession lies in the fact that the government (and in the ministry of justice) is the final arbiter of the "scope" of professional monopolies. This is illustrated by the intense lobbying spawned by the 1991 legislation merging the professions of legal adviser and lawyer. See Antoine Vauchez and Laurent Willemez, *La justice face à ses réformateurs (1980–2006): Entreprises de modernisation et logiques de résistances* (Paris: Presses Universitaires de France, 2007).

exponential increase in the numbers, from seventy-five hundred *avocats* in 1970 to over sixty-five thousand today.

Reform efforts to reposition the profession at the core of corporate counseling services have continued ever since. It was relaunched a decade ago by the report on legal professions (2009) commissioned by Nicolas Sarkozy to one of the principal figures of the Paris business bar, Jean-Michel Darrois. The report called for shortening the list of activities that are incompatible with the legal profession (in particular nonsalaried managing director of commercial companies).[18] It was followed by another report on the international legal competitiveness of Paris law firms (2011), written by the former president of the French financial regulation agency, who recommended the merger of lawyers and in-house legal counsel, a highly sensitive issue with regard to the traditional professional ideals of independence.[19] The so-called Macron Act for Growth, Activity, and Equal Economic Opportunity of August 6, 2015, adopted when Emmanuel Macron was still minister of the economy, was also a step in this direction, allowing lawyers to practice in multiprofession partnerships—for example, with their longtime competitors in the field of corporate counseling services, namely certified accountants (*experts-comptables*).

In the course of these successive reforms the figure of the lawyer-barrister whose practice is mostly centered in courts progressively gave way to that of the "Swiss knife lawyer," a jack-of-all-trades capable of filling a broad array of functions: legal and tax adviser, public affairs specialist, lobbyist before French and European public institutions, as well as international arbiter, mediator, business and fiduciary agent, estate executor, nonsalaried managing director of a commercial company, not to mention member of Parliament or university professor. This progressive loosening of the many professional rules restricting lawyers' activities is not merely a technical issue. At stake in the set of incompatibility rules is the possibility for lawyers to combine their professional activity with other positions in economic, legal, political, and academic fields, thereby endowing them with the social and political capacity to reach out into a variety of fields, and circulate in-between them. In other words, four decades of reform of the legal profession have considerably reinforced what Laurent Willemez has

---

18. The report also advocated fewer bans on lawyers' activities (in particular with nonsalaried managing director positions in a commercial company) to enable lawyers to hold their own with "competing vendors such as banks, insurance companies, secondary health insurance providers, legal advisory companies, debt collection companies, accounting firms and business management consultants."

19. On these mutations, see also Christophe Jamin, "Services juridiques: La fin des professions?," *Pouvoirs* 140 (2012): 33–47.

quite aptly termed the "fluidity" of the title of lawyer:[20] that is, the capacity that it confers (in varying degrees depending on time and place) to, simultaneously or successively, work in and circulate across a great variety of social and professional milieux.[21]

A CORPORATIZATION OF PARIS BAR

The big bang that set in motion the creation of the French business bar came in the 1990s, when the profession of *conseillers juridiques* merged with the bar, and American and British law firms arrived in Paris.[22] The December 1990 law stipulating a merger of the professions of *conseils juridiques* and *avocats* had its importance. It had the effect of opening the bar to tax specialists who had for years been organized around a handful of major legal counseling firms, such as CMS Bureau Francis Lefebvre and Fidal, each employing several dozen partners and employees. This in turn transformed the politics within the legal profession consolidating the segment of the bar working with corporate clients: a specific professional association was even constituted, the *Association nationale des avocats conseils d'entreprises*, which seeks to represent and voice at the Paris bar association the interests of this emerging group of *avocats d'affaires*.[23]

In parallel to the insertion of *conseils juridiques* into the profession, big American and British law firms made a much-noted entry (Linklaters, Allen & Overy, Freshfields, Sherman Sterling, among others). In the wake of renewed attention to the European single market agenda in the late 1980s, these firms opened offices in the major European cities—Paris, Milan, Frankfort, or Brussels.[24] From the outset, they upended the quasi monopoly that had been the prerogative of the handful of French corporate law firms. In fact, the following years were marked by a long succession of enticements, poaching, and headhunting hires—in 1998 no fewer than sixteen partners left Gide—and regroupings and mergers; see the alliance between the French firm Rambaud Martel and the American firm Orrick in 2006, which ultimately led to the disappearance of certain historic firms from the Paris scene, such as Coudert Frères that was definitively shuttered in 2005.

---

20. Laurent Willemez, "La 'République des avocats': 1848; le mythe, le modèle et son endossement," in *La Profession politique, XIXe–XXe siècles*, ed. Michel Offerlé (Paris: Belin, 1999), 201–29.

21. Antoine Vauchez, "Une élite d'intermédiaires: Genèse d'un capital juridique européen (1950–1970)," *Actes de la recherche en sciences sociales* 166–67 (2007): 54–65.

22. On the general transformations of the legal profession, see John Flood, "Megalawyering in the Global Order," *International Journal of the Legal Profession* 3 (1996): 169–213.

23. "Création d'un 'grand syndicat' du barreau d'affaires," *Les Échos*, February 24, 1992.

24. Susanne Lace, "Mergers, Mergers Everywhere: Constructing the Global Law Firm in Germany," in *Legal Professions: Work, Structure and Organisation*, ed. Jerry Van Hoy (Greenwich: JIA Press, 2001), 51–75.

This reshuffling was accompanied by a profound transformation of the models of worth and wealth within the legal profession. With the 1990 merger and the arrival of large US law firms, the new entrepreneurial values and managerial techniques were imposed in the Paris bar, bringing logics of profitability and business development at the core of the professional activity. A competitive recruitment market emerged in parallel, characterized by a steady flow of hires (between 150 and 250 partners change firms each year in Paris), a stark break with the traditional sedentary professional model.[25] This shift, narrowing the gap between this segment of the profession and the corporate world, was further amplified by the flourishing of a new specialized press (*Lettre des juristes d'affaires, Lemondedudroit.com, Décideurs Magazine*, and other specialized sites) that brought to the Paris bar a whole new universe of representations typical of the business world.[26] This press pays much attention to coups and other big deals, salutes firm mergers and alliances, and avidly chronicles transfers of partners in the Parisian law associates market. In addition, these new media contributed to the development of new criteria and procedures for the assessment of lawyers' quality. Traditionally, the "set of rules (total prohibition on personal advertising) precluded the formation of a system of public information on lawyers' qualities and fees." With the rise of these new media and blogs, a vast array of guides, distinctions, and awards developed. Mostly constructed on the basis of reputational surveys of clients and members of the profession (Chambers, Legal 500, etc.), they challenged the traditional economy of a profession hitherto dominated by interpersonal and localized judgment of professional excellence.[27]

A business bar was born. Its perimeters can be outlined in different ways, depending on the type of clientele taken into account, the structure of the entity, or the degree of specialization in various types of disputes.[28] But the basic structure is always the same, organized around three main poles, geographically concentrated in the Paris bar association as well as in the Hauts-de-Seine bar whose jurisdiction includes *La Défense* business district west of Paris where most large French corporations have their headquarters. The first pole is constituted by the former legal departments of the Big Four accounting and audit firms, which were formally separated from their parent entities in the wake of the Enron

---

25. Data compiled by DayOne consulting firm which tracks "trends in the law marketplace," essentially based on a close reading of the professional press. See "Dix ans de mouvements d'avocats associés," http://www.village-justice.com/.

26. Powell, "La nouvelle presse juridique et les métiers du droit."

27. On this, see Lucien Karpik, *Valuing the Unique: The Economics of Singularities* (Princeton, NJ: Princeton University Press, 2010).

28. Christian Bessy, *L'organisation des activités des avocats* (Paris: LGDJ, 2015).

affair. Today, they remain concentrated in the Hauts-de-Seine bar that owes its reputation as the "premier business bar in France" to their membership.[29] These firms include Ernst & Young with its eponymous law firm; Landwell & Associés, recently renamed PwC-société d'avocats; Taj, linked to the Deloitte firm; and Fidal, the French top business law firm in volume of billings as well as in the number of lawyers.[30] The second pole of the business bar is made up of international corporate law firms, the great majority of which are Anglo-American (Baker & McKenzie, Cleary Gottlieb Stein & Hamilton, Clifford Chance, Orrick Rambaud Martel, Willkie Farr & Gallagher, etc.). There are also several "national champions" in this field, of which Gide and CMS Bureau Francis Lefebvre (close to a hundred partners each); like their Anglo-American counterparts, they are implanted in many countries, including a strong rooting in northern Africa, and count up to a hundred partners each. Third come medium-sized corporate law firms, most often French, with fewer staff and branches abroad, more specialized positioning, and most often led by the "patrician elite" of the Paris business bar, in the image of Bredin Prat, Darrois Villey, or Veil Jourde (between fifteen and fifty partners).[31] While it remains difficult to determine the exact proportions of this business bar within the legal profession, there can be no doubt about its economic success. The total volume of estimated billings for the top one hundred business law firms has grown by 41 percent over the last decade, from 2.46 to 3.47 billion euros in 2013.[32] In the "discreet hierarchy" of the legal profession, that connects fields of legal specialization (fiscal, financial crime, international, intellectual property, etc.), type of clientele, and level of revenue, this segment of the bar is placed at the top of the professional pyramid and possesses the rare possibility of combining good clients, substantial cases, and high income.[33] As an ultimate sign of recognition, members of this business bar, long absent from bodies representing the profession and not often seen in professional electoral campaigns for the Council of Order, have gradually acquired positions of some importance, as seen in the election of Jean-Marie Burguburu as president of the

---

29. "L'irrésistible ascension du barreau des Hauts-de-Seine," *La Gazette du palais*, September 18, 2012.

30. In 2014, Fidal had twice the gross billings (322 million euros) and twice as many staff (1,200 lawyers) as the second largest law firm in Paris.

31. On the notion of the patrician elite as applied to the legal profession, see Michael Powell, *From Patrician to Professional Elite: The Transformation of the New York City Bar Association* (New York: Sage, 1988).

32. These figures are drawn from annual questionnaire surveys of law firms conducted by the professional journal *Décideurs stratégie finance droit* (July–August 2014): 70–87.

33. On this "discreet hierarchy," see John Heinz and Edward Laumann, *Urban Lawyers: The New Social Structure of the Bar* (Chicago: University of Chicago Press, 2005).

Paris bar association (2002–2003), likewise Jean Castelain (2010–2011), whose careers are closely associated with this new facet of the profession.[34]

Between the Public Law of Business and the Private Business of Public Affairs

This portraying of the rise of Paris business bar would be incomplete if it did not take into account its many connections with the liberal and regulatory evolution of the state. In their upward trajectory, business lawyers soon encountered public institutions that were themselves in a sweeping process of change. Far from limiting the levers of public intervention, the regulatory turn taken by the state would yield above all a wider palette of instruments (including sanctions, restrictions, incentives, approvals, authorizations, nominations) through which public entities (whether French or European) determine the conditions under which private operators participate in various markets, in industry, banking, finance, health care, telecoms, and so forth. While this transformation was spread out over three decades, there was a rapid acceleration in the late 1990s, driven by the vast opening of competition of "public monopolies."[35] The public turn of EU competitive policy "away from its traditional concern with private conduct and toward the problem of government interference with the competitive process" resulted in an intense legislative activity promoting the liberalization of sectors such as telecoms, energy and transport, banking and finance, where public undertaking had been historically strong, particularly in France. The many EU legislative packages adopted from the late 1990s onward (railways packages in 2001, 2004, and 2013, postal service directives in 1997 and 2002, telecoms package in 2002, electricity sector in 1996, etc.) placed public and private firms on the same legal footing, from the point of view of authorization procedures, oversight of competition and state aid, regulations regarding mergers and acquisitions, financial operations, equity transactions, fiscal matters, and so on.

Along this hybrid public-private legal regime, a new form of public oversight of markets emerged through regulatory agencies in charge of securing undistorted competition. The development of this "public fabric of private markets" profoundly modified the structure of economic competition. It became just as

---

34. Ibid.
35. The public turn of EU competition policy characterizes the period when the European Commission moved "away from its traditional concern with private conduct and toward the problem of government interference with the competitive process" and targeted more specifically public monopolies: David Gerber, *Law and Competition in Twentieth Century Europe: Protecting Prometheus* (Oxford: Oxford University Press, 1998), 382.

important for big companies to weigh in on the rewriting of the rules and to protect, via adroit formulations, their market from new entrants as to pursue technological or commercial innovation.[36] The major economic and financial operations of corporations (divestitures, mergers and acquisitions, licensing, etc.) are now also largely legal battles, conducted simultaneously before a variety of public institutions whether they are ministries, Commission's Directorate General, regulatory agencies, specialized courts, and so forth. As they put the various political, administrative, and judicial poles of this public fabric of private markets at the core of their professional services to their corporate clients, law firms have played an essential part in the rise of both the regulatory state and the related new market for counsel and influence, at the crossroads of regulatory law and public affairs.

BETWEEN REGULATORY AND COMPLIANCE: HOW CORPORATE LAWYERS BECAME STATE EXPERTS

In a context of strong competition from other corporate counseling professions, notably certified accountants and notaries, the uninterrupted wave of legislation to liberalize and reregulate the economy has fueled an intense movement of professional innovation among Paris law firms. From regulatory to legal expertise in public-private partnerships, from transactional skills, lobbying, investor-state arbitration, and compliance to constitutional disputes, a whole set of new services developed from the 1990s onward.[37] Across their diversity, these specialties have a common trait, in that they implicate lawyers' capacity to be familiar with, to influence or advise the state, and more broadly the whole array of public institutions implicated in the regulatory turn of policies (the European Union, publicly owned companies, regulatory agencies, etc.).

The main law firms in Paris followed this trend by highlighting the multidisciplinarity that enabled them to handle this constant intermingling of public law and private law aspects in legal domains as diverse as environmental law, banking and financial services, energy infrastructure (electricity, nuclear power, etc.), transport (road, rail, air), or telecommunications. A whole new range of services was on offer as a complement to their more traditional expertise on merger and acquisitions, restructuring and insolvency, or tax. At the turn of the 1990s, public law departments started to blossom in corporate law firms. As says one partner, "public law is a full-fledged department in law firms. International

---

36. Y. Dezalay, *Marchands de droit*.

37. Unless otherwise noted, quotations in this chapter are drawn from a corpus of documents compiled from law firms' websites consulted between 2014 and 2017.

law firms understood this quite well. All Paris firms now have a team devoted to administrative law, to public-private partnerships (PPP), to public law or regulatory matters."[38] The exact contours of these departments vary from one firm to the next of course, depending on the size of the firm and its areas of specialization. In addition to tax issues, most often a department in its own right, these departments may be called "competition, European law, and economic regulations," "governments and public sector," "regulatory," "public and regulatory affairs," "French public law and government affairs practice," "major projects— PPP—public law of business," or "public law, regulatory, and competition law." But beyond these various circumstances and headings, Paris corporate law firms all now claim to be able "to handle the most complex situations involving private and public law, for business and institutional clients" and propose "services combining corporate and regulatory action." They vaunt their full range of legal services, "pre-litigation and litigation, transactional and jurisdictional, national and international," via "negotiation of complex projects on a European scale," mastery of the multiple public, legal, and financial procedures that are specific to "complex public contracts" (drafting and monitoring contracts, project finance, dispute resolution, advice on restructuring, arbitration). They also present their unique capacity to anticipate "the stakes from the point of view of national and European competition authorities (State aid) and taxation"—all of which requires deep knowledge of the EU framework and "familiarity with negotiations with the European Commission and EU agencies."

Along with this multidisciplinary legal expertise, knowledge of public institutions and their regulations have emerged as a specific subcategory of competence among business lawyers. This new specialty, often called compliance, has been promoted by a small group of *avocats d'affaires* within the Paris bar who have created a "Cercle de la Compliance" and, like Anglo-American law firms, vaunt the commercial advantages and reputational benefits obtained by companies when they adopt standards of "ethical and transparent governance" and show their good will with respect to norms of corporate ethics and social responsibility (CSR).[39] The exact shape of this new expertise is still in flux, but it is always a matter of advising companies on public regulations and criminal law related to tax fraud, discrimination, health and safety standards, environmental

---

38. Fabrice Cassin, "Entretien: Que sont-ils devenus?," *La Gazette de l'Institut de droit public des affaires* 16 (2016).

39. On the genesis of this market in deontology, see Murielle Cœurdray, "La conversion d'un savoir judiciaire en un capital symbolique au service de multinationales françaises," *Droit et société* 72 (2009): 411–32.

issues, personal data, corruption and money laundering, business ethics, and so forth. The heavy sentences levied on French and German companies by United States regulatory authorities,[40] and the growing number of international covenants and initiatives in these domains have spurred consolidation of new expertise based on knowledge of public standards. (Internationally, these measures include the Foreign Corrupt Practices Act adopted by the United States in the late 1970s, the UK Bribery Act of 2010, the G20 Anti-corruption Action Plan, and the anti-corruption clause of the International Chamber of Commerce, among others. Within France, the so-called Sapin II Law on Economic Crimes of November 2016 consolidated this "compliance turn" making the implementation of compliance programmes legally binding for firms, and creating a French antibribery agency to control the implementation of compliance programmes within companies).

In the palette of new public law services, law firms have also invested in an expertise in constitutional law in the context of the opening in July 2008 of a new legal procedure before the *Conseil constitutionnel*, the so-called *Question prioritaire de constitutionnalité* (QPC) that allows citizens and legal persons that are party to a lawsuit to ask the *Conseil constitutionnel* to review whether the law applied in the case is constitutional. It may seem surprising to come across the *avocats d'affaires* in the halls of the constitutional court at Palais-Royal. After all, this leading measure of the revised French constitution adopted in July 2008, came initially charged with vast *political* promise. By opening this new constitutional review procedure, it was expected that the debate over "rights and freedoms guaranteed by the Constitution" would no longer be left to opposition members of Parliament (who can request a constitutional review immediately after the vote of a new law) or constitutional law professors (who traditionally send memos to the *Conseil*). As civil society would be able to directly intervene before the *Conseil constitutionnel*, the latter would hence become the "protective shield of the essential rights of the Republic," and even the instrument of a "continuous democracy" that shifts the balance of power to the benefit of the citizenry.

In matter of fact, this new constitutional stage was soon the scene of much activity. In just over five years, some ten thousand QPCs have been registered. Although few cases ultimately come before the constitutional court,[41] it nonetheless

---

40. See the 2014 case in which BNP Paribas was fined 60 million euros by the United States for fraudulent use of public aid.

41. *Questions prioritaires de constitutionnalité* have to be sent first before the *Conseil d'État* or the *Cour de cassation* who act as filters and only send the "most serious cases" over to the *Conseil constitutionnel*.

rules on between sixty and eighty questions each year. A "constitutional reflex" has taken root. Few detailed studies have yet been conducted on this issue, but many signs indicate that business lawyers, more than any other group, have found this terrain to be propitious for their litigation strategies. Previously, they had no particular reason to take an interest in the Constitution or the jurisprudence of the *Conseil constitutionnel*. But the considerable potential of the new legal recourse rapidly gave them cause to rethink. Compared with ordinary legal procedures, the QPC is inexpensive, very simple, and extremely fast (under six months). And it can be formidably effective, going as far as pure and simple dismissal of the case. The EADS trial spectacularly revealed the potential of QPC procedure. This high-profile corporate inquiry brought German carmaker Daimler and the French media conglomerate Lagardère to criminal court on allegations of insider trading in the 2006 sale of shares in the European aerospace and defense group EADS. In October 2014, as the trial had barely started, EADS lawyers filed a QPC claiming that the "non bis in idem" principle (a principle drawn from article 8 of the French *Déclaration des droits de l'homme et du citoyen*)[42] had not been respected given that the finance regulation agency had already settled the case in 2009, thereby leading to the suspension of the trial to wait for a decision of the *Conseil constitutionnel* in the case. In March 2015, *Conseil constitutionnel* proved defense lawyers right with the immediate effect that the EADS trial was definitively called off, suddenly bringing it to an end.

This spectacular cancellation of this decade-long set of judicial inquiries confirmed that the "Rights and freedoms guaranteed by the Constitution" were becoming an integral part of business lawyers' litigation arsenal. These business lawyers did not stop short with a desultory appeal to economic freedoms (the freedom of enterprise, property rights, contractual freedom). They also frequently invoked the fundamental principles of the procedure, in the name of equality, or articles of the Declaration of the Rights of Man and the Citizen (1789), to contest variously the General Tax Code, or the Monetary and Financial Code, or the Labor Code. And here, there seem to be infinite possibilities as the QPC made it possible for the first time to question the constitutionality of all statute laws—in particular the ones that predated the Fifth Republic or had so far escaped the control of the constitutional court.[43]

---

42. Article 8 of the 1789 *Déclaration des droits de l'homme et du citoyen* states that: "The Law must prescribe only the punishments that are strictly and evidently necessary; and no one may be punished except by virtue of a Law drawn up and promulgated before the offense is committed, and legally applied."

43. Before the institution of the *Question prioritaire de constitutionnalité* in 2010, the constitutional review *exclusively* concerned statute laws that had just been adopted by the Parliament

While tax lawyers were initially the most active, the practice rapidly spread to all business law, leading to the emergence of a *droit constitutionnel des affaires*. Law firms were quick to include this specialty in the list of services offered to their clients.[44] Armed with constitutional expertise that they fortified on occasion by recruiting former members of the *Conseil d'État* or the *Conseil constitutionnel*, these firms are now in a position to pursue long-term legal strategies, deciphering the inflections of this highly technical jurisprudence, immediately seizing the opportunities it offers, and now and again attempting innovative and even risky stratagems that might consolidate this *droit public des affaires* that they have so actively brought into existence.

As the state pursues its liberal and regulatory evolution, this new constitutional area of dispute around rights and freedoms offers in proportion a great many possibilities to private players, who can directly take part in redefining the role of public institutions in market governance.[45] This reshapes the form of a constitutional trial, which had long been beyond the reach of the influence wielded by corporations and interest groups. Previously they had been obliged to channel their interests through the *portes étroites*, a term designating the informal practice of firms, interest groups, or NGOs to send legal briefs to the *Conseil constitutionnel* when Parliament or the executive branch solicited the *Conseil*'s verdict on a piece of legislation.[46] Far from leading the *Conseil constitutionnel* to take on grand decisions on issues of human rights, the QPC seems to have above all created a new battlefield of microconstitutional issues with considerable legal and economic effects in the areas of taxation and corporate law, as well as on the capacity of government agencies (Ministry of the Economy, competition regulatory agency, etc.) to regulate markets.[47] In giving business lawyers an additional opportunity to weigh on public regulation of the economy, "the QPC has little

---

(so-called a priori review before promulgation), thereby impeding retroactive questioning of the constitutionality of the statute laws.

44. "Les avocats mobilisés sur la Question prioritaire de constitutionnalité," *Lettre des juristes d'affaires*, June 7, 2010.

45. See "Question prioritaire de constitutionnalité et droit des affaires," *Les Petites affiches*, September 2011.

46. In an interesting journalistic investigation of the so-called *portes étroites* practice, Mathilde Mathieu reports that no less than twenty-four briefs were submitted by law professors and law firms with regard to the so-called Macron Act for economic growth and equal opportunity of August 6, 2015. Mathilde Mathieu, "Dans les coulisses du Conseil constitutionnel, cible des lobbies," Médiapart (blog), October 12, 2015.

47. On this, see Stéphanie Hennette-Vauchez, "Les droits et libertés que la constitution garantit: *Quiproquo* sur la Question prioritaire de constitutionnalité?," *Revue des droits de l'homme* 10 (2016).

by little changed the balance of power between companies and public bodies," as recently noted by a member of the *Conseil d'État*.[48]

WIELDING INFLUENCE

In this new context, with public regulation at the heart of law firms' expertise, the patrician elite of the Paris bar had some cards in their hands, starting with their long-standing ties with regulators. By virtue of their social and professional proximity to national political, administrative, and judicial elites, the first generation of Paris *avocats d'affaires* (Jeantet; Loyrette; Bredin, Prat; Darrois; Veil; among others) were in good position to take advantage of this public turn of the bar.[49] Along the path of their trajectories, often starting with their prestigious high schools, and then higher education, in particular at Sciences Po, and the select clubs of the power elite (for example *Le Cercle interallié* or *Le Siècle*, to which Jean Loyrette and Jean Veil belonged), they established strong personal ties that often extended later on into the terrain of legal counsel and defense. For instance, Jean-Michel Darrois, founding partner of one of the principal business law firms in Paris, is a longtime friend of former prime minister and current president of the *Conseil constitutionnel*, Laurent Fabius, whom he knows from their days at Sciences Po, and Darrois took on his defense in the late 1990s in the contaminated blood products trial before the *Cour de justice de la République* (*ad hoc* court established to try cases of ministerial misconduct). He also willingly acknowledges that he has long been close to Alain Minc, a longtime influential member of the French banking elite, who "really helped" him by giving his name "as the first choice when he was asked for the name of a lawyer."[50] While it may be difficult to systematically account for the role of social capital in securing one's central position in the business bar, family capital can act as a proxy. It is hard not to note the pervasive presence among prominent *avocats d'affaires* of key French legal dynasties that possess, in various proportions and degrees depending on the generation and siblings, experience in public service, the private sector, the judiciary and academia. Suffice it to consider the family pedigree of this managing partner of an important Paris law firm whose parents were both members of the *Conseil d'État*, whose grandmother was a prominent international law professor, and great-grandfather, president of the

---

48. Charles Touboul, "Juger l'action économique, c'est encore agir sur l'économie," *Revue française de droit administratif* 1 (2016): 83.

49. On the notion of the patrician elite in the legal profession, we refer readers to Powell, *From Patrician to Professional Elite.*

50. Jean-Michel Darrois, quoted in Christophe Perrin and Laurence Gaune, eds., *Parcours d'avocat(e)s* (Paris: Le Cavalier bleu, 2010), 43.

International Court of Justice. Another illustration is a partner in the Jeantet firm, one of the most prominent competition law lawyers in Paris, who is the sister of a former minister of cultural affairs, daughter of a member of the *Conseil d'État* and granddaughter of a law professor who was one of the four judges at Nuremberg. No wonder why the professional press points at the fact that "her proximity to public players is one of her assets."[51]

However, as legal and public affairs counseling professionalized, this capital of relationships in the heart of the political, administrative, and judiciary elite was no longer sufficient. The arrival of US and UK law firms challenged the traditionally central position of the patricians of the Paris bar. The former could claim a competitive advantage on their mastery of the various national and international sites of public regulation; and a capacity to wield influence across the *whole* normative process, from drafting legislative bills and amendments, to the implementation of rules via lobbying of government ministries and regulatory bodies, and ensuring legal assistance and representation in national and European courts. As these law firms positioned themselves as veritable hubs, offering multiple avenues of contact with regulators (whether judges, legislators, or bureaucrats), they contributed to the professionalizing of the traditional roles of counsel and influence.[52] The historical business law firms of the Paris bar initially coldly spurned the more aggressive lobbyist strategies of the multinational law firms that were so contrary to the traditional mores of the profession, but they soon had to adapt to the new reality. They chose to highlight their competence in terms of niche and luxury products, describing themselves variously as the "Rolls-Royce of competition" or "a house of legal *haute couture* [sic]," and in turn engaged in the new lobbying practices developed by American and British lawyers. Symbolizing this shift, in May 2011, five of the most solid firms of the Paris business bar (August & Debouzy, Granrut Société d'avocats, Jeantet associés, Lexidia Société d'avocats, and Vogel & Vogel) formed the *Association des avocats lobbyistes* (AAL) "to encourage and foster lobbying practices in the profession." The same year lobbying was given full recognition and included in the activities listed in the "national internal rules" of the profession, following the impetus given by business lawyer Jean Castelain, as he became president of the Paris bar association.[53]

---

51. "La fidèle: Loraine Donnedieu de Vabres," *Lettre des juristes d'affaires*, December 15, 2008, 46–50.

52. Laurens, *Bureaucrats and Business Lobbyists*.

53. "Les avocats et le lobbying: Un gisement d'opportunités," *Le Monde du droit*, February 1, 2008; Philippe Portier, "Des avocats revendiquent (enfin?) leur rôle de lobbyistes," *Option Droit & Affaires*, June 8, 2011.

And so, the new multidisciplinary range of services grew to include "administrative and parliamentary lobbying in the interest of private businesses as well as public entities, such as local authorities." One of the founders of AAL, a partner in one of the principal business law firms in Paris, explains lobbying by lawyers in these terms: "Providing counsel to a client stops with the case file; it is legal advice. Lobbying goes beyond the lawyer/client relationship. When I advise a client I give information on the legal framework of an investment, I draw up contracts, I negotiate the contract with a third party. When I tell a client that we are going to lobby for their issue, it goes much farther. There is not just one interlocutor—the lawyer for the other party. Instead there are multiple targets: we tell the client we are going to tackle them all together—we attack the politicians, the administration, other interest groups. This means 'attack' in quotes: we concentrate our forces to persuade them. Lobbying is an extension of legal counsel."[54] One firm proposes "to intercede with administrative offices, the government and Parliament before legislation and regulations are issued, to construct legal arguments in support of our clients' interests, to present them to authorities and transpose them into proposals for bills or amendments." Another firm with a worldwide presence presents its public policy department in these terms: it "regularly advises clients on the European and British legislative process, starting with the choice of procedure, timing of legislation, stages of parliamentary work and the institutions involved. It is essential to understand the context in order to influence emerging legislation. Political intelligence, monitoring, the legislative process and drafting of documents, corporate strategy and risk evaluation, early knowledge of regulatory developments, the capacity to alert clients to the implications of government proposals, etc." It should be said however that the professionalization of lobbying has in no way impeded the more traditional forms of influence, which remain in place, often entrusted to former political figures who are called upon to act as intermediaries and to ensure the conciliation that may be necessary when negotiating and executing large international contracts. The press has reported on these special quasi-diplomatic assignments carried out by figures who are often former ministers, for instance Pascal Clément, who joined a firm whose principal partner stated that the new arrival "excelled particularly in defending the interests of French companies and major corporate groups in their sometimes rocky relationships with certain foreign States." Likewise, the connections of former prime minister Dominique de Villepin or former *Élysée* secretary general at the time of Sarkozy's presidency, Claude Guéant, both of them turned

---

54. Interview quoted in Coraline Schornstein, *Les Avocats-lobbyistes: Émergence, légitimité, incertitudes* (Master's thesis, Université Paris 2, 2015), 53.

business lawyers, have proved to be useful to French companies, accompanying them in international negotiations, notably in the context of mediation between French companies and foreign states, especially with French-speaking Africa, in strategic sectors such as energy, oil, and telecommunications[55].

CREDENTIALIZING THE CORPORATE BAR'S PUBLIC-SPIRITEDNESS

As the proximity between corporate law firms and political, administrative, and judicial authorities has become a prime field for competition between firms, they have developed full-blown strategies to build a reputation of "public-ness." These strategies range from snatching up former regulators (political figures, high-level civil servants, judges, etc.) to vaunting the civic merits of the firm (support for the sciences, philanthropic action, pro bono work, etc.), or taking an active part to public debates through memos, op-eds, bill proposals, and so forth.

There is no point in distinguishing here between brand development and acquisition of professional expertise and so on. In the environment of the business bar, the symbolic and the economic are closely intertwined. As a matter of fact, the race to acquire symbolic capital attesting to a civic and disinterested stance is one of the areas in which economic competition within the business bar has grown more intense.[56] The international law firms have invested heavily in building a reputation in the public sector, hoping to appear well connected to national regulators, on the same footing as the Paris firms. Even the choice of geographic location in the French capital marks their desire to display closeness to the seats of power. Looking for legitimacy on the political and administrative plane, the Anglo-American firms set up offices in palatial surroundings that vie with those of the government, and turned to the most prominent architects (such as Wilmotte and Portzamparc, among others) to fit them out. Like White & Case, Clifford Chance opened its office on the Place Vendôme in 2010, just opposite the Justice Ministry building. Thus it was just a symbolic step across the street when Laurent Vallée, a member of the *Conseil d'État*, left the firm in April 2010 to become the head of Civil Law Department at the ministry. In another example, DayJones rents premises that used to house the United States consulate at the Place de la Concorde, and greets

---

55. Emeline Cazi and Ariane Chemin, "Un businessman nommé Villepin," *Le Monde*, January 11, 2013.

56. On these markets in which symbolic valuation plays an essential role, see Julien Duval, "Les enjeux symboliques des échanges économiques," *Revue française de socio-économie* 10, no. 2 (2012): 13–28.

clients in the room where Napoleon's foreign affairs minister, Talleyrand, died, as one of the firm's partners proudly told us.

This quest also includes action to showcase the civic spirit and public virtues of the firms. While this type of engagement used to be individual and discreet, and directly correlated to the respectability inherent to the professions, investment in a disinterested civic image and reputation is now handled by the firms themselves, and is an essential feature of their signature. In the way of the Hogan Lovells firm that displays its civic commitment, business law firms sponsor the arts, make donations to humanitarian groups, contribute to action to protect the environment, and support scientific research by funding dissertation awards or endowing chairs in academic institutions. French firms pursue the same ends, like the Gide firm that has created its own "Gide Pro Bono" fund and emphasizes its corporate social responsibility policy. In this way, lawyers' civic commitment typical of the *barreau classique* (legal aid, income-scaled fees, etc.) has been replaced by pro bono policies imported from the world of American law firms, and which are part and parcel of the firm's communication policy.[57]

In this light, we can see clearly why being chosen to advise the state also has critical symbolic importance for these firms. By building close ties to public institutions, these law firms gain access to a new clientele, of course, but they also construct a valuable reputation that has currency, and at a good price, with their private-sector clients. In 1986, when the Gide firm was hired to help the Ministry of the Economy draft privatization bills, its founding partner Jean Loyrette complained of the financial conditions of this collaboration: "all these operations are not very profitable; the Treasury is stingy," he confided to *Le Monde*, but he later recognized that "these operations are prestigious, and we hope for returns."[58] The publicity accorded to experience in the public sector, an essential aspect of law firms' commercial strategy, is intended to attract private companies who deal with public entities, just as much as it is addressed to an institutional clientele looking for legal services. This is seen in the fact that the firms' websites and promotional literature underscore their knowledge of and work for the public sector. White & Case proudly announces a partner "who is regularly consulted by public authorities for presentation of new legislative bills"; Clifford Chance states that "the firm is highly appreciated and serves a broad range of eminent

---

57. Robert Granfield and Lynn Mather, eds., *Private Lawyers and the Public Interest: The Evolving Role of Pro Bono in the Legal Profession* (Oxford: Oxford University Press, 2009). On pro bono in France, see Charles Bosvieux-Onyekwelu, "Profit, temps d'emploi et plus-value morale: Le travail *pro bono* dans les multinationales du droit en France," *Socio-économie du travail* 60, no. 4 (2019).

58. Jean Loyrette quoted in "Ubiquistes avocats," *Le Monde*, November 25, 1986.

clients, including several European States, and [advises] the European Financial Stability Facility on sovereign debt"; Gide proudly claims to be "the habitual advisor of the State and major public establishments." This display of public expertise is now reflected in the internal organization of the firms, which have progressively made room for poles devoted to "Public and regulatory affairs," "Public law," "Public economic law and competition law," "Public, regulatory, and competition affairs," "Compliance," somehow mirroring the very structure of French and European public institutions. Some firms speak of their "regulatory activity," others of their services related to "the French Directorate General for Competition, Consumption and Repression of Fraud," or to "representation before French regulatory authorities (*Agence de régulation des communications électroniques et des postes,* CRE, *Conseil supérieur de l'audiovisuel,* ARAF, AFSSAPS, CEPS, etc.)." Still others mention their expertise in global governmental relations, or "counsel and representation of sovereign States," the basis for "assistance to countries, their government ministries and public entities" with respect to debt, privatization, and "regulatory system" restructuring. Positioning themselves as veritable "auxiliaries of public service," to quote one firm's website, the firms claim to be equipped to advise states in all their steps of organizational transformation and policy (selling shares of state-owned companies, creation of new structures, and modernization of procedures at all levels—statutes, agencies, and human resources).

Building a reputation of proximity with political, administrative, and judicial elites appears as a key competitive advantage. Consider this introduction that opens the Veil Jourde website: "What do people think of us? That we know how to handle the most complex situations, and that we know a great many public and private-sector players who direct or oversee business activity."[59] Or the rankings and awards based on opinions expressed by professional peers (*The American Lawyer, Legal 500, Chambers Europe,* etc.); for instance the Bredin Prat tax department is credited with "unparalleled transaction expertise and excellent relations with fiscal authorities."

It is in this framework that in the 1990s firms began to compete vigorously to recruit from among the ranks of political and administrative elites.[60] A survey of all moves and transfers by partners shows that for the period 2006–2014 more than one-third (34 percent) of outside hires came from political and administrative sectors, a quite substantial proportion, even when compared to the

---

59. Home page of the Veil Jourde law firm website, accessed December 2018.

60. Frédéric Foucard, "Le recrutement de personnalités chez les professionnels du droit," *Droit et patrimoine,* May 1993, 74.

52 percent of hires from the legal departments of private companies.[61] Once again, the Gide firm is a precursor in this respect; in the last two decades, the firm has hired an *inspecteur des finances*, four members of the *Conseil d'État*, a member of the *Cour des comptes*, a former president of the Paris Administrative Court, a former minister of foreign affairs, a former deputy secretary general of the political party, a president of the then majority party in the National Assembly, and three former members of the cabinets of EU commissioners. This accumulation of political and administrative capital has no doubt contributed to the singular status of the Gide firm, which has become over the years "not a law firm, but an institution," in the words of one of our interviewees (interview no. 14, man, *Conseil d'État*, ENA graduate, public law).[62] Initially, the fact of taking on an *énarque* (graduates of the *École nationale d'administration*, ENA) was most likely a matter of distinction, reserved for the most prominent firms; one of our respondents noted the following about a big Paris firm in the 1990s: "[the founder of the firm] wanted a member of each of the elite corps. He already had the *Cour des comptes*, he wanted someone from the *Conseil d'État*, and he had his eye on a fellow from the *Inspection des finances*," France's three state *grands corps*. Progressively, the hiring of a high-level civil servant became a mandatory step for the firms that claimed to be full-service law firms: "Nowadays, for a certain number of firms, they have to have their *conseiller d'État*, and clients demand it as well. I've heard clients, they want there to be one in the team" (interview no. 9, man, *Conseil d'État*, ENA graduate, public law).

BOX 1. / August & Debouzy, a regal law firm

August & Debouzy is often presented as a success story of the Paris bar. The firm started with six lawyers in 1995, and now numbers over one hundred. The firm was born out of an atypical association between a thirty-three-year-old ENA graduate, Olivier Debouzy, and a young business lawyer, Gilles August, educated at ESSEC business school and in an American law school. Debouzy had a brief career at the Foreign Affairs Ministry and at the Atomic Energy State Agency; he died prematurely in 2010. The founders both claimed to be inspired by "the Washington model of law firms," and presented "administrative and parliamentary lobbying" as one of their prime areas of

---

61. The survey conducted by the DayOne consulting firm is not without bias, because it is based solely on data from the professional press, which tends to underrepresent "escapees" from technical sectors and pay more attention to hires from the upper echelons of the administration and political positions. See DayOne, "Dix ans de mouvements d'avocats associés," 2015, https://www.dayone-consulting.com/fr-actualites-paris/10-ans-de-mouvements-davocats-associes/.

62. Excerpts from our interviews are tagged to indicate the gender of the correspondent, the state professional graduate school (*École nationale d'administration, École nationale des impôts*), possible membership to *Conseil d'État*, and specialization in law practice (tax, competition, etc.).

competence:[63] August & Debouzy represents the interests of companies before French and EU administrations and legislators, and "proposes to companies its array of cutting-edge competence in all fields of corporate law, public law and lobbying."[64] As the firm's website indicates, one of its specific assets has been the systematic recruitment of high-level politicians and bureaucrats: "thanks to the various areas of expertise and competence of its lawyers, several of whom have held political or administrative responsibilities, August & Debouzy advises companies and professional groups, monitoring the legislative and regulatory changes that affect their business or activity."

The son of a former close associate of former French president Jacques Chirac, and "firmly right-wing," Gilles August had Claude Chirac (Jacques Chirac's daughter) as a client when he was still at his first firm. More recently, he was "close to Dominique Strauss-Kahn, and lawyer for (former minister) Jérôme Cahuzac."[65] As for his partner, Olivier Debouzy, member of the *Le Siècle* elite club, he maintained close ties in the political and administrative milieux throughout his career as lawyer. A member of the consultative council at RAND Corporation Europe (1999–2006), he participated in the work of the expert committee that produced the government's white paper on nuclear power in 1993, and was a member of the group of experts for the white paper on defense in 2008; at one point, the press mentioned him as a possible director of the *Direction générale de la sécurité extérieure*.[66] This strong implantation in the defense industry enabled the firm to handle, for instance, the transformation of the DCN (French industrial group specialized in naval defense) into a private company backed by public capital, in 2003. At the reception held at the Palais de Chaillot for the fifteenth anniversary of the law firm in 2010, guests could rub elbows with chief of defense, Admiral Edouard Guillaud, with Admiral Alain Oudot de Dainville, chairman of ODAS (a formerly state-owned turned private company in charge of promotion of French exports in the domain of defense, security, and high-tech fields), "the reorganization of which had been piloted by August & Debouzy," and with Charles Edelstenne, CEO of Dassault Aviation (an international French aircraft company with strong specialization in defense).[67]

The firm's "Public, regulatory and environment" pole also came to be over the years a privileged point of entry through which high-level civil servants joined the business bar. Among these were three ambassadors, a former prime minister, a former director of the cabinet of the minister of defense, a former prefect, a former cabinet director to President Nicolas Sarkozy, and so on. Far from being hidden, this back-and-forth circulation is emphasized as a distinctive trait of the firm. As put forward on the law firm's website: "August & Debouzy has always chosen lawyers from a broad range of backgrounds: former heads of companies, ministers and ambassadors, high-level civil servants, etc." This rich diversity of profiles, strategically chosen among conservative as well as socialist ranks, has "shaped the firm's signature: to give our clients more than just the law."[68]

---

63. http://www.august-debouzy.com/, accessed December 2018.
64. Ibid.
65. "Gilles August et associés, un cabinet très politique," *Le Monde*, December 21, 2012.
66. *Le Point*, April 19, 2010.
67. *La lettre A*, October 8, 2010.
68. http://www.august-debouzy.com, accessed December 2018.

The major international and Paris business law firms have since then continually had recourse to those who are in a position to have special access to politics and government, and who have firsthand knowledge of courts' internal dynamics (whether judicial, administrative, constitutional, European). The gains to be had by hiring former public decision makers are not limited to the address books compiled in the course of political and administrative functions, as is often asserted. These hires are also part of promotion and communication strategies that aim to bolster the image of the firms "that can afford an *énarque*." When in 2009 Orrick Rambaud Martel hired Alain Juillet, a former civil servant in charge of economic intelligence, shortly after having welcomed the former minister of justice Pascal Clément, the international firm announced its strong Paris implantation: "these profiles ideally fill out our service offer, and anchor our brand more firmly at the local level." Likewise, the powers of influence and persuasion usually attributed to former public decision makers can prove especially useful for the new lobbying activities undertaken by business law firms. The hiring of high-level civil servants also signifies the purchase of the technical competence acquired in the course their careers—legislative drafting, regulatory practice, oversight missions, jurisdictional functions, and so forth. In short, law firms have many good reasons to hire these "escapees": access to political and administrative networks, expertise in bureaucracy, authoritativeness, brand reputation, and so on. Again, it would be pointless to distinguish between skills and technical know-how, and similar, that might be truly needed by the firms, and what might be purely symbolic and reputational, as the two facets are continuously intertwined in the specific economy of law firms in that changing context. In interviews, many civil-servants-turned-lawyers cite in particular their capacity to understand how an administration works and to navigate through it, and their practical mastery of the rules and mores specific to the various sectors of public action. It is not solely a "commerce of relationships [but also] a deep knowledge of administrations and their psychology. One does not approach an administration at the top of one's voice, for example" (interview no. 19, man, *Conseil d'État*, ENA graduate, public law). This is emphasized by a former tax inspector: "It would be a mistake to think that they are buying an address book. This might be the case for certain very political profiles, but I don't have a political profile, I have a technical profile, and it is not at all my address book that they bought. . . . And it would be an error to do so, because in the administration people do move around quite a lot, and someone's address book, I don't know how long it would be valid, but certainly no more than three to five years at the most. . . . Internal knowledge of the administration, how it functions, is what counts . . . knowing how competences are distributed, sometimes along quite fine lines, between two different offices. Knowing, for instance, that an issue will fall within the purview of two offices in the central administration. That means, right off the bat, that it will take more time for the administration to react. And that is something you can say straight away to your client" (interview no. 11, man, ENI graduate, tax law). All these facets, from practical knowledge to address book and specific expertise all converge to underscore the increasing *convertibility* of the currency of resources and titles acquired in the service of the state in the business law.

All in all, the business bar that has grown up in the past two decades was not constituted *against* the state, but close alongside the very structure of the state, directly linked to its transformation, as a sort of exoskeleton of the regulatory state. Far from being exclusively entrepreneurial, the business bar continuously takes great pains to display its "public-ness" whether by promoting public virtues, exhibiting privileged relationships with government agencies, claiming an intimate knowledge of the political and administrative apparatus, and so forth. This public turn of the business bar has been all the more far-reaching in that it has played out in the time of the neoliberal turn of state policies.

The Public Sector's Private Business

The "Golden Age" of France's interventionist state is already a thing of the past. The hold that the state exercised over the French economy up to the end of the 1980s, through a substantial public sector in industry and banking, is no more. A first wave of privatization dealt a blow in August 1986, amputating sixty-five enterprises from the state (in particular banks and insurance companies), followed by a second in July 1993, with partial divestiture of twenty-one public companies in the field of transports (Air France), banking (BNP), energy (Elf), and by many others ever since. The deployment of the European single market certainly amplified this movement, triggering a powerful wave of liberalization of the telecommunications, energy, and transport sectors, and constraining the ability of the state to grant financial aid to "its" enterprises. Henceforth, the validity of state aid as defined by the European Commission and the Court of Justice of the European Union has been assessed according to the yardstick of the "private investor's test," in the name of strict equality between public and private operators. The very status of *établissement public*, a key legal category for public entities with commercial activities, is itself problematic in the eyes of EU institutions because it is assimilated to a form of state aid by the "implicit State guarantee" it conveys.[69] In addition, the European Commission's powerful Competition Directorate General consolidated a doctrine of "competitive neutrality" whereby state-owned undertakings had to be taken to the same competitive standards as private companies (for the sake of securing a level-playing market) with very few and restrictive exceptions that can be made in the "public interest."

However, these multiple realignments do not signify that public institutions have withdrawn from the economic sphere. Rather, they are the sign of a profound redeployment of the forms and justification of public intervention, which are henceforth more focused on regulation of private markets and oversight of eventual market distortion, than on coordination of a mixed economy.[70] In the wake of the December 1986 Government Order (*ordonnance*) on free competition, public institutions now are positioned above all as guardians to enforce "respect for the rules across the entire economy, without exception."[71] This new relationship to markets does not exclude Parliament and the central administration. But it does tend to circumscribe their role, transferring prerogatives to regulatory agencies that are maintained beyond the reach of the administrative hierarchy and parliamentary control. These agencies have indeed established privileged relationships with market actors, and with professional intermediaries, whether lawyers or consultants. In their quest to distance themselves from the traditional administrative style, and to establish a reputation of independence with respect to their former ministries' departments, the new agencies such as the finance regulation agency, the *Autorité des marchés financiers*, or the competition agency, the *Autorité de la concurrence*, just to name the two most important ones, have increasingly relied on the regulated sectors and on their legal representatives. The same is true for a good number of administrations themselves, eager to establish their credibility as market operators on an equal footing with the others, in public procurement as well as equity and financial operations. To do so, they have recourse to market intermediaries to secure their interventions in the private sector. In sum, far from being a free-standing phenomenon, constructed in a vacuum, the regulatory turn of the state has spawned new patterns of relations with professions and actors in the private sector, first and foremost business lawyers.

---

69. See Dominique Ritleng, "L'influence du droit de l'Union européenne sur les catégories organiques du droit administratif," in *Traité de droit administratif européen*, 2nd ed. (Brussels: Bruylant, 2014), 1063–88.

70. See particularly Henry and Pierru, "Les consultants et la réforme des services publics."

71. Bruno Lasserre, president of the *Autorité de la concurrence*, hearing before the Senate Inquiry Commission; Jacques Mézard, *Un État dans l'État: Canaliser la prolifération des autorités administratives indépendantes pour mieux les contrôler*. Paris: Sénat, 2015.

The State's Private Counsels

The recourse to private consultants by the government and, even more so, by a vast array of public entities (EU institutions, state-owned companies, regulatory agencies, and local government) is a first tracer of this neoliberal turn of policies. Truly enough, political science literature has long held that the *grands corps* in France put up resistance to the intrusion of consulting firms in the realm of the state, in contrast to the situation in Britain according to this analysis. Indeed, for a long time the French state made very little use of private consultant services. This does not mean that the state did not rely on a multitude of private channels and connections to regulate markets. Throughout the nineteenth century, Paris Chamber of Commerce and Industry, a body representing private firms, was the main supplier of economic expertise to public institutions such as the *Conseil d'État*, the Parliament, and government administrations that did not possess their own expertise.[72] But the law and lawyers have long remained marginal in this consulting market. Ministries might on occasion call upon the expertise of professors at the Paris law faculty, notably in civil and commercial law, or in the framework of large-scale private arbitration proceedings.[73] Likewise, and still today, the legal representation of the state before international courts is entrusted solely to the litigation department at the *Quai d'Orsay*.[74] As for the State Judicial Office (*Agence judiciaire de l'Etat*), the legal department in charge of representing the state before ordinary tribunals, this entity uses *avocats* only for a few recurrent cases of litigation.

BUSINESS LAWYERS AS STATE'S AGENTS

With the rising wave of consulting activity, however, the dikes began to crumble in the early years of the twenty-first century. Very little data is available that would allow us to assess the magnitude of the phenomenon, as amply shown by the difficulties encountered by the *Cour des comptes* itself when it sought to draw up an inventory of private consulting services employed by the state.[75] Famously,

---

72. Lemercier, *Un si discret pouvoir*.

73. Antoine Vauchez, "Quand les juristes faisaient la loi: Le 'moment Carbonnier' (1963–1977), son histoire et son mythe," *Parlement(s)* 11 (2009): 105–15.

74. The French state differs in this respect from other states like Great Britain or the Netherlands, which frequently entrust their defense to law firms. See Marie-Pierre Granger, "From the Margins of the European Legal Field: The Governments' Agents and Their Influence on the Development of European Union Law," in *Lawyering Europe: European Law as a Transnational Social Field*, ed. Antoine Vauchez and Bruno de Witte (Oxford: Hart, 2013), 55–74.

75. Cour des comptes, *Le Recours par l'État aux conseils extérieurs: Rapport à la commission des finances de l'État* (Paris: La Documentation française, 2014).

the Directorate General for Modernization of the State has entrusted various firms, including Capgemini, with the task of monitoring the implementation of its broad review of public expenditure from 2007 onward (the so-called *Révision générale des politiques publiques*).[76] But more important, what the 2014 report of the *Cour des comptes* eventually showed was that the government relied on outside consultants—law firms, financial advisers, or public affairs consultancies—in a large variety of domains from audit and evaluation to strategic financial counsel, communication, legal expertise, and so forth.

A full-fledged history of the state's recourse to private counseling remains to be written. However, privatizations certainly played a central role in fueling the rise of a whole counseling industry. The first act of this new deal opened in the autumn of 1981.[77] The Socialist Party had just come to power, and undertook a program to nationalize the banking and industrial sectors on a scale not seen since the Liberation. Weakened by its electoral defeat and internal divisions, the political right went into the parliamentary battle to fight the nationalization legislation in unfavorable circumstances. Giving it their all, the right wing called upon the lawyer Jean Loyrette, whom we saw fifteen years earlier in our account, when he had just founded the Gide Loyrette Nouel firm. Meanwhile, he had become one of the best specialists of the new equity techniques born in the late 1960s, especially in the field of takeover bids. When consulted by the leaders of the opposition in Parliament, his proposal was to take the dispute over the fair compensation of the "expropriated" private shareholders before international jurisdictions. In a fat two-volume opus entitled *Le Problème des nationalisations*, which would later form the basis for the opposition's filing against the nationalization law before the *Conseil constitutionnel*, Loyrette denounced the insufficient indemnities offered to shareholders, and threatened the new socialist government with multiple international trials if the foreign subsidiaries of nationalized groups were not correctly valued.[78] It was on this legal and financial terrain that the right wing won its only victory at the time, obtaining substantially higher remuneration for shareholders, in particular foreign shareholders, in the legislation that was ultimately passed in February 1982. This first success put Jean Loyrette in the cockpit to steer privatization, five years later, when the

---

76. On this point we refer to the work by Philippe Bezes and Julie Gervais listed in the bibliography.

77. Cf. Mathilde Goanec, "Quand les avocats d'affaires écrivent les lois," *Le Monde Diplomatique*, January 2013.

78. Rapports de Gide-Loyrette Nouel, Le problèmes des nationalisations, 2 vols.; and Problèmes constitutionnels et de droit international posés par le projet de loi de nationalisation, recours devant le Conseil Constitutionnel. 1981–1982. In National Archives, Ministry of Justice, Sous-direction du droit économique, File "Nationalisation."

conservatives came back to power. One year before the 1986 parliamentary elections, the right-wing parties commissioned him to write a preliminary outline of a privatization bill. Published in book form entitled *Dénationaliser: Comment réussir la privatisation*, it became the "Bible" of the right's platform.[79] The omnipresence of the Gide firm did not go unnoticed, and even before the right was returned to power the socialist MP Michel Charzat remarked that it would be "a shame to see masters Chirac, Barre and Giscard d'Estaing relinquish their power to the Loyrette firm, when it is the future of the French economy that is at stake."[80] When the overall process of privatization started in 1986, Gide was in a central position to act as legal counsel to the treasury, to banks (Saint-Gobain), and insurance companies (Paribas, AGF) in the process of privatization, acting "on both sides, in all operations."[81] Seven years later, in July 1993, when twenty-one government-owned companies were privatized, the privatization market had become an established practice within Paris business bar. While Jeantet and Gide advised on the 10 billion euro privatization of Renault, Anglo-American law firms also played a critical part, in particular Shearman & Sterling and Linklaters & Paines, which had developed in the meantime strong French practices. Given the amount of money involved, and the magnitude of the change for France's economy, these first two waves of privatizations constitute an inaugural scene bringing business lawyers, together with private bankers, at the core of state's economic and financial operations. By their involvement in the many legal aspects of privatization, business lawyers not only played a central part in this phase of profound transformation of the state's relation to markets, but also made a spectacular entrance at the very heart of the French state.

Subsequently, they would be closely associated with each of the stages of undoing the state's derogatory regime both in economic terms with regard to its position as sole shareholder, and in financial terms with regard to the state's financing circuit which rested on a dense network of public banks and deposits.[82] In 2002, a specialized body was created, the State Holdings Agency (*Agence des participations de l'État*, APE), under the aegis of the French treasury department,

---

79. Paul Fabra, "Vademecum de la privatisation," *Le Monde*, April 8, 1986; "Comment réussir la privatisation," *Le Monde*, September 29, 1986.

80. Michel Charzat, at the National Assembly, "Compte rendu intégral" [Full minutes], session of 19 November 1985, p. 4506.

81. Jean Loyrette quoted in "Ubiquistes avocats," *Le Monde*, November 25, 1986.

82. See Benjamin Lemoine, "The Politics of Public Debt Financialisation: (Re-)Inventing the Market for French Sovereign Bonds and Shaping the Public Debt Problem (1966–2012)," in *The Political Economy of Public Finance: Taxation, State Spending and Debt since the 1970s*, ed. Marc Buggeln, Martin Daunton, and Alexander Nützenadel (Cambridge: Cambridge University Press, 2017), 240–61.

but endowed with functional autonomy to manage the state's holdings.[83] This sealed the transformation.[84] With the APE, the entire "holdings doctrine" shifted, from a vision of "public holdings as an alternative to private property, to a notion of these holdings as transitory aid for the development of the private sector."[85] This new doctrine went hand in hand with new relationships with the banking and financial sectors. Hoping to be "recognized as a fully professional player," in the words of the agency's director general, but without in-house financial and legal expertise to rival that of the main market operators (private banks, law firms), APE pursued a policy of hiring staff from the private sector, to beef up the agency's expertise in the areas of European norms regarding state aid, contract law, and divestiture techniques.[86] In the same way, the APE drew upon professionals to establish its reputation and the credibility of its financial operations and attract investors; these partners, in particular law firms, soon proved to be indispensable for the successful sale of public assets. APE turned to a small group of business law firms, specialized in privatization as well as equity law, for its main operations (sales of assets, capital increases, mergers):[87] Bredin Prat advised APE on the sale of France Telecom shares in 2007;[88] DLA Piper worked with the agency to float the Areva group (French multinational company specialized in nuclear power) on the publicly traded market in 2011; more recently, in 2014, Shearman & Sterling oversaw the sale of roughly eight million shares of Airbus Group, and so on. It is not only for public assets that the state increasingly has recourse to market intermediaries to secure its equity operations. As the traditional state-centered circuit of debt financing was dismantling, market mechanisms have become the sole lever for all public authorities (state and local authorities). As a consequence, the public banking pole—from the public investment bank (*Banque public d'investissement, Caisses des dépôts et consignations*) to the strategic investment funds (*Fonds stratégique d'investissement*)—has developed approaches to financing that are more and more similar to market conditions. Relatedly, they have turned to private banks and law firms to get the necessary expertise as well as

---

83. The *Agence des participations de l'État*, still one of the largest bodies managing public shareholdings worldwide, has a portfolio of eighty-one companies for a value of around 100 billion euros in four different sectors (energy, manufacturing, services and finance, transport).

84. Bruno Bézard and Éric Preiss, "L'agence des participations de l'État," *Revue française d'administration publique* 124 (2007): 601–14.

85. Agence des participations de l'État, *Rapport de l'État actionnaire* (Paris: La Documentation française, 2009).

86. Bézard and Preiss, "L'agence des participations de l'État."

87. Cour des comptes, *Le Recours par l'État aux conseils extérieurs.*

88. *Lettre des juristes d'affaires*, July 2, 2007.

the legitimacy that would guarantee that these public institutions act as authentic private markets players.

Beyond financial and equity operations, law firms also play an increasingly strong role in the domain of public procurement. The voting of the public-private partnerships (PPP) statute law in 2004 opened up a new breach, and profoundly transformed what had been the prime province of the state alone and the prerogatives of the public authority—that is, public tenders and government contracts. This new legislation allowed all sorts of public entities (local authorities, central state administrations, public health care facilities, health services provided by major public infrastructure companies) to entrust private consortiums with missions related to financing, design, construction, and operation of large investments, in exchange for payments from the public purse over the amortization period of the private investment. These were notably investment projects for hospitals and universities, but also for major sporting and cultural venues.[89] The share of PPP in public investment, on the order of 5 percent of total investment, and the number of agreements signed—the state contracted eleven PPP in 2012, and local authorities twenty-six—might at first seem limited, but "[their] qualitative influence is felt more and more."[90] These PPP agreements were almost all related to "strategic" state projects, from the Defense Ministry's so-called Pentagon project, construction of stadiums for the Euro soccer competition in 2016, or the building of one unique huge courthouse complex in Paris, and so on.

The emergence of this new market in public procurement brought with it more widespread recourse to consultants, tasked with the accounting, financial, and legal assembling of these singularly complex projects, often undercutting the architects and construction firms that had been in the forefront in the past. Due to the scope of these projects and the highly technical nature of the financial and legal tools involved, as well as the welter of stakeholders (project owners, banks, insurance companies, construction and public works companies, subcontractors, etc.), a small number of specialized experts—accountants, tax advisers, bankers, lawyers—progressively came to occupy a central position.[91] This trend was confirmed in 2005 when a PPP support task force was created under

---

89. At the end of 2016, 60 percent of PPPs contracted by the state pertained to construction, 18 percent to the energy and waste treatment sector, 10 percent to transport, 6 percent to New Information and Communication Technologies, and 5 percent to sports and cultural facilities. (See the website of the PPP support task force at the Ministry of the Economy and Finances for a complete list of the sixty-two state public-private partnerships [PPP] and the 162 PPPs contracted by local authorities since December 2006, https://www.economie.gouv.fr/fininfra).

90. Mission d'appui aux partenariats public-privé, *Rapport d'activité 2012* (Paris: La Documentation française, 2013), 10.

91. See Deffontaines, "Les consultants dans les partenariats public-privé."

the aegis of the ministry of economy. This support team of "about ten experts" from "different backgrounds in the public and private sectors, all with varied professional experience including stints in business or in financial institutions" was charged with providing expertise to central government administrations, and to local authorities if they request it.[92] In this array, the role of law firms expanded as the legal and judiciary risks involved in this type of public procurement became more evident. This tendency was strengthened by a ruling of the *Conseil constitutionnel* in 2008, that held that PPPs were an exception to state practice, and therefore required a prior legal and financial assessment showing them to be necessary. As the decision created a significant risk of cancellation or revision of contracts in the courts, it actually contributed to bolster the role of lawyers in cementing these public-private deals.

PUBLIC RELIANCE ON THE PRIVATE LEGAL EXPERTISE

This transformation, of which we have cited just a few markers, outlines a nascent dependency of public entities on legal counsel from outside law firms. It is as yet difficult to accurately quantify this expansion of the private legal counsel market. We can, however, grasp the diverse nature of the public entities that habitually have recourse to outside counsel, and the range of domains where this service now seems to be obligatory for the state. A first cross-sectional view comes from a sample we have compiled of two hundred cases in which a public person hired a Paris business lawyer, between 2009 and 2012 (see figure 1). This sample is no doubt imperfect: it was compiled from media reporting on high-profile cases published on the professional business law website lemondedudroit.com; it over-represents large firms, which are better equipped to publicize their big deals, and therefore is made up only of the cases that these firms sought to highlight.[93] Nonetheless, it is a preliminary indicator of the penetration of private legal counsel.

This illustrates the broad range of public entities that today use the services of Paris law firms. Far from being limited to the central administrations of French government, these include many public establishments (sports federations, etc.), local authorities, and enterprises in which public bodies have holdings, as well as foreign states, often former French colonies,[94] and European and international

---

92. Mission d'appui aux partenariats public-privé, *Rapport d'activité 2012* (Paris: La Documentation française, 2013), 4.

93. Here, I would like to thank Charlotte Ducouret, intern at the time at the CESSP Research unit, who helped me gather and process these data.

94. On the Paris bar as a hub for the African legal market, see Sara Dezalay, "Lawyers in Africa: Brokers of the State, Intermediaries of Globalization; A Case-Study of the 'Africa' Bar in Paris," *Indiana Journal of Global Legal Studies* 25, no. 2 (2018): 639–69.

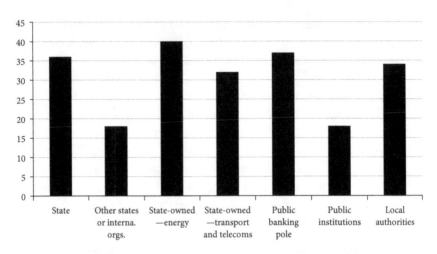

FIGURE 1 / Public entities that consulted law firms (2009–2012)
Source: Graph based on data from http://www.lemondedudroit.com
Notes:
State: government, ministries, etc.
State-owned undertaking—energy: EDF, GDF, ERDF, Areva, EADS, Safran, etc.
State-owned undertaking—transport and telecoms: France Telecom, Air France, RATP, SNCF, La Poste
Public banking pole: national organizations (e.g., *Caisse des dépôts, Banque publique d'investissement,* etc.) and extranational (e.g., European Investment Bank, European Financial Stability Facility, etc.)
Public institutions: universities, regulatory agencies, public establishments, France TV, etc.
Local authorities: local governments and sports federations

public organizations. The growth of local legal services has also been spurred by the development of PPPs that transformed the public procurement practices of territorial governments and public establishments. When in 2012 the Nord-Pas de Calais regional government decided on a socially responsible bond issue, it turned to Clifford Chance for counsel. When the public service delegation of the Palais Omnisport Paris Bercy (a major indoor sports arena and concert hall) was renewed in 2012, the City of Paris engaged the expertise of Bird & Bird. When plans were made by local authorities for a new Orly Airport–Versailles–Nanterre metro line, they consulted the legal teams of Orrick & Rambaud (2012). This list goes on. Paris business lawyers are also active across a cluster of European Union public entities. These include the European Financial Solidarity Facility, for emission of 5 billion euros in EU aid to Portugal (Clifford Chance Paris, 2011); the European Investment Bank, for assistance with implantation of the so-called "Juncker Plan" European Investment Fund in France (Gide, 2015); and counsel to the French government in its talks with EU competition authorities regarding renewal of existing hydropower concession agreements (Orrick Rambaud Martel, 2012), and so on.

Keeping the reservations mentioned above in mind, this sample also reveals the broad diversity of public activities that would now require private legal counseling. Recourse to law firms for judiciary defense of public entities is without doubt still a marginal phenomenon, excepting certain cases involving state-owned undertakings before the EU Court of Justice, and arbitration cases in major international contracts. Legal counsel is a different matter entirely, and is singularly present in the financial and equity operations of public entities in French and foreign markets. All the major banking and equity operations of the state and public enterprises (divestiture, capital raising, bond issues, public buy-out offers, etc.) now mobilize the services of law firms. This is the case, for example, for operations by the *Fonds d'investissement stratégique* (acquisitions, minority share holdings, etc.), France's sovereign wealth fund, that involve various firms in Paris (Hastings, 2011; Herbert Smith, Orrick Rambaud Martel, and Willkie Farr & Gallagher, 2012, etc.). Other examples are the *Caisse des dépôts et consignations* (France's major public sector financial institution) and ad hoc public banking structure (*Banque publique d'investissement*), which have also secured their market operations by recourse to private legal counsel. Major corporations with public shareholders are in the same situation, as seen in these examples: the sale by Renault of 14.9 percent of the capital of Volvo, for 3 billion euros (Skadden, 2010); bond issues by France Telecom for 2.5 billion euros (Jones Day, 2009); the initial public offering of France's nuclear power multinational group, Areva (DLA Piper, 2011); sale of EDF holdings (state-owned electric utility company) to supermajor oil company Total (Racine, 2012), and so on. Other cases involve more classic recourse to expertise in negotiating and drafting contracts, generally international (creation of joint ventures, concession agreements, certification applications, etc.). One can also cite: a joint venture in the Middle East created by Aircelle, a subsidiary of Safran and Air France (Baker McKenzie and Gide Loyrette Nouel, 2010); talks between Orange and the shareholders of Dailymotion (August & Debouzy, 2015); French investments in Africa, such as France Telecom's purchase of 100 percent of mobile service operator Congo China Telecom (CCT) in the Democratic Republic of Congo (Gide, 2011); Air France's creation of the new airline Air Côte d'Ivoire (August & Debouzy, 2012). Last, public procurement and especially PPP also have an important place in legal counsel to public entities—all the more significant in that they involve many different types of public clients, from ministries and local authorities to public establishments such as hospitals, universities, airports, and so on. This segment spans major public works of strategic importance: major infrastructures such as the much-contested (and now abandoned) concession contract for the Grand Ouest airport at Notre-Dame-des-Landes that involved many firms (Jean Latournerie et associés, Willkie Farr & Gallagher, Yves-René Guilloui Avocats); the construction of the new Defense Ministry building (Salans, Orrick Rambaud Martel, Hogan & Lovells, etc.); the opening of the judiciary complex in the Batignolles quarter of Paris.

In short, the presumed immunity of the French state, which was described as putting up fierce resistance to outside counsel, is no longer a valid assumption. This view fails to account for the pivotal role that business law firms have acquired as the state has taken a neoliberal turn.

The New Government of Markets

The view of this new public-private collusion would, however, be too narrow if it was only limited to direct recourse to private legal expertise by public entities. As the state has pursued its regulatory change, a new government of private markets has emerged that positions professional advisers, notably business lawyers, as key liaison agents.

The most characteristic feature of this new government of markets is the proliferation of regulatory agencies from the 1980s onward. The former leading divisions of the Ministry of the Economy and Finances (the General Directorate for Competition Policy, the Tax Department, the Treasury) have ceded an essential parcel of their powers to general—the *Autorité de la concurrence*, the *Autorité des marchés financiers*, or sector-specific authorities—the *Autorité de régulation des communications électroniques et des postes* (ARCEP), the *Commission de régulation de l'énergie* (CRE), the *Autorité de régulation des activités ferroviaires* (ARAF),[95] etc. This proliferation is all the more significant in that these agencies now have substantial powers of authorization, investigation, legal action, injunction and sanction, and oversee crucial sectors such as insurance, banking, rail transport, telecommunications, health care, broadcasting, and so forth. The *Autorité de la concurrence* and its staff of four hundred now supervises, in lieu of the Competition Directorate General at the ministry of economy, corporate mergers and buy-outs (roughly two hundred cases a year), punish illicit practices that violate competition law, and issue over a billion euros in fines each year in sectors like mobile telecommunications, construction and public works, transport, and so on. The considerable span of this expanding web of independent

---

95. See appendix 2 for a brief presentation of these regulatory authorities.

public regulators is also seen in the fact that the *Conseil d'État* itself, the supreme administrative court, recognizes that "their 'signature' sometimes inspires greater confidence than that of the State."[96]

In the course of building up their credibility as regulators independent from bureaucratic circuits of command, these agencies have developed new ties with professionals in the regulated sectors, and singularly by working through business lawyers. This can be seen first of all in the channels through which agencies acquire sectoral expertise that is relatively independent of government ministries. This knowledge has been forged by maintaining a dense network of contacts in the regulated sectors—by recruiting market professionals in the staff, by developing a network of joint working groups, by organizing multiple hearings, colloquia, and seminars, and so on. Securing a reputation of independence also implied that the agencies would display new standard operating procedures different from the conventional administrative style. The progressive import of a quasi-judicial style with public hearings and contradictory procedure played an integral part in this breakaway from state's bureaucratic ethos. In all agencies, the investigation-sanctions pole has been progressively separated from the regulatory pole, and is organized around quasi-judiciary proceedings that are designed to bolster the rights of the defense.[97] This double mutation, in expert and judicial styles, is today an essential marker of the autonomy acquired by these agencies vis-à-vis the historical administrative departments. Former head of the financial regulation authority, the *Autorité des marchés financiers*, who would later practice as a business lawyer, Jean-Pierre Jouyet says as much when he underscores that the creation of the agency in 2003 was the "condition sine qua non to regain market confidence" and "to consolidate the attractiveness of the Paris marketplace": "technical knowledge, specialization and rapidity then went hand in hand with the fundamental procedural guarantees granted to the companies under investigation."[98]

Business lawyers played an essential role in this metamorphosis. As the natural defenders of due process and sector-specific experts, they became essential partners in the rise of regulatory agencies. As recently remarked by Bruno Lasserre, current vice president of the *Conseil d'État* and former chair of the

---

96. Conseil d'État, *Rapport annuel: Les autorités administratives indépendantes* (Paris: La Documentation française, 2001), 82.

97. In 2003, the structure of the financial regulator (*Autorité des marchés financiers*) was transformed as the legal action units (investigation) and the decision-making entity (sanctions) were uncoupled.

98. Jean-Pierre Jouyet, "Le pouvoir de sanction de l'Autorité des marchés financiers," in *Études à la mémoire de Fernand-Charles Jeantet* (Paris: LGDJ, 2010).

Autorité de la concurrence, "the development of competition law has shaped a new profession on the European scale. Competition law is less and less a unilateral force, based on sanctions, and increasingly a more contractual form of law, where lawyers will take on the role of experts. Examples are the commitments procedure (to correct a behavior), the no-dispute-of-grievances procedure (transactional procedure), the clemency procedure (partial or total immunity in exchange for the company's cooperation in the investigation). These options provide lawyers with new opportunities."[99] In point of fact, the latter are now assiduous visitors at regulatory agencies. They come to defend their clients, and each case can mobilize up to several dozen lawyers as was the case for example in a dossier devoted to interbank commissions in 2012 before the *Autorité de la concurrence* that brought an armada of no less than twelve law firms. Business lawyers are also key protagonists in the small ecosystem of working groups, conferences, and publications that have grown up within or along the edges of regulatory authorities. Lawyers' careers may upon occasion take them to these regulatory agencies, either as interns (students of the Paris bar's vocational training school can in fact earn credit for an internship in a regulatory agency) or as directors in legal departments and executive committees.

And yet, these agencies have not turned into courts. While they have only a distant relationship to the administrative units they have replaced, they remain quite singular. The period preceding the creation of France's first competition agency in 1986, when lawyers went "to plead [their] cases before the departments of the Ministry of the Economy" is long past of course, but the ground rules of these spaces are still hybrid constructions, at the crossroads of judicial and bureaucratic rationale.[100] In fact, the *Conseil d'État* has itself marked the limits of this judiciarization process, in the case of the *Autorité des marchés financiers* stating that these agencies cannot claim the status of national jurisdiction but must content themselves with the term of tribunal in the meaning of article 6 of the European Convention on Human Rights (ruling of February 4, 2005, *Société Gsd Gestion*). Above all, the comportment expected in regulatory hearings is very different from that of courtroom proceedings. As one business lawyer puts it, "fancy oratory and eloquence are out of place," and lawyers act as law technicians rather than as pleaders of a cause: "here there are no judges in robes, no

---

99. "Réception de M. Bruno Lasserre, président de l'Autorité de la concurrence, et de Virginie Beaumeunier, rapporteure générale de l'Autorité de la concurrence," *Bulletin de l'ordre des avocats de Paris*, December 10, 2013, 3.

100. "L'art de plaider devant les autorités de régulation," *Lettre des juristes d'affaires*, December 15, 2008, 18–19.

courtroom, no court recorder," notes a journalist from the specialized press.[101] He adds, "before the *Autorité de la concurrence* as before the *Autorité des marchés financiers*, everyone is seated around the table without any decorum whatsoever." The emblematic question of the robe, initially raised by lawyers, was quickly set aside. Indeed, the law practiced is itself of a new kind. Administrative law with its classical notions of public authority, sovereignty, exorbitance, submission, and the general interest, on which the state had hitherto founded its specific role with regard to the private sphere, has given way to a continuous flow of norms and standards, from the EU in particular, that have sketched out the shape of a new hybrid field of law, called either *droit public des affaires* or *droit public économique*. This transversal body of regulatory law, blurring the traditional *summa divisio* between public law and private law, applies indifferently to private companies and to public enterprises, and subjects the state to the same obligations as are imposed on actors in the private sector.[102]

Truly enough, not all levers of action held by the state have been affected in the same way by the process of agencification. With respect to the regalian prerogative of taxation, the *Commission des infractions fiscales*, an administrative body charged with reviewing major cases of tax fraud continues to bear the marks of administrative style (nonmotivation of opinions issued, absence of contradictory testimony, etc.). Nonetheless, the ways the fiscal administration interacts with companies have undergone profound change, once again creating a new opening for professional counsel. Over the past two decades, a new culture of dialogue and transaction with companies has been promoted within the tax inspection body in charge at the ministry of economy of controlling France's largest corporations with a view to establishing a new climate of "business confidence."[103] This new marching order of the tax administration favored measured application of fiscal law through negotiation and correction rather than sanctions. This "relationship of trust" as the administration itself called it, puts tax lawyers in a brand-new and strategic position as indispensable intermediaries between the state and the large taxpayers.[104]

The transformation of the state ever since the mid-1980s is not merely a renewal of policy tools and procedures. By plunging into the marketplace and embracing the regulatory paradigm, public institutions have in practice woven

---

101. Ibid.

102. Ségolène Barbou des Places, "La *summa divisio* en droit communautaire," in *L'Identité en droit public*, ed. Xavier Bioy (Paris: LGDJ, 2010).

103. Alexis Spire, "La domestication de l'impôt par les classes dominantes," *Actes de la recherche en sciences sociales* 190 (2011): 58–71.

104. Ibid.

new collusive ties with the companies and intermediaries present in the market. In the end, far from evolving at a distance or in opposition to each other, the business bar and the regulatory state seem in fact to be partners. While the figure of business lawyer was invented in large part via its claim to be an expert in *public* regulation, the new regulatory government of markets forged its own credibility and instruments for intervention in the new system of alliances with market professionals, in particular business lawyers. This interdependence has shaped a space where public and private are contiguous, along the porous fringes of the regulatory state and the unfixed boundaries of the marketplace. In this steadily expanding twilight zone in which law firms and business lawyers have acquired a central position, a new form of revolving door has been invented.

2

THE PUBLIC-PRIVATE FOUNDATIONS OF THE NEOLIBERAL STATE

When in September 2007 the weekly satirical paper *Le Canard enchaîné* reported that Jean-François Copé, chair of the majority parliamentary group at the French National Assembly, had also been working for several months at the Gide law firm, this news came as a revelation of the new attraction that politicians felt for the robes of the lawyer.[1] Over the next few months the curiosity of journalists was aroused, as leading politicians were sworn into the bar at a steady pace. Numerous articles were published on this confusion of roles: within just a few weeks of each other, two incarnations of the politicoadministrative elite in France—former *Élysée* secretary general and later prime minister Dominique de Villepin and his successor in the former position, Frédéric Salat-Baroux—were admitted to the Paris bar. The former founded his own consulting firm (SAS Villepin International, January 2008) and the latter joined the highly regarded American law firm Weil Gotshal & Manges (November 2007). In 2010, two former ministers of justice were recruited by Paris law firms after their time of the ministry, following the example of a third one who two years earlier had joined the firm Orrick Rambaud Martel immediately after leaving office.

The media discussion stirred up by these so-called *pantouflages*—a slang word for the practice of civil servants and politicians joining the private sector[2]—focused almost entirely on politicians and the rising risks of conflict of interests. It therefore failed to adequately reflect the breadth and diversity of the movement that started in the 1990s between the politicoadministrative elite and major business law firms in Paris. This *pantouflage* into the business bar is intriguing, first of all because it was novel as it came after a period in the late 1980s when the flow

---

1. "Les fins de mois de Copé," *Le Canard enchaîné*, September 26, 2007.

2. It is important to note that the word "*pantouflage*" bears a different meaning than *revolving doors* as it does not imply moves back and forth but rather a *departure* from the public sector. Indeed, when it was noticed that some of these individuals were actually coming back to the public sector, a new word was coined: *retro-pantouflage*.

of exchange between political and administrative elites and the legal profession had practically dried up. As seen in the first chapter, the French Republic was no longer a lawyers' Republic (*République des avocats*) and the legal profession had long since ceased to be a breeding ground for the political elite. In addition, the traditional circuit of *pantouflage* to the private sector led historically to the big banks, strategic sectors, and companies who were close to public procurement, and never took them through law firms. Indeed, the current *pantouflage* to law firms is far from this conventional one typical of the 1970s, that prolonged, as it were, the preeminence of the state and its *grands corps* as guardians of the mixed economy *à la française*. The sudden attractiveness of the business bar also draws our attention because of its scope. Going well beyond just the most visible political figures, who were the tip of the iceberg, a much broader swathe of former section presidents at the *Conseil d'État*, *Élysée* secretaries general, members of the *Conseil d'État*, heads of tax departments, cabinet staff members, and public managers in various regulatory agencies, in short a wide cross section of the political and administrative elite is involved today in this circulation toward corporate law firms of Paris, whether they be French, British, or American.

Before even questioning what the new movement points to, one needs to provide a systematic cartography of these new French revolving doors. To this aim, we have attempted to collect all the individuals that have moved from politics and government positions to the business law firms of Paris since the early 1990s. The assumption is that by drawing a collective sociological portrait of these *pantoufleurs* (their breeding grounds, springboards, pathways, etc.), one can reveal, the way chemicals reveal a photograph, a *structural* view of the new pattern of relationships that have been consolidated at the interface between the state and markets: the type of *public* positions and resources that are prized by the business bar, and also the type of companies and law firms that hire from the public sector, and the sectoral pathways followed by recruits. As we are able to map out the total social space in which these crossovers move, on either side of the public-private border, it is possible to sketch the field of intermediation and influence that has developed over the course of two decades of the state's neoliberalization.

When Political and Administrative Elites Don the Robe

First and foremost, it is necessary to procure the methodological tools capable of describing this *pantouflage* phenomenon. Classically, political science has examined connections between society and political elites, either through the prism of pathways *into* politics, or exit routes (*pantouflage*) at the very end of a public sector career.[3] This traditional analysis in terms of entry and exit no longer suffices, however, to describe the multiple shapes and nonlinear trajectories of career moves, or the ambiguous and porous nature of the border between political and administrative spaces and professionals from the consulting industry, whether they be lawyers, lobbyists, bankers, or other. A politically centered view that sees politics as the coronation and endpoint is no longer properly focused, when a stint in a ministry or regulatory agency is often just a step along the way in careers that accumulate and combine different professional, corporate, government credentials. Likewise, the flow between the legal profession and politics is no longer a one-way street; far from it, as the direction of movement we now observe is more frequently from politics to the bar. Last, this vision masks the fact that there is now a large number of intermediate and multiple positions *across* the fields of law, government, and politics, making it impossible to reason simply in terms of point of departure and point of arrival.[4] Furthermore, the lines delimiting the top echelons of government administration, and of the political profession, are now uncertain. Fixed-term contracts have proliferated on the fringes of the civil service, particularly in regulatory agencies, cabinet offices, and public entities, while semi- and preprofessional positions are increasingly appearing in the margins of the political personnel, as local elected officials, their staff, and parliamentary assistants.[5] On top of this is the fact that the title of lawyer permits a large variety of types of practice (status of retiree with pension, honoraria, temporary omission from the bar, bar registration with occasional practice, part-time activity, etc.) that make it possible to combine the activity with other positions (law faculty, Parliament, expert committees, think tanks, etc.). In these circumstances, it is not only the move from one sector to the other that interests us, but also the circulation, back and forth, and cumulative positions and functions throughout a career.

Following this analytical framework, we have attempted to trace the professional trajectory of all individuals who started in the public sector (temporary public agent, high-level civil servant, minister or member of Parliament) before joining the bar in Paris or the Hauts-de-Seine—the latter covering the business district of La Défense, just outside of Paris, where most large French companies have their headquarters. Empirically speaking, the inquiry was far from easy as

---

3. See Dogan, "The Mandarins among the French Elites."

4. Our statistical treatment of the sample codes the "last position before becoming a lawyer," the "point of arrival in the legal profession," as well as the different positions occupied during the professional trajectory. For more details, see appendix 1.

5. Didier Demazière and Patrick Le Lidec, *Les mondes du travail politique* (Rennes: Presses Universitaires de Rennes, 2014).

there existed no established list of these *pantouflages*. It soon became evident that, beyond the usual names of a handful of prominent politicians, most of the crossovers concerned high civil servants whose coming to the business bar had drawn very little attention. It therefore required lengthy investigations into a large variety of sources that may incidentally refer to these *pantouflages* and allow us to trace professional trajectories: specialized publications *(Lettre des jurists d'affaires, Décideurs magazine*, etc.) and blogs (*Legal 500, Chambers*, etc.), law firms' websites, *Who's Who*, directories (*Annuaire de l'ordre du barreau de Paris, Annuaire de l'ENA*, etc.), and so forth. This enabled us to identify 217 individuals who have taken this pathway since 1991. While this number may seem limited, all the evidence leads us to think that it represents just a small part of the flow circulating around and through the business bar.[6] It does not include either the more traditional stream of "lawyers who go into politics," or "lawyers who go into administration," whose numbers are growing in regulatory agencies. Likewise, as we have left out large regional bar associations such as Bordeaux, Lille, Marseille, and Lyon, local flows linked to markets in local public authorities have undoubtedly escaped our attention. Neither does our sample cover circulation at intermediate levels of state employment, for instance tax inspectors who are moving in considerable numbers to firms specialized in tax law, but who rarely draw the attention of the specialized press, and whose mobility is for the most part invisible.[7] Despite these gaps in the overall count, we observe that this new crossover path has become increasingly significant over the past twenty-five years.

Crossing Over: A Chronicle

There have long been special pathways that were supposed to facilitate transfers from the state *grands corps* to the legal profession. In particular, members of the *Conseil d'État*, of the *Cour des comptes*, and of the body of judicial magistrates have been exempted from the requirements of the bar exam and professional internship since June 1972 (see article 97, box 2). However, this option at first

---

6. Although they are also civil servants, law professors who work with law firms have not been counted, nor movements within the private sector (from companies' legal departments to law firms).

7. A quick survey shows that there is long-standing and steady circulation here. For the period studied, we identified eighty-four crossovers of tax inspectors, but this flow seems to have been much heavier, as the *Commission de déontologie de la fonction publique* (CDFP)—the committee in charge of controlling moves to the private sector—mentions twenty-seven requests submitted for the year 2000 alone. Commission de déontologie de la fonction publique, *Rapport d'activité 2000* (Paris: La Documentation française, 2001).

interested only a few mavericks. The first crossover in our sample is a member of the *Conseil d'État* who at age 38 joined the Gide firm in 1979, after having been chief of staff (*directeur de cabinet*) for the industry minister. This itinerary is a singular one, in that the person already possessed professional law certification and went back to his original civil service corps as early as 1983. The few other passages in the bar were generally due to a poor class ranking at ENA,[8] earlier studies at law school, or familial ties to the profession (succession in a family firm). The only long-standing and solid chain that we have found is tax inspectors, who have regularly and for a long time joined fiscal law firms. In 1972, an equivalency was established between the *École nationale des finances publiques* (ENFIP, the state vocational school training tax inspectors) degree and a master's degree in law, thereby opening up a bridge allowing ENI graduates to migrate to the legal profession. In fact, in a context of near state monopoly on fiscal expertise, the competence of former ENFIP students was highly sought after by consulting firms such as Fidal and Francis Lefebvre, which began to regularly pay their passage through the revolving door, thus opening the gates for a flow that has not stopped since.

The 1990 merger between the *avocats* and the *conseils juridiques* dramatically changed this rather stable scenario.[9] A decree of November 27, 1991 (see box 2), adopted in the wake of the merger of the professions of lawyer and legal adviser, considerably widened the dispensatory pathway allowing civil servants to join the bar, thereby taking on the name of "bridge decree" (*décret passerelle*).

BOX 2. / Excerpts from the so-called "bridge decree" allowing for exemptions from the bar exam and training sessions in the access to the legal profession (November 27, 1991)

Art. 97: Are exempted from the degree requirements, from theoretical and practical training requirements, from the bar exam and internship:

(1) *Members and former members of the Conseil d'État, magistrates and former magistrates of the administrative courts and administrative courts of appeal.*

(2) *Magistrates and former magistrates of the Cour des comptes, regional courts of accounts, and territorial chambers of accounts in French Polynesia and New Caledonia.*

(3) *Magistrates and former magistrates of the judicial order governed by order no. 58–1270 of December 22, 1958.*

---

8. The *École nationale d'administration*, the training school for French top civil servants, ranks students at the end of their two years of studies and internships according to their results. Only the very first in the ranking can access one of the state *grands corps*: see more details in appendix 2.

9. For a full narrative of this turning point, see Karpik, *French Lawyers.*

(4) University professors charged with teaching juridical subjects.

(5) Lawyers before the *Conseil d'État* and the *Cour de cassation*.

(6) Advocates before appellate courts.

(7) Former lawyers registered with a French bar association and former legal advisers.

Art. 98: Are exempted from the requirements of theoretical and practical training and bar exam:

(1) Notaries, bailiffs, court-appointed administrators and mandataries for liquidation of companies, former court-appointed overseers and administrators, industrial property counselors, and former patent and invention counselors who have practiced in this capacity for at least five years.

(2) Associate professors, adjuncts, and teaching assistants who have a doctoral degree in law, economics, or management, and five years' experience in teaching law in their academic capacity in training and research bodies.

(3) In-house legal counsel and company lawyers with at least eight years' professional experience in the legal department of one or more companies.

(4) *Top civil servants and former civil servants, or persons assimilated into this category, who have practiced legal activities in this capacity for a period of at least eight years in a government administration, public service unit, or international organization.*

(5) Legal counselors attached for at least eight years to the legal units of a trade union or labor organization.

Persons listed in (3), (4), and (5) can qualify for exemption on the basis of different occupations listed above so long as the total cumulative period of these activities is at least **eight years**.

This decree made it possible for top "civil servants and former civil servants" to be exempted from the bar exam and internship provided they could prove eight years of "legal activity" in their previous professional positions. The text indicated however that applicants needed to have a law degree and to show eight years of juridical activities in their civil service capacity (see article 98.4, box 2). Eager to highlight the new attractions of the legal profession and its openness to new profiles and backgrounds, the Paris Bar Council provided an extensive interpretation of the decree. First, members of Parliament and ministers were considered as part of the category of top civil servants.[10] Second, their years as MP or minister were counted as "legal activity" for the eight years' requirement. Third, the "law degree" requirement was understood as also including political science and economics degrees.[11] Thereby, the initially narrow bridge turned into

---

10. The prosecutor's office can still appeal decisions by bars' admission policy, but in point of fact has almost never used this option.

11. Mathilde Mathieu and Michael Hajdenberg, "Parlementaires-avocats: Le gouvernement est passé outre les réserves du conseil d'État," Médiapart (blog), April 17, 2012, citing the cases of two

a large pathway, thereby offering unprecedented opportunities for members of political and administrative elites to move into a bar whose business dynamics was rapidly increasing.

The new professional prospects opened by the 1990 merger of the *avocats* and *conseils juridiques*, as well as the markets that were emerging in the fields of competition law, fiscal law, and privatizations, indeed attracted early moves of civil servants to the legal profession. The *pantouflages* movement steadily grew, from 14 individuals over the period 1979–1990; to 63 for 1991–2001, then 103 for 2002–2010—an average of 6 crossovers per year in the 1990s, and 10 in the first decade of the twenty-first century. The five years of the presidency of Nicolas Sarkozy (2007–2012) have a special place in this set. With the election of Sarkozy, who had been trained as a lawyer in the 1980s under a mentorship of a key figure of the Paris business bar, and had founded his own firm in 1987,[12] came a sharp upturn in *pantouflages*, with nearly one-third of the movements in the database (74 out of 217). This observation confirms studies in political science that underscore the unprecedented high rate of migration to the private sector of Sarkozy's staff and entourage, especially individuals leaving ministerial cabinet offices, and in particular members of the *grands corps* (43 percent of the latter moved to the private sector).[13] This phenomenon must also be seen in the light of the "return" of lawyers to the executive branch as Sarkozy rose to power, with four minister-lawyers (out of 32) in the first Villepin government (2005) and eight (out of 40) in the second Fillon government (2010). The leadership of the bar association unanimously lauded this renewed interest for lawyers among politics and government elites. Several presidents of the Paris Bar Council spoke enthusiastically of these new ties with the political class. One leader, Yves Repiquet, himself a business lawyer, even wrote of the *République des avocats*, briefly resuscitating this prototypical figure of legitimacy that recalls the golden age of the Third Republic, and rejoiced that a "lawyer is back at the head of the State" to carry the torch previously held by Thiers, Grévy, Loubet, Lallières, Millerand, Doumergue, Auriol, Coty, and Mitterrand.[14] Crowning this period, an amendment to the 1991 "bridge decree" was introduced in the very last weeks of Nicolas

---

former ministers (Jean Glavany and Frédéric Lefebvre) who did not have law degrees when they were admitted to the bar.

12. The career of Nicolas Sarkozy from his admission to the bar in 1983 is described in Michel Pinçon and Monique Pinçon-Charlot, *Le Président des riches* (Paris: Zone, 2010), 85–93.

13. Luc Rouban, "L'État à l'épreuve du libéralisme: Les entourages du pouvoir exécutif de 1974 à 2012," *Revue française d'administration publique* 142 (2012): 487.

14. Yves Repiquet, "Un avocat à la tête de l'État," *Bulletin: Ordre des avocats du barreau de Paris* 15 (May 15, 2007): 1.

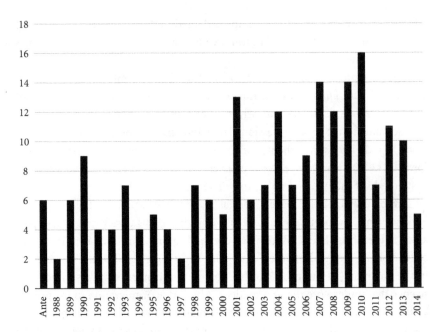

FIGURE 2 / Yearly flow of crossovers (from the public sector to law firms) (n = 207/217)
Source: authors. "Crossovers" biographical database.
Note: "Ante" refers to the whole period from 1979 to 1987. For ten individuals in the database the year of entry into the bar could not be determined.

Sarkozy's presidential term. Given the likelihood of defeat of the latter, pressure was mounting in the entourage of the prime minister and president to further facilitate *pantouflages* into the Paris business bar. The amendment grants the benefit of the dispensatory pathway to admission to the bar to anybody who can attest to "at least eight years of exercise of *public responsibilities* [and not of *legal activity* as previously required] that led them to participate directly in drafting legislation." This opened the door for crossover to all former ministers, members of Parliament, and important local elected officials, as long as they had accumulated eight years of experience in one or another of these roles. The dispensation was also extended to parliamentary assistants with eight years in this function.[15] The widening of the scope of these bar exam exemptions that secured the full convertibility of political and administrative experience in legal credentials was

---

15. While the dispensation of the bar exam for all those who had exercised eight years of "public responsibilities" was repealed by a revised decree on April 15, 2013, when François Hollande rose to power (although not without hesitation on the part of the government), the bridge option was maintained for parliamentary aides and assistants to deputies or senators.

such that important parts of the legal profession protested, fearing for the reputation and the ethics standards of the profession.

Even though the "Sarkozy moment" was a singular high point, it is consistent with the growing crossover movement. This movement continued apace after the election of François Hollande, with twenty-six crossovers in 2012–2014, a much higher rate than the average for the twenty-five years covered here. This attests to the consolidation of this new revolving door.

Neoliberal Revolving Doors

As the number of *pantouflages* to the bar grew steadily over a quarter of a century, the phenomenon spread to a progressively wider segment of politics and government administration. Initially confined to fiscal matters, other fields of law were involved as new sectors were affected by the neoliberal shift of the state from the powerful rise of competition policy (1986 government order on competition, new economic regulations legislation in 2001, modernization of the economy act in 2008) to reforms of public procurement (legislation on public-private partnerships in 2004 and 2008), public holdings and participations, and so on. Each wave of liberalization and strengthening of the regulatory state was met by a symmetrical interest of law firms for the corresponding segments of the state, leading to a progressive consolidation of the crossover movement and its diversification.

It was initially in fiscal matters that a small number of *énarques* tried out this new revolving door. Judging by articles in the professional press at the time, certain of these crossovers appear to signal a shift in the scope of possible transfer options for ENA graduates. In 1991 the former director general of the taxation office, France's highest tax civil servant, moved directly to head Bureau Francis Lefebvre, a historical fiscal consulting firm. At nearly the same time, a former deputy director of the fiscal legislation department (in charge of drafting tax laws at the ministry of economy) joined Arthur Andersen as a partner. The transfer chain of tax inspectors was already solidly in place for these firms, but these new recruits from the very top of the fiscal administration blazed a new trail that would be heavily used in later years. However, top civil servants from many other sectors would soon follow. Experts in the field of competition policy with the hiring of a former member of EU competition directorate general by the Paris branch of White & Case in 1990; experts in public procurement, such as one member of the *Cour des comptes* who moved to Gide in 1990; specialists in equity and securities operations such as one magistrate, former director of the legal department at the financial market regulatory authority, who joined Darrois Villey in 1995, and so forth.

After these multiple sectoral niches corresponding to law domains reputed to be highly technical (tax law, public procurement, competition law), in the mid-1990s came crossovers from central government structures (secretariat general of the government or of the presidency, ministries' chiefs of staff, etc.) revealing that the field of "public affairs" and "influence" was becoming a new breeding ground for *pantouflages*. Thus, a new type of entrant, less specialists than *mandarins* of the French state, came to the bar. Without claim to specific sectoral expertise, sometimes without any legal credentials at all, these new entrants could bank on their capacity to wield influence and on their knowledge of public affairs. The arrival of Jean-Pierre Jouyet in 1995 and of Hubert Védrine in 1996, from their respective positions of cabinet director to the president of the European Commission and of secretary general of the presidency in France, are emblematic. These newcomers were neither business developers who brought new clients, nor sectoral experts, but they could demonstrate unique closeness with the central spaces of political and administrative power in Paris as well as in Brussels.

As the crossover movement extended beyond specialized legal fields to the sector of influence and public affairs, politicians, also often from the ranks of the *grands corps*, plunged into the breach. In the bar, they could find a fallback position after an electoral defeat, and from these temporary positions eventually embark on a new career. As early as the 1980s, a few public figures ventured into the legal profession as a comfortable exit at the end of a career; for instance Michel Aurillac, a former minister who had been in charge of dealing with France's former colonies at the so-called *ministère de la coopération*, was admitted to the bar in 1989 and worked on African cases.[16] But it was not until the mid-1990s that the bar became the new waiting position or conversion space for the political elite.

As a preliminary assessment of the political leanings of the individuals surveyed, we constructed a left/right political indicator on the basis of electoral office and of the political color of the national governments and local executive offices in which the *pantoufleurs* held cabinet functions.[17] Interestingly enough, while no significant difference appears between center-left and center-right parties in this regard, it is the left that first opened the pathway. After the stinging defeat of the Socialist Party in the 1993 legislative elections, several figureheads of the party joined the legal profession. This was the case for socialist power

---

16. *Lettre des juristes d'affaires*, April 16, 1990.

17. We gathered information on 140 of the 217 crossovers to obtain a rough picture of the effects of political change on the flow of transfers to the law profession (see figure 3).

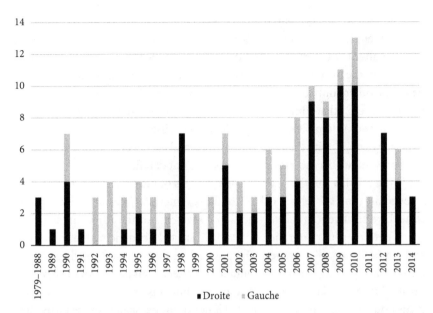

FIGURE 3 / Political leanings of crossovers (n = 140/217)
Source: authors. "Crossovers" biographical database.

couple Ségolène Royal, former minister for the environment (registered for the bar between 1994 and 1997) and François Hollande (registered for 1994 only),[18] both of them *énarques* who briefly moved to the law firm of a close friend from the Socialist Party. Former minister of industry and future IMF managing director, Dominique Strauss-Kahn also became a business lawyer in 1994, when he founded the firm DSK Consultants.[19] The stream of crossovers from politics would not soon dry up. Peaks correlated with elections came in 1992–1993, with 7 crossovers from the left-wing government out of 11 during this period, and then in 1997–1998, with 8 political crossovers, all from the right-wing government, out of 9 for the period. As the political winds shifted, and internal disgrace occurred or scandals erupted, more former ministers escaped whether from the right (e.g., former prime minister Dominique de Villepin) or the left (e.g., former prime minister Bernard Cazeneuve). Broadly speaking, the peaks in admission to

---

18. Ségolène Royal, a graduate from the ENA and prominent figure of the Socialist Party, would later be presidential candidate for the Socialist Party in 2007.

19. Dominique Strauss-Kahn was drawn into the so-called MNEF scandal (named after a large students' insurance fund) by reason of 600,000 francs in fees he received as lawyer representing the fund: "Le parquet fait enquêter sur les 600,000 francs versés à DSK par la MNEF quand il était avocat d'affaires," *Libération*, December 9, 1988.

the bar of former ministers and members of their staff typically occur just before or just after elections or internal disgrace in political parties. Whether fallback position after (or before) electoral defeat or springboard to a new career, these transfers to the business bar are part of a larger movement in which politicians penetrate other contiguous worlds (communication, think tanks, public affairs, consulting, etc.) that function as buffer zones between the squeeze and expansion of the accordion pleats of the political job market.[20]

Truly enough, with the wave of political scandals that erupted in France from 2010 onward, with a succession of affairs (tax fraud, influence peddling, etc.) on the left as much as on the right, the *pantouflages* of public servants into the private sectors (and the related risk of conflict of interests) became a salient public issue. Investigative journalists, traditional segments of the Paris bar, as well as moral entrepreneurs from the political field started denouncing the connivance and confusion of roles between the political and administrative elites and the business bar, putting at risk the reputation of reserve and probity of the law firms involved in such recruitment, and so on. In some instances, politicians and law firms would rather shun a situation that is politically damaging for the former and commercially risky for the latter. After the French satirical newspaper *le Canard enchaîné* revealed his parallel appointment as Gide partner and majority leader of the National Assembly, Jean-François Copé had to withdraw from his position in the law firm. Likewise, some members of Parliament now report in their income statement to the *Haute Autorité pour la transparence de la vie publique*, France's agency in charge of the integrity and ethics of public officials, that they have asked to be struck from the bar "so as to preclude accusations of conflict of interest."[21] But while the publicizing of politicians' *pantouflages* has illustrated the reversal of fortune that is always a risk, the bridges are solidly anchored between the top ranks of civil service and the legal profession. This movement has unceasingly expanded over the years and the lines of transfer are consolidated. Even at the height of debate about politicians donning the robes of lawyer, high-level *pantouflages* of the former director of the DGSE intelligence agency (France's FBI) to the Franco-American firm Orrick Rambaud Martel, and the move of the second in command at the tax department (DGFIP) to Ernst & Young, were discussed only very briefly in the columns of the specialized press, showing how banal transfers from the top of the state administration had become.

---

20. On the specificities of the political job market, see recent work by Demazière and Le Lidec, *Les mondes du travail politique*.

21. As indicated by Edouard Philippe in his statement of interests and assets submitted to the high authority for transparency in public life when he was a deputy in the National Assembly, 2014.

The Trials of Conversion

Readers should not imagine that the passage of civil servants and politicians to the business bar is always easy, without problems or missteps. When they join the legal profession, the *pantoufleurs* must first comply with a set of professional rules and customs that differ from those of the central government administration. Admission to the bar requires a genuine professional retooling, and success hinges on rapid acclimation to the professional norms of big business law firms. The crossovers we interviewed describe a phenomenon of culture shock. The most senior of them mention, with some delectation, the cases of those who were never able to adapt to the new constraints, and eventually left the profession, or have a marginal practice: "he doesn't like his job, he's not a lawyer. His fiscal reasoning is very interesting, but he doesn't see clients" (interview 8, man, ENA graduate, tax law). Specialized journalists also like to chronicle stories such as the one of this "Paris firm, [where] there are still painful memories of a politician (albeit of second order) that the firm had recruited—at considerable cost— and then had all sorts of trouble getting rid of, when his results proved to be inadequate."[22] Some crossover attempts have been spectacular failures, such as that of Hervé de Charette who was admitted to the bar in 2001, a few years after having served as Chirac foreign affairs minister from 1995 to 1997. He was sentenced to reimburse 200,000 euros in fees to a former client, Otor, who accused him of failing "to draft a single brief or letter to a judge, and who attended no hearing or court session" in the course of litigation with the second-ranking producer of cardboard boxes in France.[23]

The difficulties most frequently mentioned by crossovers are the liberal nature of the profession—"client relations," and the specific time frame of the trade— and the sense of loss of personal power. "What we lack the most, as *énarques* and when you've been in public service," confides this business lawyer from the *Conseil d'État*, "is often the relationship with the client. How to talk to him, give him a sense of security, present things positively, never say 'your thing is impossible,' but rather 'your case is not simple, pretty complicated, I can't promise success but I will do all I can....' That's the thing, an *énarque*, he shows up and says: 'this is a shambles.'... The second thing is the financial relationship with the client. How much to bill, how to submit the bill, when to bill ... Myself, I always ... I can't manage to write up a bill, I don't care about it" (interview 14, man, *Conseil d'État*, ENA graduate, public law). One of the first *pantoufleurs* emphasized

---

22. *Lettre des juristes d'affaires*, October 1, 1990.
23. "Les mésaventures d'Hervé de Charette, avocat novice," *Le Monde*, September 11, 2007.

his discovery of how differently this new profession worked compared to the rationale of his public service job: "I didn't bring any clientele, and I hadn't at all grasped the commercial aspects. At the *Conseil d'État*, things are simple, you have a captive market, on the contrary you have to push back against solicitations" (interview 12, man, *Conseil d'État*, arbitration and public law). "Whatever the situation, the client is brought to you, and cannot set you up in competition with the customs administration or the defense ministry" (interview 10, man, ENI graduate, tax law). A former judiciary magistrate who migrated to the Salans law firm says the same thing: "In my first meetings with clients, I was ill at ease, especially when it came to talking about fees. I still have a hard time with this merchant relationship . . . I felt like I was on the other side of the courtroom rail. I was emotional. For a fraction of a second my head spun in an identity whirl. I was on the verge of passing to the other side of the table, to the side where I was so accustomed to sitting as magistrate."[24] In addition to the commercial stance that goes along with the imperative of always being at the client's service, the *pantoufleurs* mention the pressure of the time sheet, and temporal organization that is less foreseeable than in the administration, and which demands constant availability. "What is exhausting is the fact that you never stop. The client, when he needs something, he has to find his lawyer, and if you're on vacation, it doesn't matter, you can still manage the conference call. You never let go of your Blackberry, and there is never an instant when you are not connected, when you are not thinking about the firm, its clients, about such and such a case. And that is what is exhausting, the fact that you can never take a break" (interview 17, man, ENA graduate, competition law). Another person adds: "Culture shock, it's true. Not in terms of volume of work, I used to work Saturdays before. At the *Conseil d'État*, one works more and more, the myth of the English club where one goes to work from time to time, it doesn't work like that. . . . What is true, however, is that there is a difference from the point of view of stress and the predictability of the work, in a law firm you don't know in the morning what might hit you during the day. . . . It's Friday evening for Monday morning" (interview 9, man, *Conseil d'État*, public law of business).

Many point out a sudden loss of authority: "It's very frustrating not to have power. In the administration, I banged on the table, and I could say 'That's it now, I've decided.' You have a power of influence, not of action. And that's frustrating" (interview 14, man, *Conseil d'État*, public law of business). Likewise, the nonhierarchical relationships with other associates, or inversely the subordinate

---

24. Rémi Barousse, quoted in Perrin and Gaune, *Parcours d'avocat(e)s*, 24–25.

position vis-à-vis the American or English headquarters of the firm. The discovery of this work dynamic is expressed first of all as a contrast with the administration, that may be positive or negative. First comes the observation of a different spirit or ethos, underscoring the common culture shared among graduates of certain state vocational schools or *grands corps*: "The reference framework is not at all the same between the administration and a law firm. There is an enormous advantage in the administration, which is that everybody went to the same school, ENFIP (state's vocational school for tax inspectors), so ab initio there is a sort of shared company culture. . . . You know, when you meet someone, when you recruit a young staffer, depending on the remarks and comments made about him and the interviews you have with him, you've immediately got a bead on him. . . . In the private sector, the game is reversed, here there are staff members from all sorts of universities, there are those who've been to business school and then did a graduate degree in tax law, there are economists. . . . And all that means that the culture is created by the subject matter, by the case, rather than on the basis of initial training" (interview 10, man, ENI graduate, tax law).

Despite the difficulties of conversion, a new path of *pantouflage* was nonetheless established. Structural elements certainly account for the success of this new pathway to the business bar. Among these is the widening income gap between the public elite and business lawyers over the past three decades. This growing disparity of remuneration can hardly be ignored. In our interviews, respondents often say that the prospect of earnings is *naturally pleasant* but not a determining factor in choice of career (which is more often presented as a question of personal accomplishment, and lack of challenge of the administrative environment). There is quite a lot of data, however, confirming that since the 1980s, the gap has doubled between the average salary of the top 1 percent best-paid civil servants and the corresponding segment in private firms.[25] Today only 0.05 percent of employees in the state civil service (i.e., 1,200 people) attain the average salary of the top 1 percent in the private sector.[26] These findings corroborate those of a report issued a decade earlier in 2004 that indicated that: "a director in the central administration earns on average 115,000 euros gross pay annually, three to four times less than high-level directors in the private sector."[27] The income statements of French *public managers* now published by

---

25. Marie-Christine Kessler, "L'évasion des membres du Conseil d'État vers le secteur privé," in *Le Droit administratif en question* (Paris: Presses Universitaires de France, 1993), 122–38.

26. Eva Baradji, Dorothée Olivier, and Erwan Pouliquen, "L'encadrement supérieur et dirigeant dans les trois versants de la fonction publique," *Point Stat DGAFP*, February 2015, 4.

27. Jean-Ludovic Silicani, *La Rémunération au mérite des directeurs d'administration centrale: Mobiliser les directeurs pour conduire le changement* (Paris: La Documentation française, 2004), 5.

the *Haute Autorité pour la transparence de la vie publique* illustrates this vividly. One example is Emmanuel Macron, whose salary was cut sixfold when he moved from managing associate at Banque Rothschild to the position of deputy secretary general at the Élysée Palace in 2012. Among lawyers an example is former majority leader Jean-François Copé who reported income of 313,703 euros for 2012, twice his salary as a member of Parliament. While it is always hard to evaluate the income of those in liberal professions, the average billings of partners in the top one hundred business law firms in France attain high levels, at 1,482,578 euros (2014). This figure is sharply lower for purely French firms, at 1,134,210 euros on average per partner, compared to an average 2,843,147 euros per partner in the Paris offices of American firms.[28] Looking at the figures of the national statistical institute (Insee) on high income groups (the top percentile) in the nonsalaried private sector, the legal profession is strongly present. Lawyers and notaries make up 12 percent of the category of "very high incomes in the nonsalaried private sector," representing 18,000 people with an average annual income of 243,467 euros.[29]

However, while the financial attractiveness of the business bar certainly increased the gap, it is not enough to account for the progressive consolidation of this pathway. One factor relates to internal transformations of the administration that have made circulation to and from top state's positions much easier. The move to less strict statutory constraints at the summit of the state has indeed contributed to a more porous border between the public and the private. Nonstatutory positions have steadily augmented at the summit of the state ever since the 1980s:[30] in 2012, there were 525 positions in 39 ministerial cabinets, 458 top state positions "at the discretion of the government" (ambassadors, prefects, departments' directors, etc.),[31] and 2,033 positions in regulatory agencies,[32] all which were contractual and based on direct loyalty to the government or the agency's president. The rapid development of these porous fringes of the state (where budgetary rules allow for higher wages) have made the departure to and the return from the private sector far easier.

---

28. See the survey by the professional magazine *Décideurs: Stratégie finance droit*, July–August 2014, 70–87.

29. Michel Amar, "Les très hauts salaires du secteur privé," *Insee Première* 1288, April 2010.

30. On the extension of the scope of "discretionary appointments" in the administration, see Jacques Chevallier, "L'élite politico-administrative: Une interpénétration discutée," *Pouvoirs* 80 (1997): 89–100.

31. As of December 31, 2012, according to Baradji, Olivier, and Pouliquen, "L'encadrement supérieur et dirigeant dans les trois versants de la fonction publique."

32. René Dosière and Christian Vanneste, *Rapport d'information sur les autorités administratives indépendantes: Rapport de l'Assemblée nationale no. 2925* (October 28, 2010).

In opening the way, one should also account for the role of a few pioneers who succeeded in becoming figureheads of the business bar and soon became role models as well as brokers for top civil servants aspiring to follow their tracks. By producing new representations of what was possible and feasible in the course of a political or administrative career, these examples encouraged younger individuals to follow in their turn this as yet less traveled road. The first generation of crossovers, for instance Jean-Patrice de La Laurencie in competition law, or Olivier Debouzy in public business law, both of them *énarques*, came to be recruiters in the ranks of the *grands corps* and the upper echelons of the civil service. They continued, beyond the limits of public administration, the practices of "administrative godfather," "protectors at the center of clientelistic patronage mechanisms, in an economy of support provided and favors returned."[33] As they vaunted the merits of this new career to their comrades, they helped create veritable recruitment chains for a small number of firms.[34]

A New Power Elite?

The group of 217 *pantoufleurs* to the business bar, over two-thirds of whom are still members of the bar at the time of inquiry (December 2015), may at first glance seem not very significant in size compared to the large mass of lawyers in the two bar associations (Paris and Hauts-de-Seine), or to the ranks of the political and administrative elite during this period. There are indeed 27,500 lawyers in the Paris and Hauts-de-Seine bar associations, and about 200 partners changing law firms every year.[35] The category of public managers (members of Parliament, ministers, ranking elected officials, mayors of large cities, managers of state-owned companies, cabinet staff, high-level civil servants) as enumerated by the *Haute Autorité pour la transparence de la vie publique* consists of over 10,000 people. This perspective is radically altered, however, when one considers the pivotal position in the field of power occupied by these crossovers to the private sector. This group includes 117 *énarques*; 89 former members of ministerial cabinets; 47 members of Parliament (former and current); 35 former

---

33. Jean-Michel Eymeri-Douzans, "Les bons endroits, les bons amis, les bons moments," in *L'État, le droit, le politique: Mélanges en l'honneur de Jean-Claude Colliard* (Paris: Dalloz, 2014), 7.

34. See the special issue of ENA Alumni magazine, *ENA Mensuel* 329 (2003) entitled "Lawyers: The New Challenges," which lists many cases of crossovers.

35. The professional website DayOne has counted between 150 and 250 transfers of partners per year over the past decade in Paris. See DayOne, "Dix ans de mouvements d'avocats associés," http://village-justice.com/.

ministers; 30 former directors and deputy directors in the central administration departments; 29 former cabinet chiefs of staff; 8 former presidents and secretaries general of political parties; 6 former secretaries general and deputy secretaries general of the office of the French presidency. Many of these have held more than one of these positions in the course of their career. The portrait gallery of these 217 crossovers is the description of an elite of the elite.

An Elite of the Elite

Let us start by sketching a typical or median profile of these crossovers, as compared to their counterparts in the field of politics, government, and business bar. This group possesses a distinctive set of features. First and foremost, it is a very masculine set (87 percent men), much more so than top civil servants, politicians, and partners in the business bar—who are themselves already a very unbalanced professional milieu.[36] This confirms research showing that top civil service women are less likely to cross over to the private sector, and suggests a new glass ceiling in the phenomenon.[37] It will come as no surprise that those who cross over to the private sector have impressive academic credentials.[38] A degree from Sciences Po is the best ticket for access to these border spaces: two-thirds of crossovers attended one of the nine Sciences Po institutes (eight of which are outside of Paris), and almost all of them attended Sciences Po Paris, as opposed to just 5.5 percent who went to elite business schools and 4.6 percent who have university degrees in economics. The Sciences Po degree also often comes with a law degree: 53 percent of Sciences Po Paris graduates have this double qualification. This configuration harks back to an earlier time, when law remained marginal at Sciences Po Paris and studies at one of the Paris law schools was considered a necessary complement. Yet others, mostly among the younger cohorts, have only been to Sciences Po Paris: "I did law at Sciences Po the way everyone did law at Sciences Po, that is I had marks of 19 or 20 [out of 20] in constitutional law and administrative law, and then 3 or 4 in penal, civil law, because those were not

---

36. The share of women partners in business law firms is one of the lowest in the profession. See "Femmes au barreau en 2013," *Bulletin de l'ordre des avocats du barreau de Paris*, March 2013.

37. Referring to the *Conseil d'État*, Olivia Bui Xuan has noted that women in this *grand corps* are much less mobile than their male peers, and even more so with respect to mobility outside of the administrative sphere, with the effect that women tend to make up the permanent staff of the institution, justifying the epithet "vestales of French public law," in Olivia Bui Xuan, *Les Femmes au Conseil d'État* (Paris: L'Harmattan, 2001), 179–81. See also, for a more recent survey, Luc Rouban, "L'accès des femmes aux postes dirigeants de l'État," *Revue française d'administration publique* 145 (2013): 89–108.

38. Indeed, a master's in law is required to qualify for the dispensatory procedure to enter the bar.

TABLE 1 /   Academic background of the crossovers (n = 209/217)

SCIENCES PO PARIS	126
of which Sciences Po Paris + law school	66
of which Sciences Po Paris + École normale supérieure	7
of which Sciences Po Paris + business school	9
SCIENCES PO (OUTSIDE OF PARIS)[1]	14
of which Sciences Po (outside of Paris) + law school	8
UNIVERSITY DEGREES	99
Law school	59
PhD	10
Political science	7
Economics	9
Other diploma	14
GRANDES ÉCOLES (excluding Sciences Po Paris)	12
of which École normale supérieure	4
of which engineering schools	5
of which business schools	3
Total	228

Source: authors. "Crossovers" biographical database.

Note: The total number is greater than the number of individuals because of multiple degrees in some cases (e.g., ENS + law, Grande École + law).
"Law degree" includes both the "license" and "master's" degrees, because the details are rarely given, and a more specific breakdown cannot be made.

[1] From the 1950s onward, a number of political science institutes were opened on the model of Sciences Po Paris in Aix, Bordeaux, Grenoble, Lille, Rennes, Toulouse, Strasbourg, and most recently Saint Germain en Laye.

subjects studied at Sciences Po. And overall, we passed. But I can't say I really studied law" (interview 14, man, *Conseil d'État*, public law of business). On the whole, whether they have combined law schools and Sciences Po degrees or not, their academic training situates them at a good distance from the poles of business or engineering schools.

This academic training set a track leading a majority of the sample group to the core of the state governing elite whether it is by virtue of succeeding the highly selective exam to enter the *École nationale d'administration*, as is the case for more than half of them (53 percent), or because they were called upon to join a minister's cabinet staff, often considered a sort of "second ENA" further validating one's credentials as an experienced policy maker (49 percent).[39]

---

39. Luc Rouban, "Les énarques en cabinet (1984–1996)," *Cahiers du Cevipof* 17 (1997): 31.

Another defining element of this group of *pantoufleurs* lies in its being relatively young on average, in contrast to the classic image of an end-of-career *pantouflage* moving to the private sector just a few years before or after retirement from public service. Age of admittance to bar ranges from 25 to 78 years of age, but in most cases the applicants admitted are under 50. While in the Fifth French Republic, *pantouflage* has traditionally been an end-of-career move, relatively few cases correspond to this model here. One instance is prefects—11 joined the bar after the age of 60. To be sure, joining the ranks of the liberal professions is a convenient way to bypass retirement: "One of the advantages is that as a lawyer you can go beyond the retirement age and continue to earn a good living" (interview 12, man, ENA, arbitration and public law of business). The benefits are nonnegligible for high-level civil servants, whose pension calculation excludes bonuses, meaning that their purchasing power falls considerably when their administrative career comes to an end.

But this new form of *pantouflage* is taken by younger and younger crossovers. The average crossover age is 47; in all, 59 percent of the individuals in the sample joined the business bar before they were 50, and nearly one-third (29 percent) even before they were 40. This observation confirms trends noted in other research on the *grands corps*.[40] Typically, the person who crosses over to the bar, a move that is at once "conversion and wager," is "a man in between two ages, no longer all that young but not yet well established in his career."[41] For high-level civil servants, this is a period when they are already embarked on an administrative career that is sometimes beginning to lose its luster, and for which there seem to be few opportunities for advancement in terms of salary or interesting position. "At the *Conseil d'État*, I knew that I would automatically become chamber's president in the coming years,[42] but that didn't particularly appeal to me, because I felt I was too young. . . . I really like the *Conseil d'État*, and I'll say right off the bat that I count on returning. . . . But I figured that at my age, in a position where I would be doing the same thing for practically 20 years, in the same premises, . . . [becoming a lawyer] came from the idea of doing something else before coming back" (interview 14, man, *Conseil d'État*, public law of business). "The problem with ENA," says another crossover, "is that it's great at the beginning, it's very interesting from the start, but later on it

---

40. A historical outlook is provided by Christophe Charle, "Le pantouflage en France (vers 1880–vers 1980)," *Annales: Histoire, Sciences Sociales* 42, no. 5 (1987): 1115-37.

41. Ibid., 1124.

42. There are ten chambers (so-called *sous-section*) at the *Conseil d'État*.

gets boring. . . . What do you do afterwards?" (interview 8, man, ENA graduate, tax law).

Public Springboards and Private Fallback Positions

By construction, all the *pantouﬂeurs* in our sample group began their career in state service, as a civil servant, in the parapublic sector or on a political staff. These positions do not lead equally to crossing over to the private sector, nor do they predispose one to the same career pathways, however. Four major spring-boards can be identified, correlated to different initial points of entry into the public sector. While statistically important, the springboard of legal positions is relatively limited (32.5 percent of the *pantouﬂeurs*) given the fact that we are considering a population that would later move to the business bar. Interest-ingly, magistrates in the judiciary, who specialize in civil and criminal matters, are marginal in this subgroup (6.5 percent out of the 32.5 percent),[43] when com-pared to professionals in administrative law drawn from the *Conseil d'État*, lower administrative courts, and legal affairs positions in the central administration (26 percent).

Second is the economics springboard used by those who started out in the ministry of the economy, the public banking sector, or in regulatory agencies (18 percent of crossovers). A politics springboard also appears for 13.5 percent of the *pantouﬂeurs*, represented by those who entered the public sphere in political positions, whether as elected officials or as a member of their staff (parliamen-tary assistants, local executive advisers, etc.). Last comes what could be called the "regal" springboard of ministries exercising central state prerogatives (inte-rior, defense, and foreign affairs) in which 11 percent of crossovers learned the administrative ropes. This allows us to map out the specific segments of the state that have established stable bridges with the business bar—a map that goes well beyond the remits of law positions. Symmetrically, it brings to light the institu-tions and profiles that remain relatively marginal in this circuit such as the two other *grands corps* (*Inspection des finances* and to a lesser extent the *Cour des comptes*)—not so much because they are immune from these circulations but rather because they are part of other circuits of revolving doors, notably toward banks, insurance companies, and big corporations.[44]

---

43. On the most limited (albeit increasing) number of crossovers among judicial magistrates, see Anne Boigeol, "Les magistrats 'hors les murs,'" *Droit et société* 44–45 (2000): 225–47.
44. Dudouet and Grémont, "Les grands patrons et l'État en France, 1981–2007."

TABLE 2 / Springboards: First public position held by the crossovers (n = 207/217)

Law Springboard: 32.5%	*Conseil d'État*	16.5%
	Judiciary	6.5%
	Administrative courts	5.5%
	Ministries' legal advisers	4%
Economic Springboard: 24%	Ministry of economy	14.5%
	Cour des Comptes	5.5%
	Inspection des finances	3%
	Banque de France	1%
Political Springboard: 14%	Political staff	9%
	Elected officials (local and national)	5%
Regal Springboard: 11.5%	Prefects	5.5%
	Diplomacy	4%
	Military	2%
Other: 13.5%	Other civil service corps (public hospitals, labor law inspectorate, etc.)	10.5%
	Cabinet Staff Members	3%
	TOTAL	100%

Source: authors. "Crossovers" biographical database.

Notes: Political staff: parliamentary assistants and local executive advisers.

The table also includes academics, equal to 3.5% of the total.

Now let's take a look at the fallback positions that *pantoufleurs* were able to find in the legal profession. In terms of the cartography of Paris law firms, crossovers landed in a strictly limited zone of the bar. One hundred forty firms were involved for 225 transfers (some *pantoufleurs* moved to several firms in the course of their careers), which represent only a small fraction of active law firms in Paris and the Hauts-de-Seine department. The fraction of the bar concerned can be also traced through the characteristics of these firms. Some crossovers created their own one-person firms to develop their own clientele as solo practitioners (close to 15 percent of crossovers). But they are certainly marginal cases compared to the vast majority who joined medium or large law firms; more than 40 percent of crossovers transfer to firms numbering between forty and one hundred lawyers.

The majority of the crossovers head to large firms in the Paris business bar. On the basis of the ranking of the 50 top firms published yearly by a specialized magazine, 40 of these firms were the destination of at least one crossover during the period of our study.[45] Similarly, the 20 or so Paris firms that received more than

---

45. "Décideurs 100 des cabinets d'avocats," *Décideurs*, July 16, 2014.

TABLE 3 / Fallback positions: Types of law firms hiring crossovers

TYPE OF FIRM	NUMBER OF CROSSOVERS (N=225)
Solo practitioners	32
Niche law firms (fewer than 40 lawyers)	42
Big law firms (40 and more)	151
	French law firms: 88
	Anglo-American law firms: 63

Source: authors. "Crossovers" biographical database.

four crossovers are among the biggest business law firms in Paris. Among them, one finds August & Debouzy (18) and Gide (12), the all-round champions in the "poaching" of high-level civil servants and politicians. While Anglo-American law firms are a frequent destination—close to one-third of crossovers—including firms such as Landwell, Day Jones, Allen & Overy, Clifford Chance, Bird & Bird, which regularly receive members of the political and administrative elite, one can still identify a preference for French-owned law firms. The five firms that take in the most crossovers are all members of the French business bar, and they aim to compete with the Paris offices of the major British and American firms.

Interestingly, law firms have made a special place for the *pantoufleurs* in their organization. Although few join as staff lawyers (*collaborateurs*) who are the rank and file of business law firms, they do not necessarily become partners, thereby taking direct responsibility (and risk) in the commercial success of the enterprise and its management strategy; this is the case for fewer than half of crossovers (80 out of 174 positions we were able to determine). The destination firms have proved very creative in allowing for all sorts of "à la carte" practice for prestigious figures without requiring them to either participate in board decisions or capital investment (these are nonequity partners). Likewise, they have been more than willing to accommodate short-term or even intermittent passages. Many neo-lawyers are initially positioned outside the hierarchical structure of the firms, meaning that they do not have to be measured and evaluated by the same metrics (billings, clients) as their new colleagues. This situation is most often termed a position *of counsel*, for one-fourth of crossovers, and sometimes by other even more ambiguous denominations. Some crossovers are simply "affiliated" or "domiciled" in a firm, without formally practicing law there—for example, for-mer *Élysée* secretary general and foreign affairs minister Hubert Védrine, who has been given an office at Gide without any formal position in the organigram. Some others, however, are given executive responsibilities as heads for the pub-lic law, regulatory, or fiscal poles of the business law firms (17 cases). But the *pantoufleurs* rarely get to act as managing partner, a position which is de facto reserved for professional lawyers. As a sign of their ad hoc status in the bar, none of them has taken part in the profession's representative politics, notably in the elections for Council of the Order of the Paris bar.

What this brief portrayal of the *pantoufleurs* and their trajectory in the bar has shown is how circumscribed the public-private circulation is, thereby contradicting the idea of a broad nondifferentiation between the two. There is certainly no general osmosis between the business bar and political and administrative spaces. Rather, what can be seen is a set of properties that predispose to mobility: male gender, law degree or education in a political science institute or ENA, a stint in a ministerial cabinet, membership in a party of government. But also, more broadly, the outlines of a circuit of circulation that connects specific segments of the state specialized in law, economics, and public affairs, to sectors of the legal profession.

Mapping Out the Field of Public-Private Intermediation

Upon closer look, however, the group of *pantoufleurs* is not as homogeneous as it is often casually made out to be by the press. Media attention has focused on the most high-profile political figures, the de Villepin, Cazeneuve, and other Straus Kahns, and has too often put up a screen that masks the diverse profiles of those who cross from civil service to the legal profession. The crossover population group encompasses a broad range of profiles, from former secretaries general of the Élysée Palace and former ministers to members of the *Conseil d'État* and tax inspectors, not to mention the very different specializations they possess, covering competition law, fiscal matters, public-private partnerships, public affairs, and so on. More importantly, the crossover trajectories vary considerably in terms of career positions as well as in terms of level of specialization. What the study of the 217 trajectories reveals is that this stratification of the population is highly dependent on two variables: whether the *pantoufleurs* are ENA graduates or not, and whether they have political capital or not. Analyzing in these terms the variety of trajectories and roles taken reveals the division of labor that constitutes the underpinning of France's regulatory state.

The Division of Regulatory Labor

Far from forming a homogeneous group, the crossovers have distinct profiles and career perspectives. More than half of them attended ENA (54 percent), and this is certainly the major dividing line within this set. This division can be seen most clearly from the viewpoint of academic baggage: the *énarques* have most often attended Sciences Po Paris as well, unlike those who are not ENA graduates, and who in 81 percent of cases have law school degrees. Furthermore, the ENA graduates who become lawyers, from the oldest (class of 1948) to the most recent (class of 2004), come from the most prestigious pathways for acceptance to the school. Nearly all of them matriculated at ENA via the more prestigious external entrance procedure (that is immediately after graduation: 88 percent of this group). Some had already attended other French *grandes écoles* such as the *École normale supérieure* (9.4 percent) or business schools (9 percent), thereby acquiring the "double degree" advantage that other research has described as specific to an "elite of the ENA."[46] This "elite of the elite" in terms of academic qualifications also holds for professional careers. The *énarques* who moved to the business bar have often come out ahead in the ranking set at the end of the ENA curriculum, and they frequently joined the state's *grands corps*. This breaks down as 30 percent members of the *Conseil d'État*, 10 percent from the *Cour des comptes*, and 5 percent from the *Inspection des finances*, for a total of 45 percent of crossover *énarques*. By comparison, on average just 20 percent of ENA graduates are accepted into these *grands corps* upon leaving the school.[47] If one expands this set to include the "quasi-*grand corps*" of top civil servants from the ministry of the economy and finances (22 percent), it is even clearer that the crossovers include an elite group of *énarques*. This is further confirmed by their administrative experience largely concentrated within the twin poles of the *Conseil d'État* and the ministry of economy. When considering their entire trajectory, it appears that 27 percent of crossovers have occupied a position at the ministry of economy, and 24 percent at the *Conseil d'État* (these sets in part overlap, as some crossovers did stints at both institutions).

The special status of crossover *énarques* is confirmed by the fact that they are more likely to be found in ministerial cabinets (59 percent compared to 36 percent for *non-énarques*), stay there longer, and in half of cases occupy more than one cabinet post in the course of their career.[48] *Énarques* and *non-énarques* frequently cross paths in ministerial cabinet offices. But they do not mingle, for the former tend to have executive positions, while the latter are often technical

46. Jean-Michel Eymeri, *La fabrique des énarques* (Paris: Economica, 2001), 55.

47. Ibid.

48. This proportion is considerably higher than the average percentage of ENA graduates who take cabinet positions upon leaving the school (29 percent of a class). Rouban, "Les énarques en cabinet (1984–1996)," 31.

advisers or task officers with political assignments. Of 71 *énarque* crossovers who have held cabinet positions, 30 were chief of staff or deputy chief of staff in a ministerial cabinet, or secretary general or deputy secretary general of the presidency at the Élysée Palace.

Observing the total trajectory of these two subsets of crossovers, one can see a differentiated geography of circulation: the key points of passage for *énarque* crossovers form a tightly coherent configuration of executive staff offices in ministerial cabinets, the *Conseil d'État*, the ministry of the economy and finances, and to a lesser extent the regal domains of the state (defense, interior, foreign affairs). Inversely, *non-énarques* follow more varied itineraries, some political in nature, others more technical, often in regulatory agencies or government legal departments.

A second line of division is traced within the crossover group, according to their degree of proximity to the field of politics. Two types of itineraries are seen: those directly connected to the political job market, including elected officials

TABLE 4 /   Highest cabinet staff position held by crossovers (n = 105/217)

	NON-ÉNARQUES	ÉNARQUES
Adviser	25	33
Chief of staff (and deputy)	10	31
Élysée palace secretary general (and deputy)	0	6
Total	**35**	**70**

Source: authors. "Crossovers" biographical database.

TABLE 5 /   Points of passage of crossovers during their careers

	NON-ÉNARQUES	ÉNARQUES
Ministerial Cabinets	36	59
of which president's and prime minister's cabinets	9	23
Parliamentary Assemblies	56	14.5
Local Government	46	25
Major Corporations	10	19
Ministry of the Economy	15	37
Conseil d'État	15	37.5
Regal Ministries	18	28
(interior, defense, foreign affairs)		
Regulatory Agencies	18	17
Government Legal Departments	13	3

Source: author.

Read: 28 percent of ENA graduates in the Crossovers' database have worked in the "regal ministries" at one point of their career. As individuals have occupied several posts, they are counted more than once in the table.

and political staffers, and the other defined by accumulation of bureaucratic and technical capital. On the one hand, former ministers and members of Parliament make up 27.7 percent of crossovers (11 percent have successively been MP and minister); and on the other hand, the remaining two-thirds of crossovers have never been in political positions (66.3 percent). The political pole is dominated by non–ENA graduates, proportionally more numerous: while only 14.5 percent of crossover *énarques* are former ministers or MPs, this figure is significantly higher among *non-énarques*, 34 percent of whom are former deputies or senators. The administrative pole is made up of those who are more distant from the political elite: 31.3 percent of crossovers have never held elective office, nor a position in a ministerial cabinet or on a political staff. This is a group of public policy specialists, spanning fiscal matters, public procurement, competition policy and securities, and dealing with regulated sectors (telecommunications, transportation, energy, etc.) and strategic policies (defense, international contracts, etc.). Whether they are graduates of ENA or not, these administrators tend to emphasize their professional experience and technical expertise.

This two-pronged division defines the structure and hierarchy of the crossover group, by academic background (ENA graduate or not) and political capital (work in politics or not). These two variables mark a strong internal differentiation within the group, depending on their training, the posts they have held in government, their points of passage into the private sector, and the positions that they can legitimately expect to occupy in the private sector, and in law firms in particular. These variables configure the possibilities and probabilities for the mobility of crossovers, and define classes of trajectories that can be summarized in four ideal types representing a variable combination of resources and forms of legitimacy. None of these exists in a pure state, of course, nor should they be seen as representations of reality; rather they form a stylized picture of the most *salient differences* and *polarities* within the group of *pantoufleurs* (in terms of training and professional trajectory).

Reading table 6 from the upper right, where political and bureaucratic capital are combined and added up, the highest ranked group is the "Mandarins,"

TABLE 6 / Types of crossovers' profiles

POLITICAL CAPITAL? ENA GRADUATE?	WEAK	STRONG
Yes	Regulators	Mandarins
No	Technicians	Politicals

Source: authors.

a term used to designate top-ranking civil servants who come mostly from the state's *grands corps* and have had close connections to members of the government. By virtue of their position in the central spaces of state power—for example, ministerial cabinets, secretariat general of the government, secretariat general of the presidency, and so forth—these individuals incarnate the politicoadministrative elite. Closely connected to the regimen of alternating parties and the spoils system that goes with it at the highest level of the state, they generally stay only a short time in the bar, in the course of careers characterized by great mobility and stints in France's largest corporations. Armed with generalist and transversal skills and competence, they are naturally found on the public affairs market. Their experience at the top of government endows them with prestige and a reputation that leads them directly to extrahierarchical positions in cabinets that are better suited to their status and to the sensitive matters that they will follow. This is the case of Jean-Pierre Jouyet, a member of the Inspection des finances *grand corps* who briefly joined Jeantet law firm (1995–1997), after having served as deputy cabinet director to the president of the European Commission, Jacques Delors, and before going on to become successively president of the *Autorité des marchés financiers* (France's finance regulator), secretary of state for European affairs, director of the Treasury, secretary general of the presidency during the term of François Hollande, and now France's ambassador in London.

Alongside this state nobility, there is the "Regulators" group, made up of ENA graduates who have held directorial positions in the administration of economic or technical ministries, or in agencies, without ever having taken a directly political position or belonged to a political entourage for any length of time. These top civil servants have exercised the most central functions in the regulatory state, whether as executive public officers (ministry of the economy, and agencies), as judges (*Conseil d'État*, judiciary) or as members of the executive staff offices (cabinet chief of staff, etc.). At the end of their public careers, they have accumulated in-depth knowledge of the administrative, legal, and judicial workings of the regulatory state. One example is the itinerary of Patrick Hubert, 1987 ENA graduate and former member of the *Conseil d'État*, who served as chief of staff to the ministry of justice and was nominated to be *rapporteur général* (chief investigator) to the competition authority, before joining the Clifford Chance firm in 2004, where he became a partner in 2007, working in the "Public law, environment and competition" department and frequently pleading before the *Autorité de la concurrence.*

The top part of table 6, either as "Regulators" or "Mandarins," describes the directorial pole of the regulatory state. An *énarque* who was one of the most highly visible business lawyers until his untimely death gave an illustration in the ENA alumni review:

> It was not just happenstance that so many *énarques* chose to become lawyers. Unlike *normaliens* [graduates of *École normale supérieure*], *énarques* are not intellectuals, and unlike *polytechnicians* [graduates of *École Polytechnique* engineering school], they do not identify with a network: they are *men of power*. The fact that they have spread into legal professions shows that power has shifted from States to corporations, and from armies to financiers and legal advisors. *Énarques* are the canary in the mine, alerting us to a change, that while it has not attracted much attention in France, is nonetheless real and significant.[49]

This citation can of course be classed as the semidescriptive, semiprophetic musings of a "convert," but it clearly underscores the pivotal position occupied by this group in the state.

The singular features of these "men of power" are even more clearly revealed by comparison of the top of table 6 with the lower half, the *non-énarques*. First of all are the "Politicals" who have conducted their public career in the entourage of elected officials, in parliamentary assemblies or in government staff. Like former ministers of justice or the economy (as well as the related web of junior ministries in trade, small business, industry, budget, etc.) or former members of Parliament who sat on the finance or legislation committees, they are the actors of the political scene that surrounds the regulatory state. Their capital of political experience plus practical knowledge of the machinery of writing bills and producing administrative rules are qualities they can market. While in most instances it is very hard to precisely identify the tasks they are given in law firms, which are generally listed in vague categories of negotiation, arbitration, or mediation, these individuals constitute a considerable commercial asset for law firms, who readily publicize them: "If one of my foreign clients wants to invest in a particular area in France . . . I can ask [Georges Tron, a long-term MP] to get information from the government and find out whether it's on the list of priorities. And then, as a member of the finances committee, he can inform us about the drafting of new legislation," explains the managing partner of one law firm.[50] Another lawyer describes the arrival at the firm of a Socialist Party member of Parliament in these terms: "he was on the National Assembly legislative committee for ten

---

49. Olivier Debouzy, "Les avocats et le rôle du droit dans la société française," in "Lawyers: The New Challenges," special issue, *ENA Mensuel: La revue des anciens élèves de l'ENA* 329 (2003).

50. Quoted in "Georges Tron: pour moi ça a été la double peine," *Le Parisien*, September 17, 2012.

years, that's a major asset," he says. "But what interests us is his address book, we are not allowed to solicit clients in our profession. So, the personal contacts of an MP are essential."[51] As they have turned the business bar into a new holding space to wait out the low tides of the vagaries of elections, it is frequent that these political crossovers stay only a short time. They share with the mandarins their dependence on the political job market and its seesaw movement. But, lacking the bureaucratic capital held by the state nobility, their careers in law firms are often ephemeral, or rocky. This distinguishes them from the majority of crossovers, for whom this transition is often a permanent move.[52] This is emphasized by a partner in a firm that took in a former minister: "Of course at the beginning he was enshrined in the glory of his status as former minister, and that makes some things possible, but ten years later, if he hasn't really become a lawyer, it doesn't work any more" (interview 22, man, partner, penal business law).

Last, there are the "Technicians" of the regulatory state, an eminently disparate group that covers a wide range of functions in state and state-related functions, from tax inspection in charge of controlling the largest firms to investigative functions in the wide set of regulatory agencies or courts, and legal functions in technical ministries (environment, health, etc.), and so forth. Taken as a whole, this part of the *pantoufleurs* group reveals another layer of the regulatory state, a technical stratum, and shows the new currency value of these oversight and investigative positions for large corporations and market intermediaries. These are often single-sector itineraries characterized by accumulation of a *specific* bureaucratic capital in areas ranging from taxation to public procurement, sectoral market regulation, and so on. These careers are less subject to shifting political winds, and unfold at an intermediate level of the administrative hierarchy. Professional transition to the bar is all the more durable in that these individuals do not have the political and social capital that would enable them to jump to other professional domains.

Despite their differences, these four typical profiles are ultimately facets of one and the same regulatory state. Together they form a picture of the division of labor in the work of regulation, tying public managers of economic departments to political professionals specialized in producing regulatory legislation, and likening the state nobility to technicians with expertise in the different poles of regulatory action.

---

51. Quoted in *Le Monde*, October 13, 2009.
52. If one excludes crossovers from the past two years (2013–2015), because their moves are too recent to judge whether they are permanent or not, 70 percent of crossovers were still practicing law in December 2016.

Circuits of Public-Private Circulation

Mapping out the trajectories of *pantoufleurs* also makes it possible to draw the different *sector-specific* circuits of the regulatory state. Competition policy, public-private partnerships, fiscal law, securities and banking transactions, and so on, form as many pockets of circulation where Regulators and Mandarins, Politicals and Technicians cross paths and collaborate. While it may be useful for analytical purposes to distinguish these different sectoral circuits, they are in fact often intertwined; the individuals may slip from one domain to another as new bridges are created by successive waves of liberalization. This relative fuzziness is inherent in the very nature of the emerging public law of business (*droit public des affaires*), in which case files routinely cut across the habitual lines of legal specialization: "Here I have a file that involves securities law, financial law, corporate, settlements and redress, public and tax law—five disciplines! The file I worked on this morning spans social, corporate and public law, you see, it's rare that I have a case. . . . In fiscal law one can work alone, in public law one must necessarily work with someone else" (interview 14, man, *Conseil d'État*, public law of business). In fact, crossovers often declare areas of specialization that are intentionally broad ("public law," "arbitration," etc.) or present a portfolio of expertise that calls upon a wide range of expertise (fiscal, competition, securities, economic intelligence, etc.). Still, while they may intermingle in practice, these sectoral circuits delineate specific pathways for converting public assets and experience into the private sector.

The long-standing *fiscal circuit of public-private circulation* has expanded considerably in the past two decades. More than one-fourth of the crossovers in our sample (27 percent) passed through this circuit at one time or another in their trajectory. As described above, the competence and skills of tax inspectors were sought by legal and fiscal consulting firms even before 1991, and these firms regularly paid the compensation due by inspectors who had not put in the statutory eight years of public service. At a time when specialized university degrees were very rare, the only place "where you learned fiscal law was in government tax centers and at Fiduciaire de France [an accounting firm], which right off the bat restricted the sources of recruitment for the private sector."[53] A number of veritable supply chains came into being, linking graduates of ENFIP (state professional school for tax inspectors) and today also *énarques* with experience at tax departments, to law firms and consultancies such as CMS Bureau Francis

---

53. Tax lawyer with Linklaters & Paines quoted in Bruna Basini, "Mon conseiller fiscal est un transfuge," *L'Expansion*, October 12, 2000.

Lefebvre, or Ernst & Young avocats. Firms specialized in fiscal matters almost always have on their roster at least one former tax inspector or *énarque* with a fiscal background. Typically the paths of circulation in this fiscal pole connect political positions—such as special rapporteur of the budget in parliamentary assemblies or secretary of state for the budget, positions at the *Direction générale des Finances publiques* (DGFIP), the important department in charge of drafting fiscal legislation or controlling its implementation at the ministry of economy—to jobs in the tax departments of large companies and law firms.[54]

The trajectory of someone like Dominique Vuillemot illustrates the relationships established between these poles: born in 1954, a graduate of Sciences Po and of ENA (1980)—where he met François Hollande for whom he would organize expert committees during the 2012 presidential campaign. Vuillemot entered the ministry of the economy and finances upon graduation from ENA, and held the position of head of staff at DGFIP from 1986 to 1990. From this post, he "crossed over" in 1990, and joined the legal consulting firm Coopers & Lybrand, where he practiced for some ten years and published many technical works on fiscal matters in Europe. In 1999, he founded his own law firm specialized in fiscal law, and actively pursued the opportunities that the *Question prioritaire de constitutionnalité* has opened up for tax lawyers before the *Conseil constitutionnel*.

Also in the domain of traditional state prerogatives, the *public procurement circuit* flourished anew with the development of public-private partnerships (PPP) throughout the first decade of the twenty-first century. This circuit connects many positions and institutions: prefects, local elected officials, territorial civil servants, employees of the Grand Paris and La Défense (EPAD) infrastructure development corporations, project developers such as the Lyon–Turin train line, and executives in public works and energy infrastructure corporations, and so forth. While major PPP and public law teams in Paris firms are found in this circuit, niche firms are also involved, less visible, not necessarily based in Paris, but highly specialized. Once example is the case of Bruno Kern. With a master's degree in private law from the University of Strasbourg and a graduate degree in political science from Sciences Po Paris, Bruno Kern began his career on the staff of Socialist Party elected officials and ministers, combining "ministerial cabinet and the position of elected official over a period of 13 years," as stated on his firm's website. After serving as parliamentary assistant to a Socialist Party senator, and technical adviser in various ministries, he became chief

54. Alexis Spire and Katia Weidenfeld, *L'impunité fiscale. Quand l'État brade sa souveraineté* (Paris La Découverte, 2015).

of staff at the ministry for "social affairs" (1991–1992), then at the ministry in charge of major infrastructure work (1992–1993), and ultimately legal counsel at the interministerial mission on major infrastructure (1993). When the conservative right returned to power, Kern left politics and became a lawyer, in charge of the "Public and environment law" department at the Arthur Andersen audit firm. Seven years later, in 2000, he founded his own firm, Bruno Kern et associés (BKA), which from the outset was positioned in the field of local government law, with three former high-level territorial civil servants on the roster. With a staff of some fifteen lawyers and employees, BKA has become a leading reference in law regarding local government authorities and is classed as excellent in its subfield of local government by the specialized blogs and magazines. BKA claims on its website that "600 public decision makers" have used its services, including "20 ministries, central government offices and public establishments," but above all "11 regional governments, 30 departments, 60 intermunicipal authorities and 350 city governments."

A *competition circuit* also gradually grew in importance, to the point that one-fourth of *pantoufleurs* have passed through it at some point of their career. The initial pillar of this pole was the development of a powerful corpus of EU competition law that has steadily gained in force as the energy, transportation, and telecommunications sectors have been liberalized.[55] In the course of the period 2000–2010, this policy branched out into national poles with a European network of national competition authorities all put under the auspices of the EU competition directorate. This sectoral circuit of expertise connects the European Commission (its competition directorate and legal department of the Commission); the European Court of Justice (its clerks and judges); the French *Autorité de la concurrence* and the related web of sector-specific regulatory agencies in the field of energy (*Commission de régulation de l'énergie*—CRE), telecommunication (*Autorité de régulation des communications électroniques et des postes*—ARCEP), and transport (*Autorité de régulation des activités ferroviaires*—ARAF); and the government department in charge of implementing competition rules (DGCCRF); as well as lawyers in the EU law and competition departments of large Paris and Brussels law firms.

The career of Jean-Patrice de La Laurencie is a perfect illustration of this wide-ranging circuit of competition and regulatory expertise. Born in 1943, a

---

55. On the centrality of the competition policy in the field of EU polity, see Lola Avril, "Le costume sous la robe: Les avocats en professionnels multi-carte de l'État régulateur (1957–2019)" (PhD diss., Université Paris 1 Sorbonne, 2019). See also Kiran Patel and Heike Schweitzer, eds., *The Historical Foundations of EU Competition Law* (Oxford: Oxford University Press, 2013).

graduate of Sciences Po Paris, matriculated at ENA in 1970, La Laurencie began his career at the permanent French delegation to the European Communities, before joining the competition department of the ministry of economy (1981–1983), then the cabinet of Jacques Delors when the latter became minister of the economy. As department head at the ministry's competition unit, he worked on drafting the founding act of French competition regulation, the 1986 government order on "price deregulation and free competition." In 1990, he was admitted to the bar and joined the American law firm Couderc Frères as a partner, where he created from scratch a competition department. Later, he worked in two other firms (White & Case, Norton Rose) before setting up as independent counsel.

Less consolidated, yet very lucrative, is the *securities and financial affairs circuit* that emerged through the successive waves of privatizations as well as with the increasing dependence of public entities on private capital markets. The main sites of expertise include the vast financial pole of the state (*Caisse des dépôts et consignations, Banque public d'investissement, Agence des participations de l'État*), EU financial institutions (the European Bank for Reconstruction and Development, the Eurogroup), specialized administrations (treasury office), banking regulatory authorities (*Autorité des marchés financiers, Autorité du contrôle prudentiel*), securities law departments in law firms, and the legal services of Paris large private banks and insurance companies (Lazard, CIC, among others).

The itinerary of Anne Maréchal is quite interesting in this respect. After studying EU law, she joined the competition policy department at the ministry of the economy in 1990. Promoted to the rank of civil administrator (top civil servant) after having passed through the ENA, she worked in the fiscal legislation department from 1993 to 1996, and then moved to the French securities exchange agency where she was the head of the market division from 1996 to 1999. "Poached" by August & Debouzy in 1999 where she headed the securities law department, she later held the same position at Herbert Smith and then at DLA Piper, where she was in charge of taking France's multinational nuclear power company, Areva, public. Coming full circle, in 2015 she was brought back into public service as director of the legal department of the financial regulator, the *Autorité des marchés financiers*.

Last, we see also the emergence of a *circuit that includes the regal domains of the state circuit* spanning across numerous positions in foreign affairs and state security (20 percent of crossovers appear in this space). Here, one can find former ambassadors, leaders of major defense groups, members of the central administration at the defense and interior ministries, several former ministers of foreign affairs (Hubert Védrine, Hervé de Charrette, Dominique de Villepin) and of the interior (Claude Guéant, Bernard Cazeneuve, etc.), and members of their cabinets, who often engage in a variety of politically sensitive markets from international contracts (in particular African issues) to defense-related issues but also general experience in the broad domain of public affairs.

A good illustration of this type of itinerary is the career of Dominique De Combles De Nayves. Born in 1954, a graduate of Sciences Po Paris, he entered ENA in 1985 in the same class as Olivier Debouzy, and followed a similar career path. After stints in the economic affairs division at the foreign affairs ministry and in the cabinet of foreign affairs minister Claude Cheysson, he moved to the *Cour des comptes* (1986–1989), then to various posts in the ministry of international cooperation (mostly African issues), and from 1998 to 2001 headed the cabinet of the minister of defense. After serving as the French ambassador in Budapest, he was hired by his former classmate at August & Debouzy, where he worked from 2004 to 2014 (with an interruption of three years when he was secretary general at the *Cour des comptes*). This did not prevent him from working on a white paper on French foreign policy, or on the commission monitoring a reform of the ministry of foreign affairs. In 2014, he founded Dunaud, Clarenc, Combles & Associés with two other lawyers, where he specialized in defense and security, information and data technology, communications, nuclear power, energy.

This listing of circuits of public-private circulation connecting political and administrative spheres to the business bar is far from exhaustive. Further investigation should be carried out in technical domains, such as health care and pharmaceuticals, intellectual property, transport and environment, and others. Still, this initial list reveals a new cartography of the state, one that highlights the archipelago of political and administrative positions that have gained market currency with the neoliberal turn of public policies. It signals the many public-private hubs and related revolving doors that have prospered across the state in its relation to markets. When considered all together, these numerous leopard spots that have multiplied and solidified over the past two decades provide an unprecedented topographical survey of the social and professional underpinnings of the state regulatory, one that sits precisely across the public-private divide. This bird's-eye outlook into the social structure of the regulatory state now calls for more fine-grained and qualitative analysis of the types of practices and worldviews that have consolidated within the remit of this field of public-private intermediation.

3

THE HOLLOWING OUT OF
THE PUBLIC INTEREST

Mapping the geography of this new crossover pathway has revealed a field of public-private circulation that is often made invisible by the diversity of the policy domains involved as well as of its denizens' institutional and professional affiliations. The success of the bridge, opened up some twenty-five years ago, connecting the political and administrative elites to the corporate law, is seen in the disparate set of players (politicians, staff of cabinet offices, top-level bureaucrats, regulators, business lawyers, corporate executives) who now navigate both sides of the public-private divide. The lines delimiting this gray zone, at the intersection of government, politics, law, and business, are still fuzzy and contested as the conflicts of interest issue has gained saliency in the public debate. But the field's effect—or in other words, the pull of its gravity—is strong enough to diffuse its reform lexicon of public-private partnerships, and trigger the proliferation of clubs, think tanks, and other colloquia that espouse the credo of moving beyond the binary partition between public and private.

We do not intend to deliver an exhaustive topography of this zone that has emerged at the margins of the state. Its ramifications extend well beyond the field of law, particularly if one ventures into the accounting, financial, or banking activities of the state. Rather, our aim is to trace the growing expansion and autonomy of the interstitial space bordering on government, politics, and business—and thereby assess its transformative effects on categories and principles of vision of the state and its role vis-à-vis markets.

This dynamic development can be seen by following the trail of this group of mobile and multipositioned civil servants or politicians who turned corporate lawyers. As they invent new professional know-how and career paths, they personify, more than any other group, the dynamics of this interstitial space. They collectively act as brokers between the various poles of this field, create points of convergence, and actively disseminate new ways of thinking of the state and its role vis-à-vis markets. The density of this field of public-private intermediation can also be measured by looking at a diverse range of seemingly secondary platforms, including professional colloquia, sector-specific congresses, and other policy-oriented meetings and discussion series that are explicitly aimed at bring-ing together public and private professionals. These arenas provide participants with opportunities to liberate themselves from their respective institutional or professional loyalties and to profess the virtues of public-private synergies.

When it comes to assessing the transformative effects of this growing field of public-private intermediation, one should not look for consensus or osmosis of public-sector and private-sector professions and institutions. Instead, we sug-gest considering the production and consolidation of a new *common sense* of state reform shared by all the field's denizens regarding its new regulatory role as promoter of competitive markets, and its public-private social and profes-sional foundations. This chapter looks at its propagation at the very core of the public bastions where state categories are shaped and legitimated—for example, law schools, regulatory agencies, and the *Conseil d'État*, which have in large part incorporated the public-private paradigm into legal doctrine, judicial case law, and bureaucratic categories.

A New Policy Common Sense

Following the intuition that a field is always personified by the players who most thoroughly incarnate the properties, itineraries, and attitudes that are deemed to be relevant therein, one must first track the protagonists who have traveled the new paths between public and private, and in some instances blazed the trail. Their trajectories reveal a collection of seemingly secondary platforms (clubs, congresses, colloquia) that constitute neutral locations where the new common knowledge of the public-private partnership is formed.[1]

Professional Synergies and Competitive Advantages

As they circulate in-between the public and the private, the crossovers produce new representations of this relationship. Interestingly enough, the ex–civil ser-vants do not view their new lawyer trade as a rupture or change of state. Instead they prefer to see it as a kind of continuation of their public service mission, just like this *énarque*-turned-lawyer who feels he is still "defending the public interest in the private sector" (interview 25, man, ENA graduate, former minister, public

---

1. Stephen Barley, "Building an Institutional Field to Corral a Government."

law and lobbying). In the same way, when a former deputy director in a regulatory agency discusses his transition to the corporate department in a British law
firm, he underscores that the move is "a natural prolongation of [his] former
functions on the regulatory side" (interview 23, man, ENA graduate, securities
law). The BKA Selas (Bruno Kern & Associés) website highlights its associates'
"experience in high-level government administration, Parliament and local government authorities," and ultimately adopts the jargon of administrative law to
define its commercial position: the firm's members conceive their trade as that of
"public service adjuncts" in that they emphasize their advisory role in "assistance
to public decision making."[2] In the words of one member of the *Conseil d'État*, it
is as if they "continue to advise the State, but more effectively [*sic*]," and indeed
fulfill "as lobbyist in Brussels, a public service function."[3] While this discourse
is certainly representative of the "collective bad faith by which a group puts on
blinkers and refuses to see the foundations of its existence and its power,"[4] (i.e.,
the distinctive brokering position it occupies and the profits that it offers), it
would be a mistake to take this representation as nothing more than dissembling.
In so doing, one would ignore the existence of an established field of public-
private practices—a space that produces and refers to its own norms and models
of excellence. If these players affirm high and low that the public interest can
henceforth be served in a variety of public or private ways, it is because the liminal space that they have helped build has furnished fertile ground for new beliefs
regarding the many benefits expected from partnerships and synergies between
the public and private spheres: administrative efficacy and efficiency, reduction
of public spending, new "breathing room [*sic*]" in public service, and so forth. It
is true that many elements in their new professional practice connote a continuity of practices and forms of action. Frédéric Salat-Baroux, former secretary
general of the presidency under Jacques Chirac, for instance, is in French Public
Law and Government Affairs Practice with Weil & Gotshall. Laurent Deruy, former member of the *Cour des comptes*, works in the Government & Public Sector
department at Gide, "regularly advising and representing in court French and
foreign public institutions and private corporations." Do they not after all continue to serve the state when they are called upon to defend France's main public sector financial institution (*Caisse des dépôts et consignations*), a historically

---

2. http://www.brunokernavocats.fr/, accessed September 2019.
3. Olivier Debouzy, "Lobbying: The French Way," *Notes de l'Ifri* 54 (2003): 8.
4. Pierre Bourdieu, *The State Nobility: Elite Schools in the Field of Power* (Stanford, CA: Stanford
University Press, 1996).

state-owned electric utilities company (EDF), or Paris transport authority (RATP)? The belief is widely shared among the crossovers:

> I find myself in meetings with former colleagues from the *Conseil d'État* who are cabinet staff members and we are actually doing the same job; that's what I am saying to my colleagues who stayed at the *Conseil d'État*: I really still have the impression that I am advising the State but in a more efficient manner than what it is possible to do in the ministries' legal departments, because when there is a dossier which involves a large company facing financial or economic difficulties, then one needs experts in bankruptcy law, labor law, public law, financial law, competition law, etc. . . . If one commissions a law firm as ours, it is a guarantee to have excellence in all these domains and a capacity to mobilize up to a dozen lawyers, a sort of bulldozer . . . and this, the administration departments cannot do, they have neither expertise nor the labor force, except maybe in the ministry of the economy; so we are in reality complementary . . . that's why I am saying to my colleagues at the *Conseil d'État* who don't understand why the State is calling upon law firms. (interview 14, man, *Conseil d'État*, ENA graduate, public law of business)

Truly enough, these former civil servants are the natural leaders of the "Public law, Compliance, Regulatory, and Competition departments that have proliferated in the past twenty years in Paris corporate law firms, and in the private sector they continue to assume the sectoral attributions they had in the public sectors. Interestingly, far from being shameful, their state experience is proudly put forward in their law firms' webpages as it seems to attest to the strength of their track record; their state credentials are even often displayed on business cards that identify them as "attorney at law—former ENA graduate" or "attorney at law—former minister."

In fact, these civil-servants-turned-lawyers do indeed maintain a degree of proximity with the administrative world, which in turn recognizes them as natural interlocutors and readily keeps the door open for them:

> [being a former *énarque*] makes it easier for me to talk with the administration. . . . They know I am not a lawyer like the others. First of all, I will never try to hoodwink them, I will never talk misleading nonsense to them, and I will never do anything that is contrary to my convictions, and thirdly, I will always hold the public interest in the greatest respect. And those are things that people know, that they feel, and it can be

useful. [The same person adds:] when I go to make a pitch, to advise the State or a local authority, I have a plus, not because I am a former public servant, but simply because people feel that I still have the sense of public service. (interview 14, man, *Conseil d'État*, ENA graduate, public law of business)

If representatives of the private sector are seen as intruders in the state, as it would appear in the demurrals of the rapporteurs from the *Cour des comptes* concerning the role of a handful of firms, such as Cap Gemini and McKinsey & Cie, in implementing the overhaul of public policies over the past decade (*Révision générale des politiques publiques*, RGPP),[5] this hostility may wane when a former civil servant comes forward, "when these interests are represented by someone who is himself a member of a *grand corps*, or more modestly, a former graduate of one of the elite schools, who has crossed over to the other side, as they say. In fact, French-style lobbying is never more effective than when it takes place between graduates of Polytechnique or ENA, or better still between former members of an elite corps . . . to be effective a lobbyist must never appear to be one, that is to say they must be able to talk with their interlocutors about something else that has nothing to do with their mandate, up to the moment when, as a gesture of friendship, your comrade will do you a favor or will consider the arguments proffered, but 'in an incidental manner.'"[6] This "French-style lobbying" here formalized by the cofounder of August & Debouzy corporate law firm can easily make its way into the core of the state apparatus, all the more so as it appears in the guise of a network of solidarity between former classmates, of a "friendly society" of members of an elite group of former colleagues in government. Inversely, these same networks can prove useful within the bar—witness this member of the *Conseil d'État* who is satisfied with his decision to recruit his hirees from his original public service corps: "my co-associate was (also) a member of the *Conseil d'État*, that makes things considerably simpler, you start a sentence, they can finish it, one has the same reflexes, the same habits. So it's practical" (interview 14, man, *Conseil d'État*, ENA graduate, public law of business).

Knowing this, it is no surprise that the crossovers remain connected to the state and continue to navigate around its periphery. They are often the ones called upon to represent the private sector in the many working groups and experts' committees set up by ministries or regulatory agencies when drafting new pieces of legislation or bringing together proposals for policy reform. In this

---

5. Cour des comptes, *Le Recours par l'État aux conseils extérieurs*, 30–31.
6. Debouzy, "Lobbying: The French Way."

way, the ties and friendships forged in the administration are perpetuated across the public-private divide. One *énarque*-turned-lawyer explains how he has kept up many working relationships with former colleagues:

> for the State, I work when they ask for my opinions, but free of charge. But that's ... unofficial; I'm consulted by public authorities, by the *Conseil d'État*. . . . They come to see me, to ask me first if I'm familiar with the case file or not, and if I have any bias in the matter. Then, I am often cited by public rapporteurs at the *Conseil d'État*. . . . Upon occasion I have given my opinion, or corrected draft texts. I have corrected administrative instructions. (interview 8, man, ENA, lawyer, tax law)

Far from *leaving* the public sphere for the private sector, these top civil servants act as intermediaries straddling both sectors, with the capacity to pass through the walls as it were. They see public action as accountable to the expectations and even the demands of the private sector, and they see the latter as a natural adjunct to public authority. They alternate between developing the public affairs of private companies, and handling the private business of the state. For example, a former member of the *Conseil d'État*, who after a stint directing the public affairs pole at the Gide corporate law firm, returned to the *Conseil d'État* at Palais-Royal for a couple of years (1998–2000), and then took over management of the private property assets of the City of Paris. It would seem that these "ex's" have never been more at ease than in these cases mingling public and private, that they often consider them to be "the most attractive cases" of their career and their "most outstanding feat of accomplishment," for instance the introduction to the stock market of France's nuclear power multinational company Areva, handled by an *énarque*-turned-lawyer at DLA Piper, a case file that "involves both public and private law, securities and equity law, with at stake the market introduction of Areva shares and the need to retire investment certificates."[7] In this domain the *énarque*-turned-lawyer could make the most of her career experience as "former market manager at the financial regulator (*Autorité des marchés financiers*), combining expertise in these areas that in our university system are found in separate academic departments."[8] And when private interests become the public interest, when the future of French economy is at stake, the crossovers are once again in the forefront, defending the Paris marketplace and its

---

7. Isabelle Lefort, "Il faut un cursus deux fois supérieur à celui d'un homme pour réussir. Entretien avec Anne Maréchal," *La Tribune*, June 10, 2011.

8. Frédérique Garrouste, "Anne Maréchal conjugue le droit public à la Bourse chez DLA Piper," *L'Agefi Hebdo*, July 7, 2011.

international attractiveness in committees such as the "Paris Europlace" committee that pools public and private energy bringing together businesspeople, corporate lawyers, and high-level civil servants. In a word, today there are "state lawyers" just as in economic activity there are "state CEOs" who maintain multiple symbolic and professional ties with the state.[9]

Hubs of Public-Private Sociability

The emerging field of public-private influence has also been boosted by an unprecedented proliferation of thank tanks, clubs, and colloquia that posit transcending the public-private divide as the *raison d'être* of their activity. A dense public-private sociability has traditionally flourished in elite clubs (Cercle interallié, Le Siècle, etc.) and think tanks (Cercle des économistes, Terra Nova, Institut Montaigne, etc.); however, over the past twenty years it has spread through a constellation of sector-specific networks that offer talks, workshops, and other conventions. This nebula came into being first and foremost as a by-product of the activity of law publishing houses and corporate lawyers' societies (in fiscal law, intellectual property, etc.), which actively promoted these small sectoral public-private gatherings quite early on, establishing annual events such as the *Rencontres Lamy* devoted to competition law, other talks on fiscal law, or the *Club des PPP* (public-private partnerships) convention that has been held every year since 2006. Universities followed close behind. Numerous colloquia are organized around the Regulation chair established at Sciences Po Paris in 2000, and later at Université Paris-Dauphine. Last, these budding communities have been bolstered by regulatory agencies and public institutions themselves as they hoped to develop new relationships with market professionals in their respective policy fields. The financial regulator started a series of talks in 1998 (now known as the annual AMF talks), the Competition Policy department of ministry of economy hosts yearly competition law workshops, the *Autorité de la concurrence* has its European Days; even the *Conseil d'État* has set up since 2007 a conference series on public economic law.

These clubs, think tanks, and annual conferences have multiplied over the past decade: while they may be constituted around different objects and specialties, they share analogous public-private structures and are often linked together in multiple networks and the mesh of interpersonal relationships. The opening presentation of the 2008 *Conseil d'État* cycle of talks devoted to public economic

---

9. Dudouet and Grémont, "Les grands patrons et l'État en France, 1981–2007."

law gives a clear idea of the group of participants that the organizers had in mind: the cycle "is aimed at an audience of legal departments of State and local authority government offices, independent administrative authorities, public and private enterprises, professional organizations that represent companies, specialized lawyers and academics, as well as civil servants in charge of competition matters and State subsidies in national and EU administrations, appointees and staff of administrative jurisdictions and the specialized press."[10]

This interstitial position at the intersection of the different (public and private, academic and practice-oriented) spheres of law is exactly the same as the one chosen by the *Club des Juristes* network, created in 2007 as the "premiere French law think tank." Funded by large companies and law firms, the club has organized or participated ever since in a flurry of events in the field of law (*La Nuit de l'éloquence*, book awards, the legal publications book fair, etc.) and emerged as a major forum for reflection and development of propositions on French law and French legal professions.[11] Under the sign of breaking down barriers between public- and private-sector players, corporate lawyers, professors, and magistrates come together in this context, including leading figures of the corporate bar (Jean-Michel Darrois, Jean Veil, Daniel Soulez-Larivière, etc.), regulators (the presiding judge of the Paris commercial court, the president of the *Autorité des marchés financiers*), and regulated entities represented by the legal directors of the largest French corporate groups in the field of banking (Société Générale), media (Canal+), defense (Lagardère, Thalès), mass retail (Carrefour), and so forth. This constellation of participants and networks that promote exchange of experience and views across the borders of the public and private spheres is hardly a unified whole; it is traversed by multiple inter- and intraprofessional rivalries that make it impossible to see in this set a "community" or a single group.

The multiplication of these forums, however, is in itself a factor that works to autonomize and reinforce a field of public-private intermediation. These meetings give participants a chance to exchange their views, and also an opportunity to moderate conflict and competition, by identifying forms of agreement

---

10. Conseil d'État, *Colloque sur Les Aides d'État, École nationale d'administration*, March 14, 2008, http:// www.conseil-etat.fr/.

11. The *Club des juristes* claims to have exerted significant influence in a number of areas: reform of the code of criminal procedure; introduction of the prior constitutional question before the *Conseil constitutionnel* (QPC); the 2009 Darrois Report on the future of legal professions commissioned by Nicolas Sarkozy; debate on the issue of "environmental harm." Laurence Neuer, "Think tank ou la fabrique d'idées 'prêt-à-réformer,'" *La Semaine juridique* 44–45 (October 28, 2013): 1996–99.

on the diagnosis, stakes, and room for possible reform action.[12] As participants are invited to update their policy knowledge and shed their prior judgments, the public and private sectors are practically and symbolically brought together. Taking a closer look at one of these venues, the *Club des PPP* that gathers public and private specialists of these partnerships, it is possible to see the type of exchange that takes place and the representations that are forged therein. This crossroads space is first presented as a place for feedback on previous Public-Private Partnerships' contracts and acquisition of information on the state of the market.[13] Participants take away high-quality information on reforms that are underway, on major pending issues, forthcoming regulatory decisions, and even the leanings of future courts' case law. Just as attending the annual talks of the French financial regulator (AMF) enables participants to understand that "at the moment the AMF sanctions committee is inclined to seek 'soft' agreements to resolve litigation,"[14] at the *Club des PPP* conventions, participants can gauge whether incoming governments intend to cut back on PPP or not. The booths and exhibits of the annual Club meetings highlight "best practices" in various sectors (local transport, energy and waste, roadway infrastructure, sports and cultural facilities, etc.), successes are rewarded (PPP awards), and attendees gather current information on technical trends in law as well as new promising markets such as the ones in Africa. These forums also serve to reassure and recharge the energy of participants, by disseminating new forms of justification in moments of crisis. In 2013, for instance, a year after a more critical Socialist Party rose back to power, the organizers point at the renewed necessity of PPPs: "as public money dries up, cooperation between the public sector and the private sector is more than ever necessary." Better: it is also stated that "public-private know-how in France is one of our greatest strengths for exports." This tone prevails, even if, a sign of the times, it is conceded that "a critical and constructive assessment of public procurement tools is necessary," and "legislative changes to the [PPP] instrument are needed to make it more attractive."

Further, what makes these venues so dynamic and flourishing are the many transactions and exchanges that they favor across the public-private borders. By attending the PPP convention, in the company of local elected officials from major urban areas, presidents of mayors' associations, civil servants from the PPP

---

12. For a portrait of another similar club, see Julie Gervais, "Les sommets très privés de l'État: Le 'Club des acteurs de la modernisation' et l'hybridation des élites," *Actes de la recherche en sciences sociales* 194 (2012): 4–21.

13. Club des Partenariats public-privé, "Lettre des 7e rencontres internationales des PPP," 2013 (on file with the author).

14. "Les Entretiens de l'AMF," *Lettre des juristes d'affaires*, October 6, 2008.

government task force, the director of the national urban renewal state agency (ANRU), heads of PPP departments in large corporations specialized in utilities and infrastructures such as Veolia and Vinci, along with law firms and banks, participants can meet with competitors and clients, project owners and colleagues, and sometimes can take advantage of "stands [that allow] more discreet exchanges between public and private players."[15] It is in these venues, in meetings between directors of administration departments, executives of large companies and law firms, that individual reputations are consolidated. This is a privileged space, where address books are constituted and turned into client portfolio. New opportunities for professional transition can also be found through these contacts and networks, or in the words of one of our respondents, ways "to bridge [one's] career" toward new institutional horizons, whether public or private. Access to these arenas supposes some form of "election" or cooptation, either by virtue of institutional status, representativeness acquired in professional groups, client portfolio, and so on.

In return participation has an overdrive effect: the visibility gained further reinforces the mobility of those involved, enabling them to accumulate an astonishing range of positions and credentials (professional, editorial, academic, institutional, etc.) and giving shape to the specific form of authority (akin to that of "notables") operative in this field of public-private encounters. Of course, not all participants become these notables able to concentrate such a portfolio of resources. Full integration in these hybrid venues calls for an "open mind" and a willingness to compromise with those who would ordinarily be opponents. It requires a shared intent in seeking to overcome professional and institutional barriers, and achieve greater openness between the public and private sectors, in a quest for more effective public action. Most often, this is secured by the fact that the selected rarely belong to just one profession or represent the narrow interests of a single group. Their presence in the panels attests to their capacity to transcend the corporatist interests of their original group and to take part in the collective work to define a common ground between public and private players. While those in the private sector make concessions as they recognize the specific features and rationales of public action, public regulators also need to demonstrate their willingness to absorb the logic of business and the values of the private sector.

As a result, the annual talks and conventions are often the theater of convergence of viewpoints between stakeholders, whether regulators or regulated

---

15. Club des Partenariats public-privé, "Lettre des 7e rencontres internationales des PPP."

entities, professors or practitioners, corporate lawyers or civil servants. In the species of a pragmatic discussion that purports to be detached from any political ideology or professional corporatist interest, is constituted a body of knowledge and beliefs on the future of public regulation. Here one finds the efficacy that characterizes "neutral venues" as coined by Luc Boltanski and Pierre Bourdieu to describe these reform circles or expert committees intentionally crafted to move beyond partisan politics that turn specific political choices into seemingly apolitical policy proposals.[16] While differences and competing views persist, often expressed in euphemisms, a common sense of reform is progressively built up in these spaces, and this is undoubtedly one of the most striking indicators that the field of public-private mediation is gaining in autonomy.

Strikingly enough, the first type of agreement that is delineated in these liminal spaces is the joint recognition that the existence of the public-private divide is an unavoidable framework that must be accepted by all realistic players, even if the exact lines of the divide are to be profoundly redrawn. In the course of these talks and conventions, numerous little rituals and rules of precedence actually mark out the distance to be maintained, and remind all those present of the irrefutable existence of this demarcation line. Although this is indeed the shared framework and the words used are surprisingly unchanged (public, private, public interest, state), the content they refer to has been profoundly redefined. Ultimately a new map is being drawn: the proper dividing line and distribution of roles marks out the domain of the state reduced to its sovereign prerogatives, and the other functions of the state for which public management in its traditional forms are no longer appropriate or sufficient. This "renewed vision of economic regulation"[17] assumes that the "blockage" of the "administered economy" must be done away with, in order to take into account "the emergence of new imperatives," starting with "anchoring [government authorities and entities] in a market economy" and therefore "ensuring greater respect for the economic component of the public interest."[18] Most observers underscore the cumbersome nature of traditional administrative law, equated with a system of privilege that should no longer persist in the relationship between the state and companies. Many decry "the illusion held by government and the administration that they incarnate the public interest, which by definition cannot coincide with private

---

16. Luc Boltanski and Pierre Bourdieu, "La production de l'idéologie dominante," *Actes de la recherche en sciences sociales* 2 (1976): 3–73.

17. JeanMarc Sauvé, "Corriger, équilibrer, orienter: Une vision renouvelée de la régulation économique," École nationale d'administration, September 24, 2013, http://www.conseil-etat.fr/. M. Sauvé is a former vice president of the Council of State.

18. Ibid.

interests."[19] They may also insist on the need to take the "attractiveness of public law" into account, when legal systems are now put in competition.[20] All contest that the state is the sole representative of the public interest. "My position is anti-hypocrisy," says one crossover, an ENA graduate and former minister, "the State is not alone in defending public values" (interview 25, man, ENA, former minister, tax law). These arguments include "integration, in the notion of public interest, of demands for proper market functioning, and in particular for fair competition." With this new definition, the very notion of public interest takes on a new meaning. In the words of Council of State member Marie-Dominique Hagelsteen, prematurely deceased in 2012 after a career as legal affairs director at Elf, and then president of the Competition Council from 1998 to 2004: "competition policy is meaningless unless it serves the public interest, that is if it extends criteria of efficacy and relevance to a broad set of public policy measures."[21] Thereby, in the course of exchange of views, the denizens of this public-private field have collectively shaped a common sense of state reform that gives a new scope to the public-private joint venture and its specialists, now elevated to the role of leaders of the transition of the supposedly archaic French state into the waters of competitive European markets.

Entrenching the Public-Private Worldview

By many regards, these bold constructions, forged in the heart of the field of public-private influence, are heretical when looked at from the point of view of the traditional canons of French public law doctrine and case law. The very notion of a continuous dialogue and crossover to formulate the public interest, as advocated in the nebula of clubs and colloquia, flatly contradicts the *summa divisio* of public law and private law. Far from abstract or speculative musings on the theory of the state, these various steps to entrench public-private synergy cut to the social and cognitive base of many professional and institutional identities that are historically tied to the autonomy of the state. Here one follows how the new doctrines of public-private hybridization made their way into the state legal and bureaucratic operating procedures, by virtue of partial homologation in law

---

19. Debouzy, "Lobbying: The French Way."

20. Laurent Deruy, "Adapter le droit administratif français pour le rendre plus attractif," *Semaine juridique*, April 16, 2007, 2095.

21. Marie-Dominique Hagelsteen, quoted by Sauvé, "Corriger, équilibrer, orienter: Une vision renouvelée de la régulation économique," 6.

faculties, government, and courts. Three key entry points have been selected that allow us to assess the propagation of these public-private views into the state: the birth of a branch of law, the public law of business (*droit public des affaires*), which undermines the traditional scholarly divide; the rise of a figure of public leadership, that of the regulator, that cuts across the political versus bureaucracy demarcating line; and the repositioning of the *Conseil d'État* at the very core of the emerging French regulatory state.

Blurring the Scholarly Lines

Along the chain of talks, meetings, and colloquia, new knowledge and instruments have emerged, heralding a new brand of law straddling public and private matters—despite doctrinal controversy as to the labels they should receive (*droit de la régulation, droit public des affaires*, or even *droit public du marché*). A body of *droit public économique* has long existed; this subject matter was taught at Sciences Po as early as 1946, by a member of the *Conseil d'État*. The subject was developed in a noted work on the *ordre public économique* by professors René Farjat and Berthold Goldman (1963), and was finally included in law schools course load in the 1970s, giving rise to a steady stream of manuals and textbooks. Even then, this discipline gave hints of the first forms of transcending the frontal opposition between public law and private law. It pointed to the use of solutions devised by private players, such as contracts, by public authorities, instead of the traditional unilateral approach. But, as merely a subset of public law, the *droit public économique* focused essentially on the regimen of public utilities companies and the specific forms of administrative policing of the economy.

As the sphere of state-owned companies shrank and the scope of regulatory agencies grew, new scholarly thinking emerged. Various labels appeared that tried to make sense of the new rapport between the public and the private domains. Interestingly, the denomination, *droit public des affaires* (public law of business) which still sounded at the time like a terrible oxymoron to the ears of French legal scholars, first emerged from the world of legal practice as the Paris bar created in the late 1980s an *Institut de droit public des affaires* (IDPA) within its professional training school. Yet, while the founders of this institute had a clear intuition that the tectonic plates of public and private law were shifting at fast pace, none had a clear idea of what it actually entailed:

> Lafarge [president of Paris Bar Council in 1987–1988] wanted to break the Paris bar out of its routine, and to affirm that it should see law as a market. At the time, this was a revolutionary attitude: law was a science.

And not a market that one developed, where one prospected. The idea of Lafarge was to create institutes to develop certain fields: there were three subjects, public law, information technology and social law. . . . He needed a name for the institute at Paris 1, so I invented "public business law" because it was a contradiction in terms. I went to see the president and I suggested "public business law." He said to me "What's that, public law of business?" and I said "I don't know," he replied "Perfect, I'll buy that." (interview 6, man, lawyer, public law of business)

For a long time, this denomination of the institute remained an exotic curiosity. At the end of the 1990s, one still found statements that pointed at this "relatively new expression" as "somewhat surprising," forcing "jurists to make use of their imaginations."[22] This is however also the period when the notion of *droit public des affaires* makes its way into regular legal chronicles of specialized publishers: led by a little group of public law professors, Lamy publishing house initiated a special series in 1997 that would soon be followed by the *Lettre juris-classeur* in 1998.[23] In parallel, a competing label actually emerges, that of *droit de la régulation*, which is consecrated by the creation in 2000 of a specialized chair at Sciences Po Paris, at the instigation of a professor of private law, Marie-Anne Frison-Roche. Frison-Roche was very active on the doctrinal front from the outset, and characterized this new field of law as an "autonomous branch" that "was erected above and beyond the distinction between public law and private law." The new discipline aimed "to emancipate (itself) from the habitual distinctions of the legal system, and in particular the distinctions between public law and private law." This discipline would "furnish justification for seemingly heretical solutions that are usually criticized on the basis of the old classifications,"[24] solutions that arise in the sectors where the central government has lost the ability to act in a regulatory capacity. Beyond the diversity of labels, all these scholarly undertakings converge however in transcending the doctrinal dualism,[25] and in

22. Claude Deves, "Droit public des affaires et collectivités locales," *Les Petites Affiches* 75 (April 15, 1999): 35.

23. Other transversal legal domains emerged at the same time like penal business law (*droit pénal des affaires*) which began to come into its own as political corruption cases emerged and new investigation units assigned to financial crime were created within prosecutors' offices.

24. See for example the dispute between Marie-Anne Frison-Roche, "Droit et économie de la régulation," in *Les Risques de regulation* (Paris: Dalloz, 2001), 610, and Laurence Boy, "Réflexion sur le 'droit de la régulation,'" *Recueil Dalloz*, 2001, 3031; and Raymond Martin, "Le droit en branches," *Recueil Dalloz*, 2002, 1703.

25. Didier Truchet, "La distinction du droit public et du droit privé dans le droit économique," in *The Public Law/Private Law Divide: Une entente assez cordiale?*, ed. Mark Freedland and Jean-Bernard Auby (Oxford: Hart, 2006), 49–59.

seeking to aggregate under a unique scholarly umbrella, the heterogeneous set of policies and procedures related to market regulation and to new modes of state action as an economic agent (public procurement law, law of state holdings and participations, etc.).[26] In their attempts to provide a common rationale for this dispersed ensemble, all these scholarly attempts converged in giving EU competition law the defining role—as it actively professes to be indifferent to the public or private nature of institutions and enterprises.[27] And while the notion of an *ordre public économique*, which traditionally justifies the state policing interventions in the economy, would continue to serve as the cornerstone of these scholarly constructions, its essence is fundamentally changed as it now lies, at least in part, in the promotion of competitive markets.[28]

In parallel to these scholarly undertakings, a figure of public leadership emerged, that of the regulator,[29] a broad umbrella that includes many sorts of public managers active in organizing markets: ministers in the economic pole of government, heads of market and competition watchdog authorities, EU commissioners, high-level civil servants at the finance and economy ministry, and even members of Parliament who sit on economic committees (e.g., general rapporteurs of budget legislation), or judges from the economic chambers. By its wide scope, this emerging figure blurs the traditional distribution of tasks at the summit of the state, between political and administrative functions and their respective missions of political orientation and execution. In so doing, it outlines the shape of a new politicoadministrative elite. What initially brought this transformation to light were the large judicial inquiries and trials that emerged from the early 1990s onward in the domain of economic and financial crimes. What prosecutors in financial courts and penal lawyers unearthed in the maelstrom of politicofinancial affairs was the increasing blurring of the political and administrative chains of command in which state-owned companies, ministers, chiefs of staff, top civil servants as well as members of Parliament were involved. It is not the place here to retell the litany of scandals (Crédit Lyonnais, Elf, Clearstream,

---

26. It was not until 2009, however, that this subject was enshrined in law textbooks, with the publication of a volume on *Droit public des affaires* by Sophie Nicinski (Paris: Lextenso, 2009).

27. Maryvonne Hecquard-Theron, "La notion d'État en droit communautaire," *Revue trimestrielle de droit européen* 26, no. 4 (1990): 693–711.

28. Initially taught at Sciences Po Paris and to some extent in business schools that had a long history of courses in fiscal law and regulatory law, these new disciplines gradually found a place in the heart of the curriculum offered in university law faculties. See in particular Émilie Biland, "Quand les managers mettent la robe: Les grandes écoles de commerce sur le marché de la formation juridique," *Droit et société* 83, no. 1 (2013): 49–65.

29. See the many publications connected to the so-called Regulation chair at Sciences Po Paris in the first decade of the twenty-first century.

Bettencourt, Karachi, Cahuzac, Adidas-Tapie, etc.) that have marked the past nearly three decades. Yet, all point out the muddling of the responsibilities of political and administrative officers with a transfer of responsibility to high-level civil servants and ministerial offices, thereby lessening the political accountability of ministers and prime ministers themselves.[30] The blossoming of independent regulatory agencies further undermined the separation of the political and the bureaucratic: as they gained power and autonomy within the state, their respective presidents—most often drawn from the ranks of public service—progressively assumed a more visible and openly political role, sometimes standing in direct opposition to government of the time. Taking this increasing overlap of political and administrative functions into account, consulting firms provided new services to their corporate clients beyond the mere lobbying of legislators and ministers (whether French or European) toward a whole range of "regulators" spanning from regulatory agencies to state departments and supreme courts. As seen above, the Paris bar itself took part in this blurring, accepting either political or administrative experience as proof of the eight years of legal activity required to accede to the dispensatory qualification to join the bar offered in the 1991 decree. Likewise, anti-corruption NGOs have adjusted their aim, calling for legislation to sanction conflict of interest that would apply to all types of personnel in the public sector, both political appointees and administrative staff. When a full-fledged public ethics authority, the *Haute Autorité pour la transparence de la vie publique,* was created in 2013, it itself crafted a new category to define its target: that of *dirigeants publics* that brought under the same umbrella ministers, members of Parliament, members of the EU Parliament, local elected officials, plus staff of cabinet offices, independent administrative authorities, directors and executives of public entities (public companies, etc.), a total of more than ten thousand people. Justified by a more realistic apprehension of the state governing elites, this new legal category concept further questioned the traditional separation between the political and the bureaucratic realms.[31] Exalted by the

---

30. The growing confusion surrounding political and administrative accountability was described by Olivier Beaud, *Le Sang contaminé: Essai critique sur la criminalisation de la responsabilité des gouvernants* (Paris: Presses Universitaires de France, 1999).

31. As stated in the High Authority's annual report: "The number of elected officials and titular civil servants required to submit a statement has grown considerably, from roughly 3,500 individuals to now 8,000 people subject to this procedure. For the most part, these are elected officials (notably mayors and presiding officers of groups of municipalities of over 20,000 population); 1,600 titular employees in public positions (government appointees, cabinet staff, and 260 staff at independent administrative authorities); and 2,600 directors of public establishments and enterprises owned by the State or local authorities." Haute Autorité pour la transparence de la vie publique, *Renouer la confiance: Rapport annuel* (Paris: La Documentation française, 2015), 16.

policies of new public management, targeted by lobbyists' strategies to gain influence, investigated by judges, overseen by the regulator in charge of public ethics, scrutinized by anti-corruption activists and authorities, the hybrid figure of regulator has thus been progressively consecrated, thereby undermining another cornerstone of French constitutional law, namely the demarcating line between the political and the bureaucratic.

The *Conseil d'État*'s Invisible Hand

The *Conseil d'État* is hardly a stranger to the field of public-private intermediation. On the contrary, as a state *grand corps* populating the top levels of government, the supreme administrative court and the organic intellectual of state's architecture, the *Conseil d'État* has played a pivotal role therein. Even though in its annual reports the institution shows concern for a loss of unity in the state, its members have indeed played a key role in the muddling of borderlines, both as the first "professionals of independent regulatory authorities"[32] and as one of the main recruitment pools for crossovers moving to the corporate bar—to the point that some members of the *corps* are worried that the institution might become a "second training ground of the Paris bar."[33]

In the postwar period, those leaving the *Conseil d'État* generally gave their preference to the banking and insurance sectors. Departures were rare, and far less frequent than in the early days of the Third Republic in France: "in the 20 years following the end of WWII, only some 20 members left the *Conseil* for the private sector."[34] Inversely, the *Conseil d'État* successfully penetrated the nationalized sector and secured many "private hunting grounds" among public utilities state companies (SNCF, EDF, GDF Suez, RATP, etc.).[35] The rate of crossover to the private sector only began to accelerate in the mid-1980s, and

---

32. Jacques Mézard, *Un État dans l'État: Canaliser la prolifération des autorités administratives indépendantes pour mieux les contrôler; Rapport du Sénat* (Paris: Sénat, 2015).

33. The former deputy secretary general of the *Conseil d'État*, Benoît Ribadeau Dumas, indicates that "the institution frowns upon this trend, at least since it has become too pronounced, and has tried to halt it, unsuccessfully." Benoît Ribadeau Dumas, "Les carrières dans et hors le Conseil d'État," *Pouvoirs* 123 (2007): 73–88.

34. Kessler, "L'évasion des membres du Conseil d'État vers le secteur privé."

35. While Bruno Latour's ethnography of the *Conseil d'État* makes a point not to position it in the French field of power, he does provide interesting data on the amount and the variety of political, bureaucratic, economic experiences that its members acquire outside of the supreme administrative court: Bruno Latour, *The Making of Law: An Ethnography of the Conseil d'État* (Cambridge: Polity, 2009).

then rose exponentially in the 1990s.[36] This acceleration closely follows the economic retreat of the state capacities, with the privatization of the public banking and industrial sectors (1986 and 1993) and the growing impact of EU competition policy and control of state aid. While the crossover rate stood at 14 percent for the 1958–1968 period (14 percent of the members of the *Conseil d'État* had moved at least once to the private sector), it moved to 29 percent for the period 1990–2000.[37] While it is difficult to assess the figures accurately (depending on whether one counts the *conseillers d'État* who retired or those who have resigned from public service), some recent research estimates that 23.5 percent of the *corps* were employed in the private sector in 2013.[38]

This apparent contradiction between its role as legal guardian of the unity of the state, and the position of active participant in the growing porosity of public-private borders is revelatory of the *Conseil d'État* Janus face. This institution is indeed at once the supreme jurisdiction of administrative law, charged with the task of ensuring the legal consistency of the law of the state, and a state *grand corps* concerned for the professional future of its members and gripped in competition with its historic rivals at the *Cour des comptes* and the *Inspection des finances.* Yet, both aspects are two sides of the same medal: the capacity of members of the *Conseil d'État* to circulate within and outside of the state (and occupy all sorts of leading positions in regulatory agencies, large companies, law firms, etc.) depends essentially on the value and importance granted to administrative law, which constitutes the fundamental competency of the members of this *corps.* Inversely, the recognized utility of administrative law is inseparably tied to the capacity of its specialists, first among them members of the *Conseil d'État*, to extend its institutional jurisdiction and disseminate its influence within and outside the state. Thus the European and liberal turn of the state from the mid-1980s onward has posed a threat of obsolescence to administrative law, and directly challenges the capacity of members of the *Conseil d'État* to move beyond the walls of the Palais-Royal. From this point of view, the impressive aggiornamento of doctrine and jurisprudence it has undertaken in this context, which has profoundly reshaped its relationship to markets and to the public interest, can be analyzed sociologically as work to maintain, and even enlarge, the social validity

---

36. Luc Rouban, "Le Conseil d'État, 1958–2008: Sociologie d'un grand corps," *Cahiers du Cevipof* 49 (2008): 82.

37. In the course of the same period, this crossover rate remained stable, at a significantly higher level, for the Inspectorate General of Finances: ibid.

38. Catherine Teitgen-Colly, "Déontologie et pantouflage dans la haute fonction publique: L'exemple du Conseil d'État," in *Mélanges en l'honneur de Professeur Gérard Marcou* (Paris: IRJS, 2017).

of administrative law, and by extension the value and currency of the title of *conseiller d'État* in both the public and private spheres.

THE RISE OF THE PRIVATE "INTÉRÊT GÉNÉRAL"

The history of the realignment of the *Conseil d'État* in the context of the rise of the regulatory state remains to be written. There is no doubt however that starting in the 1980s, the Palais-Royal institution faced unprecedented intellectual and political challenges that took administrative law as the ultimate symbol of the state's resistance to modernization.[39] The questioning of the legitimacy of this derogatory branch of law took the form of multiple invitations to open the doors to private law. In the 1990s, voices like that of magistrate Patrice Maynial in his report to the prime minister urged the institution to adapt to the new deal of European law embodied by the single market, and to due process, and to accept the regulatory model of new public management, in lieu of the classical public order rules.[40] Faced with the menace of obsolescence of administrative law, the *Conseil d'État* gradually accepted a radical questioning of its founding principles and pleaded for a progressive revision of its founding principles. As its former head Jean-Marc Sauvé remarks today, "the administrative judge cannot be situated outside of the times, nor feign ignorance of his share of responsibility in the evolution of society."[41]

In fact, the *Conseil d'État* has undertaken over the past two decades a veritable cultural revolution, which can be traced through the successive editions of its annual report that has unceasingly reworked the major concepts of administrative law (*intérêt general, ordre public économique, service public*), in the light of the challenges outlined above. In this context, two rulings of November 3, 1997, *Société Million et Marais*, and of March 26, 1999, *EDA v. Aéroport de Paris*, are significant milestones. Both decisions mark fundamental stages in the redefinition of administrative law, subjecting public entities to competition law, and hence to the competitive market model in the first case, and treating "public authorities in charge of the public domain as an enterprise" in the second case.[42]

---

39. Françoise Dubois, Maurice Enguéléguélé, and Marc Loiselle, "La contestation du droit administratif dans le champ intellectuel et politique," in *Le Droit administratif en mutation* (Paris: Presses Universitaires de France, 1993), 149–74.

40. Patrice Maynial, *Le Droit du côté de la vie: Réflexions sur la fonction juridique de l'État; Rapport au Premier ministre* (Paris: La Documentation française, 1996), 73.

41. Jean-Marc Sauvé, "La valorisation économique des propriétés des personnes publiques," Entretiens du Conseil d'État en droit public économique, July 6, 2011, http://www.conseil-etat.fr/.

42. See the enlightening remarks by Jacques Caillosse on the impact of these two rulings: "Personnes publiques et concurrence: Quels enjeux théoriques?," *Actualité juridique: Droit administrative* 14 (2016): 761.

The annual reports issued by the *Conseil d'État* put this new jurisprudence into systemic form and consolidated the paradigm shift contained in these rulings. Certain formulas contained in the 2002 report on the topic "Public authorities and competition" are still quoted today: "promotion of public service starts with full recognition of the broad framework of free competition in which it is called to act"; "the vast majority of public authorities have recognized that they are anchored in a market economy"; and so on.[43] The inflection of direction continued with the "Talks on public economic law" starting in 2007, an event held yearly on topics such as "Public authorities and competition," "A renewed vision of economic regulation," "State aid," and so forth.

In this series of public reports and conferences, an ever greater distance from the old administration model is established,[44] and in correlation a transformation of the essential concepts of administrative law. This is in particular the case for the notion of the "*intérêt général*," the traditional cornerstone of administrative law, that the *Conseil d'État* undertook to actively redefine, shaping a new meaning that some observers have called "neomodern." The days when it could be written that "the definition and pursuit of the *intérêt général* is a State monopoly"[45] are now long past. While the *Conseil d'État* still sees this notion as the fundamental pillar of the legitimacy of administrative action, it is no longer an overarching top-down construction. Better yet, a private *intérêt général* has come to light, equated with the new public welfare now seen in proper competitive functioning of markets.[46] A breach had been opened early on when the *Conseil d'État* conceded, in its *Ville de Sochaux* ruling in June 1971, that the *intérêt général* could be obtained by satisfaction of private interests, in this case those of the large car company Peugeot. But it was with new European theories of competition that this redefinition of the notion truly took shape. As the head of the *Conseil d'État* readily recognizes, the Palais-Royal institution embraced over just a few years the whole "market competition" paradigm that to a large degree had been formally stated at the European Union level. "Administrative judges have, step by step, adopted most of the major theories of competition law in their arguments. One can refer to the theory of essential facilities, for

---

43. Conseil d'État, *Collectivités publiques et concurrence: Rapport public* (Paris: La Documentation française, 2002).

44. See the contributions gathered in Pascal Mbongo and Olivier Renaudie, eds., *Le rapport public annuel du Conseil d'État: Entre science du droit et discours institutionnel* (Paris: Cujas, 2010), 125–44.

45. Didier Truchet, *La Fonction de l'intérêt général dans la jurisprudence du Conseil d'État* (Paris: LGDJ, 1977), 19.

46. See Guylain Clamour, *Intérêt général et concurrence: Essai sur la pérennité du droit public en économie de marché* (Paris: Dalloz, 2006).

instance or to that of automatic abuse of dominant position."[47] This is the path followed by the *Conseil d'État* in its rulings in the *Million et Marais* case in 1997 and the *Sarl Somatour* case in 2002, erecting free competition as one essential component of the *intérêt général*. This new conception of the public interest is not different, exterior, or an alternative to that of competitive market. On the contrary, it is defined as closely aligned with it, intimately tied to its intrinsic requirements and needs. As competitive markets came to dominate as the new normative paradigm,[48] the *Conseil d'État* was drawn into a profound revision of the founding precepts of administrative law. Donning the garb of theoreticians of free competition and new forms of public-private competition, the *conseillers d'État* brought new validity to a body of knowledge threatened by the attrition of the public sphere and the ascendancy of the private management model. By contributing to a relative desacralization of public entities, by dismantling some of the legal and regulatory barriers that held the private sector at bay, by providing full recognition to the competition paradigm at the core of the *intérêt général*,[49] they also created the conditions making it possible to give new value to the title and experience of administrative magistrate in the emerging regulatory state (as well as in its private sector supporting groups).

PROFESSIONALS IN REGULATORY AGENCIES

It would be a mistake, however, to see this cultural revolution at the *Conseil d'État* as merely a process of adaptation to the market economy. It must also be understood in relation to the realignment of the Palais-Royal institution at the heart of the emerging regulatory state. It should be noted that starting in the 1980s and becoming more pronounced in the 1990s, there was a move to reorganize the legal functions of the state, with the *Conseil d'État* as one of the prime drivers. Its members were the standard bearers of a call for legal simplification and rationalization of administration[50], and thus played a key role in the emergence of legal affairs directorates in government ministries,[51] in which hitherto scattered legal and litigation offices were merged. This movement was engaged at the defense,

---

47. Jean-Marc Sauvé, "Pouvoirs publics et concurrence," Entretiens du Conseil d'État en droit public économique, May 2010, http://www.conseil-etat.fr/.

48. See Nicolas Jabko, *Playing the Market: A Political Strategy for Uniting Europe, 1985–2005* (Ithaca, NY: Cornell University Press, 2006).

49. Clamour, *Intérêt général et concurrence*, 234.

50. On the central role of the *Conseil d'État* in the emergence of the criticism of "normative inflation," and the related call for more *sécurité juridique*, see Rachel Vanneuville, "Les enjeux politico-juridiques des discours sur l'inflation normative," *Parlement(s)* 11 (2009): 80–91.

51. The organizational reform of administrative structures necessitated a decree taken *en Conseil d'État* (meaning that an Opinion of the *Conseil d'État* is mandatory), henceforth seen as the chief

education and research, agriculture, and foreign affairs ministries.[52] It was especially strong at the ministry of the economy, where a legal affairs directorate was created in 1998, marking a brand-new interest in legal regulation of economic matters. The concentration of legal activities within ministries ultimately put the *Conseil d'État* at the heart of the new state legal function, and made its members the natural titular agents for these new positions.

A similar repositioning is also found in the role of the *Conseil* in the development of regulatory agencies. The proliferation of so-called independent administrative authorities in the state apparatus has multiplied the sources of public regulation, and the *Conseil* could not remain indifferent to this development. With its role as guardian of state unity at heart, the *Conseil* early on issued warnings on the risk of a dangerous drift.[53] It suggested rationalizing agencies' legal regime across diverse sectors of activity, joined in this effort by the *Cour des comptes*, which for its part was naturally worried about the risk of disorder in accounting practices. Following its words with action, the *Conseil d'État* built up a position as safety barrier to counter the proliferation of statutory acts creating regulatory agencies that were not always clearly useful or robust, in the eyes of the legislators themselves. In jurisprudence elaborated from 1981 onward, it qualified the action of these agencies as administrative in nature, and not grounded in private law. From the outset, it placed most of the agencies within the purview of administrative law (unless expressly stipulated otherwise by statutes, as for the *Autorité de la concurrence*). In so doing, the *Conseil* gave itself the duty to ensure jurisdictional oversight of agencies that were steadily extending the scope of their regulatory intervention in the private sector of the economy.

As it was progressively expanding its (legal) control over the archipelago of regulatory agencies, the *Conseil* moved toward a softer stance, even singing the praises of these agencies:

> the creation of independent administrative authorities is undeniably a stimulant for the apparatus of the State as a whole: it forces the administration to compare the approaches of public and private law; it brings people from different backgrounds together to work in collegial bodies. It can help attenuate the reciprocal noncomprehension between the public and private sectors. Last, it enhances the necessary updating

architect of the central government administration. See Jacques Chevallier, "Le Conseil d'État, au cœur de l'État," *Pouvoirs* 123 (2007): 5–17.

52. See Colera, *Les services juridiques des administrations*.

53. Conseil d'État, *Les autorités administratives indépendantes: Rapport annuel* (Paris: La Documentation française, 2001).

of general thinking on the notion of public mediation in its broadest sense, that is to say on the characteristics of the intermediate bodies to which the representatives of national sovereignty can legitimately delegate the tasks and procedures of regulation of civil society.[54]

As it posed itself as the ultimate guarantor of the honor of a state that would lose face if it were torn apart by the centrifugal forces of the proliferating agencies, the *Conseil d'État* progressively "rewrote the grand narrative of the State,"[55] firmly consolidating its position at the core of the regulatory turn of the state. Underscoring "the risks of rendering these agencies subservient to operations in the sector,"[56] and the fact that stakeholders are less able to resist the pressure of private interests, the *Conseil* enshrines the *grands corps* as the best guardians of the independence of regulatory agencies. As stated Jean-Marc Sauvé, at the time head of the institution: "the best way to prevent the risk [of conflict of interest or penal infraction] is clearly to delve into the pool of the highest jurisdictions"[57] when it comes to recruit regulators. These words had weight, it would seem, judging by the fact that the *grands corps* have indeed emerged as the most natural recruitment pool for these new institutions, and today are seen as "the most natural agencies' professionals."[58] The figures are edifying: among the 544 appointees sitting on the collegial boards of these institutions, 167 come from the *Conseil d'État*, the *Cour des comptes* and the judicial body, and out of 40 presidents, 24 are members of these three groups. In addition to occupying a high proportion of agencies' board seats and presidencies, members of the *Conseil d'État* also contribute to the daily work of these agencies through temporary assignments (sometimes called "*ménages*" or "side gigs") as rapporteur or counselor to these authorities.

This pivotal position within the very heart of these agencies is of substantial importance, considering that these authorities are frontier institutions on the border between the public and the private. A stint in one of these agencies is an experience that familiarizes the participants with the exigencies of market

---

54. Ibid.

55. On this point, see Jacques Caillosse, "Le discours de la réforme administrative," in *Le rapport public annuel du Conseil d'État: Entre science du droit et discours institutionnel*, ed. Pascal Mbongo and Olivier Renaudie (Paris: Cujas, 2010), 125–44.

56. Rapport du Conseil d'État, 2001, quoted in Françoise Dreyfus, "Les autorités administratives indépendantes: De l'intérêt général à celui des grands corps," in *Perspectives du droit public: Mélanges offerts à Jean-Claude Hélin* (Paris: Litec, 2004), 219–27.

57. Jean-Marc Sauvé, head of the *Conseil d'État* from 2006 to 2018, quoted in the Senate report by Mézard, *Un État dans l'État*, 48.

58. Ibid.

professionals and inculcates the utility of public-private partnerships; and it has strong currency in the private sector, especially for those who hold key positions such as secretary general, legal affairs officer, or collegial board member.

These authorities often serve as a gateway to the private sector and to a more traditional transition to major listed corporations: 17 percent of crossovers in our sample had worked in one or another of these agencies, such as one former director general and one rapporteur of the *Autorité de la concurrence*, both members of the *Conseil d'État*, who went on to join corporate law firms after their tenure on the side of the regulator. Furthermore, the agencies provide an option (not much used for the moment) for top civil servants to return to state employ after trying their luck in the corporate law bar. The hybrid public-private identity that is claimed by these institutions implies not only that they recruit lawyers, legal advisers, and other profiles from the private sector, it also creates the possibility of a return to the public sector for crossovers, a so-called *retro-pantouflage* that was previously not an option. The passage to the private sector that had been deemed irreversible, would appear to be less so, thanks to the opening up of these porous spaces that in part escape the legal and financial constraints of traditional public service.

This explains the paradox formulated by a former deputy secretary general at the *Conseil*, now chief of staff of the prime minister, who underscores that "the *Conseil d'État* very rapidly imposed its presence in the independent administrative authorities, even as it regularly criticized their proliferation."[59] In a context that saw its reach under threat due to the deregulation turn of policies, the *Conseil d'État* wove a new fabric of relations along the fringes of the economy, government administration, and politics that has breathed new life into a *corps* that appeared to be in danger of decline. This transformation went hand in hand with a vast revision of administrative law that led, in successive steps, to an in-depth reframing of its founding concepts, and to a process of normalization with regard to the precepts of the market economy and free competition. In this way, the *Conseil* variously scrambled and rewrote the code of public-private interaction, and played alternating roles as principled protector of the honor of the state, so that it would not "lose face,"[60] and as concrete operator of its regulatory and liberal evolution. The *Conseil d'État* was thus solidly ensconced in the midst of the dynamic forces at work to transform the public-private divide.

Overall, as might be clear from this chapter, the field of public-private interaction is much more than just simply a space for crossovers and circulation.

---

59. Ribadeau Dumas, "Les carrières dans et hors le Conseil d'État," 84.
60. Pierre Bourdieu, *On the State: Lectures at the Collège de France* (Cambridge: Polity, 2015).

Through its own gravitational force, it has a powerful transformative effect on key notions of the state, as well as on its circuit of legitimacy. It is undoubtedly true that the players in this field are not always strong enough to weigh directly on politics and impose their legislative agenda.[61] But they perturb the conventional cardinal points of the state compass and redefine from inside its elites as well as core categories. As the result, one cannot dispense with an inquiry into the political implications and consequences for democracy that stem from this fast-expanding field of public-private intermediation.

----

61. See, however, the afterword added to this edition of the book, which analyzes Macron's ascendency to power as the formal entry into politics of these new public-private elites.

4

A BLACK HOLE IN DEMOCRACY?

The neoliberal remodeling of the French state has not only profoundly renewed the government's role vis-à-vis markets. It has also spurred public institutions to cultivate new collusive ties with companies and market intermediaries and to weave a new system of alliances at their periphery. A field of public-private influence has grown up in the interstices, and has grown steadily as the shift to a neoliberal policy agenda has consolidated in Paris as in Brussels. However, we have not yet been able to collectively assess the political and democratic consequences of this major transformation. The "burning obligation" of managerial modernization of the state, a refrain obsessively repeated since the early 1990s, has dulled our capacity to discern in this new public-private partnership anything other than a quest for bureaucratic efficiency or an economic objective to enhance the global competitiveness of the "enterprise France." Is there nothing else at stake here? Even the critics have too often suggested just this, by framing their questions within the bounds of these very policies; rather than assessing the toolbox itself, the public conversation has remained focused on the cost overruns of PPPs, and debates over individual conflicts of interest of regulators, and so forth.

Of course, political and moral outrage was voiced in the wake of the scandals that emerged in the first decade of the twenty-first century, ranging from the conflicts of interest of Sarkozy's closest financial adviser turned banker, the tax fraud committed by Hollande's budget minister, Jérôme Cahuzac, or the many failures to act of the successive governments in the Tapie-Adidas arbitration (see box 4 below). But the main effect of the scandalist framing of these cases was to reduce them to matters of *individual* deviation from the norm of a political and administrative system deemed to suffer from very little corruption. This viewpoint undoubtedly made it easier to resolve the crises, treating the scandals by identifying individual judicial accountability in each case, and deploying a new arsenal of deontological reforms for the public sector. The reinforcement of policies to prevent conflict of interest will not in itself suffice, however, to rise to the challenge: the juridical and individualizing perspective of the conflict of interest lens underestimates the *systemic* nature of the blurring of boundaries and its broad political effects. With the eyes glued to a corrupt transaction or a specific conflict of interest, one loses sight of the system as a whole, and runs the risk of not perceiving the political costs and the prejudice to democracy linked to the emergence of a field of public-private influence, whose effects are probably more diffuse and less spectacular but no less corrosive for our democracies. Much more than just an incidental shortcoming in relation to professional norms and ethics, these affairs more broadly highlight the conditions in which the public interest is defined today.[1] In failing to measure the structural intermingling of business and state actors, all the periodic attempts to construct Chinese walls are much like a play of shadow theater.

In drawing up an inventory of the corrosive political effects of the blurring of the public-private boundary line, as we intend to do here, one may be taxed with engaging in an exercise of nostalgia for the "strong State" *à la française*; or even of archaism as it means opposing the modernization of the country and being death to the profound "respiration" of the state coming from its newfound public-private lungs. However, by examining public-private partnerships only through the lens of modernization and competitiveness, one fails to see that we are standing at the very edge of democratic space, in the space where the public interest—which must continually be armed against the inegalitarian tendencies that spring up at the heart of capitalism—is defined. It is certainly not easy to identify let alone measure the costs. While the profits to be gained by the professionals of intermediation, in particular corporate lawyers, from this fuzzy public-private line are readily identifiable, the collective costs remain largely out of sight. Meanwhile this borderline area has grown steadily larger and has all the features of a "black hole" in the power structure, positioned in the blind spot of public oversight, be it political or administrative, and of professional regulations. In short, it is time to conceive a new policy of separation to strengthen the bodies in charge of overseeing this border space and to protect the public sphere from the ever-growing threats to its autonomy.

A Politics beyond Reach

The formation of a field of public-private influence in between the market, politics, and government administration has given rise to a gray area that is sufficiently distanced from political and bureaucratic tutelary supervision and at the same time protected by the rules of professional confidentiality and self-regulation

---

1. John Galbraith, *The Economics of Innocent Fraud* (Boston: Houghton Mifflin, 2004), 32–34.

that are the prerogative of liberal professions. Between a Parliament unequipped to deal with the proliferation of regulatory agencies, the Paris bar eager to bolster the economic attractiveness of the legal profession, and a public administration in which the elite corps, starting with the *Conseil d'État*, are both judge and party to the crossover between public service and private activity, this new field of public-private intermediation largely escapes the public eye and control.

Legal Privilege?

It should be clear by now that corporate lawyers are today a pivotal group connecting the neoliberalized part of the state and the market. And yet, while they do now play a critical part all along the norm-building process, in their roles as lobbyist, representative, legal adviser, and attorney, they bear no direct responsibility for their structuring role in policies. By virtue of its organization as a liberal profession, the legal profession has indeed remained out of public sight and beyond the reach of political and administrative control.

Secrecy and confidentiality are the cardinal virtues of the profession. The profession's national bylaws state that confidentiality in the lawyer-client relationship is a broad public principle that is "general, absolute and without limitation in time," and applies to all paper documents, emails, correspondence with clients, with colleagues in the profession, notes on meetings and discussions, the client's identity, the lawyer's date book, and so forth. Quite surprisingly, while lawyer-client confidentiality privileges are historically linked to the rights of the defense, this principle has remained unchanged despite the transformation that has taken the legal profession far from the courtroom, and into the business of providing advice and purveying influence. In the aftermath of the 1990 merger between the *avocats* and the *conseils juridiques* that widely expanded the scope of the legal profession, the *Cour de cassation* made a show of resistance (see chapter 1), and issued a restrictive interpretation of confidentiality privileges that it saw as limited to the exercise of defense action before the courts—and not to the activity of drafting documents or acting as negotiator. This interpretation was swept away, however, by legislation enacted in April 1997 giving lawyers a broad jurisdictional immunity, whether acting as defense lawyer or corporate agent. These confidentiality privileges in effect ensure a sort of juridical extraterritoriality for the legal profession[2] and constitute a decisive comparative advantage, and even (to quote one former head of the Paris bar) a "formidable marketing

---

2. On this point, see Georges-Albert Dal, *Le Secret profession de l'avocat dans la jurisprudence européenne* (Brussels: Larcier, 2011), 114.

tool"[3] for corporate law firms as they compete with lobbyists, expert accountants, and consulting firms.

Clinging tightly to its defense of self-regulation, the profession has fiercely opposed all attempts to change the status quo. This is true at the EU level, where lawyers have been the most reticent and the least numerous of all professions to sign onto the Transparency Register established by the European Commission and Parliament.[4] This is also true of the various EU directives adopted in the first decade of the twenty-first century to combat money laundering and which aimed to push back against this tradition of secrecy. Consequently, an obligation to submit a "declaration of suspicion" is now imposed on lawyers in the exercise of their counseling activity; they must spontaneously report to the president of their bar association any facts or circumstances that could lead to suspect money laundering operations. The president of the bar acts as an ethical filter and must decide whether the case should be forwarded to Tracfin, the anti-money-laundering unit at the ministry of the economy that is in charge of investigating such operations. But while over the years since 2004 four EU directives have been enacted and transposed into national legislation, the representatives of the legal profession have unceasingly fought to maintain a broad definition of the scope of confidentiality privileges. Even today the profession stands out for its "absence of participation" in the money laundering alert mechanism, to quote the acerbic assessment of the Tracfin unit.[5] As the profession has been called upon to become the "intelligence service for the justice system and various financial administrations (customs, taxation, social security)" regarding questions related to partial or total dissimulation of professional activity, underreporting or misuse of income or sales revenue, tax fraud and fraudulent avoidance of social charges,[6] the lawyers' boycott has been confirmed: Tracfin received just one "declaration of suspicion" from lawyers in 2014, a figure to be compared with the 1,040 declarations submitted by notaries for the same year.[7] This is all the more problematic in that the instance in charge of sanctioning failures to submit declarations is none other than the bar council itself and its disciplinary commission!

Alongside the lawyer-client privilege, the second fundamental pillar of the legal profession in France is self-regulation of professional ethics and deontology.

---

3. "Déontologie, esprit d'entreprise: Faut-il choisir?," *Les Petites Affiches*, March 11, 2015.

4. Christian Lahusen, "Law and Lawyers in the Brussels World of Commercial Consultants," in Vauchez and de Witte, *Lawyering Europe*, 177–93.

5. Tracfin, *Rapport annuel d'activité 2011* (Paris: Ministère de l'économie et des finances, 2012), 45.

6. Tracfin, "Tracfin 2014: 1 avocat pour 1 soupçon," http://www.cercle-du-barreau.org/.

7. Marine Babonneau, "Lutte contre le blanchiment: Les avocats toujours mauvais élèves," *Dalloz Actualité*, April 20, 2015.

The disciplinary regime applicable to lawyers was modified in 2005 under a reform intended to bring it into compliance with the "fair trial" standards promoted by the European Court of Human Rights. But in practice only minimal requirements of publicity and transparency have been imposed.[8] In the opinion of even some eminent members of the profession, disciplinary action continues to be characterized by its opacity: "unlike many other professions, starting with magistrates, there are no national statistics and there exists no way to track disciplinary action,"[9] nor even an annual report listing complaints, the behaviors in question and the sanctions given, as is the case for the magistrates' disciplinary chamber.[10] The general public, the very body that the professional has historically claimed to speak for and defend against the arbitrary decisions of the state, is kept completely in the dark. Litigants cannot register a complaint with the bar's disciplinary council, and must make do with an appeal to the president of the bar; they have no rights allowing them to take part in a procedure of which they are simply informed. A recent survey conducted by Sophie Harnay and the EconomiX team provides data for an initial assessment of ethics and disciplinary practices in the Paris bar.[11] Even beyond the punishment meted out by the disciplinary council, which can scarcely be called severe, this research reveals the extraordinary place of an "informal justice, the hidden face of disciplinary action," that is conducted upstream of the council. It is the president of the bar and the members of the bar council who filter complaints from clients and colleagues, and decide which ones warrant initiating a disciplinary procedure. So while the annual frequency of complaints is very high—22.6 percent of Paris lawyers have been the object of complaints for breaches of the ethical code—"only 4 [cases] in 1,000 lead to a formal disciplinary procedure." The bar presidents and members of disciplinary commissions prefer the so-called paternal admonishment, a simple reprimand that the bar president can address to a lawyer without any conditions of form or procedure. The "familial nature" and "paternal spirit of the bar's jurisdiction" (to use expressions taken from professional ethics handbooks) continue to permeate the way the profession exercises control over its members and their practices. These attitudes keep the bar, its dysfunctional aspects and deontological issues,

---

8. Likewise, the deontological and professional code of the Paris bar cannot be accessed by the general public on the bar's website, nor can the pages that refer to the bar's ethics commission.

9. Thierry Wickers, *La Grande transformation des avocats* (Paris: Dalloz, 2014), 122.

10. Researchers who have examined the disciplinary practices of the Paris bar also point to "significant difficulty in accessing data": Camille Chaserant and Sophie Harnay, "La déontologie professionnelle en pratique: Enquête sur l'activité disciplinaire de la profession d'avocat," *Revue française de socio-économie* 16 (2016): 119–39.

11. Ibid.

out of public sight, and allow it to conduct its affairs in a partially public setting that is marked above all by the usages of the legal club.

The state is not exempt from responsibility here, as it can, via the office of the public prosecutor, file complaints with the disciplinary commissions and appeal their decisions. Although the available data is sparse, the EconomiX survey shows that the prosecutor's office pursues disciplinary action primarily in the cases of lawyers who have been charged in criminal proceedings. Other mechanisms also exist, intended to prevent conflicts of interest or benefiting from "unlawful advantage" by former civil servants who have crossed over to the bar, but their effectiveness often stops at the doors of the law firm. As an example, there is a waiting time during which former public servants are banned from "drawing up arguments and pleading against the government administrations overseen by the ministerial department to which they belonged." But this ban, based on the individual responsibility of former civil servants, is hard and even impossible to enforce in large firms with many lawyers working together as a team. As one lawyer remarks, there are no rules against sending another lawyer from the firm to work with companies that a former tax inspector in the firm had audited (interview no. 11, man, ENI graduate, tax law).[12]

Public Ethics' Default Lines

It is true that the state has not been entirely immobile. A series of scandals that emerged ever since 2008 involving ministers and top civil servants has triggered a "deontological moment" that resulted in the proliferation of norms and standards and the creation of new institutions to prevent and sanction conflicts of interest. An ethics committee was created at the Senate as early as 2009, followed by the appointment of an ethics officer at the National Assembly in 2011, charged with advising the members of the Assembly on these matters. An independent authority in charge of public ethics was instituted in 2013, the *Haute Autorité pour la transparence de la vie publique* (HATVP, or High Authority for transparency in public life), with a view to identify conflicts of interest and personal enrichment of politicians and top ranked bureaucrats, by gathering and publicizing statements of assets and interests. While progressively expanding the scope of its control to more than fifteen thousand *dirigeants publics*, the Authority was granted special access to tax administration; it is also charged now with

---

12. In addition to this is the fact, reported in work by various researchers, that both the administration and judges are lenient with intermediaries (lawyers, expert accountants), who are rarely charged. Spire and Weidenfeld, *L'impunité fiscale: Quand l'État brade sa souveraineté.*

reviewing, preventively, the fiscal circumstances of the incoming members of government cabinets. And last, under the Sapin II legislation passed in December 2016 to promote transparency, fight corruption, and modernize the French economy, a new agency endowed with the power to investigate and to issue sanctions was created, the National Agency for the Prevention and Detection of Corruption (*Agence nationale de prévention et de détection de la corruption*). The Sapin II legislation also asked the HATVP to keep a transparency registry of lobbyists modeled in many ways on the EU example.

On paper, this array of arms in the new ethics arsenal looks complete. In fact, however, it risks being ineffective. The measures taken fail to avoid the pitfalls of legislation adopted in a panic, leading to a disorderly jumble of ethics watchdogs—two ethics officers in Parliament, the civil service ethics commission, HATVP, and now the corruption prevention agency. Their articulation is neither simple or clear, and may even be counterproductive.[13] The scopes of the various instances largely overlap, in terms of their competence as well as the categories of public persons they are meant to oversee. Indeed, this complex, perhaps unintelligible, architecture has its share of incoherent and bizarre features. There is a certain inconsistency of statutes, as the High Authority is legally independent of the government, but this is not the case for the *Commission de déontologie de la fonction publique* (CDFP)—hereafter, the *commission de déontologie*, the civil service ethics commission in charge of assessing the lawfulness of *pantouflage* to the private sector.[14] Nor is the ethics officer (the so-called *déontologue*) of the National Assembly independent with respect to the office of the president of the Assembly. The roles of these bodies are also distributed somewhat incoherently, as the High Authority is endowed with powers to review the statements of assets submitted to the tax administration by elected officials and ministers, but the *commission de déontologie* does not have equivalent powers regarding high-level civil servants. Last, a lack of coherence persists due to different prevention and oversight strategies pursued by these instances, calling for considerable work to moderate, arbitrate, and coordinate these bodies.

On a more fundamental level, the supervision of the public-private border continues to be characterized by self-regulation, partial transparency, and soft law (without sanctions). The history of the *commission de déontologie*, which

---

13. Pierre Lascoumes and Carla Nagels, *Sociologie des élites délinquantes: De la criminalité en col blanc à la corruption politique* (Paris: Armand Colin, 2014).

14. Following a new law of August 2020 on civil service, the Commission de déontologie de la fonction publique has eventually been integrated within the HATVP, thereby benefiting from its independent statute.

has always been presided over by a member of the *Conseil d'État*, is emblematic. Under the legislation enacted January 29, 1993, to prevent corruption and promote transparency, in cases of crossover of a civil servant to the private sector, the *commission de déontologie* must issue a prior opinion on the compatibility, in terms of penal liability and ethical responsibility, of the new activity with the activity of the civil servant in the three years preceding the transition.[15] In addition to the progressive enlargement of its scope to include employees in cabinet offices, since the enactment of legislation on the rights and obligations of civil servants (April 21, 2016), the *commission de déontologie* has "powers to seek information" (which are not investigative powers, however).[16] This legislation stipulates that government administrations must monitor the activity of civil servants who have been permitted to move to the private sector, but with "reservations." But the *commission de déontologie* has neither the powers nor the means to ensure that former civil servants respect the constraints imposed on them. Most significantly, the control mechanism remains a secret internal process, even for the highest-level civil servants (cabinet officers, directors of administrative divisions, etc.), despite the fact that groups such as Transparency International have called for publication of the commission's opinions. An emblematic example is the spectacular departure of Bruno Bézard, director general of the Treasury at the time (May 2016), for a Chinese investment fund; the opinion, and eventual reservations, of the *commission de déontologie* were not made public.

In actual fact, the contentious cases are generally settled by a discussion, without publicity or sanctions, between the crossover candidate, the ethics commission and his or her original administrative branch. Nothing is more revealing of the inadequate oversight of these crossovers than the fierce resistance put up by the executive branch, in the spring of 2016, in opposition to repeated attempts by a number of parliamentarians from the Socialist Party to place the ethics commission within the purview of the *Haute Autorité pour la transparence de la vie publique,* for crossovers to the private sector concerning members of cabinet offices, collaborators of the President of the Republic, and other staff employed at

---

15. "In the first instance [penal liability] the task is to verify that the private-sector activity envisioned by the public employee does not place the latter in contravention with the Penal Code (e.g., working in a company that the former civil servant had to control in his previous State functions); the second instance [ethical responsibility] ascertains that the private-sector activity does not impinge on the dignity of the former administrative functions or jeopardize the normal operations, independence and neutrality of the public service." Olivia Bui Xuan, "La moralisation de la vie publique," *Droit administratif,* 2014, 10–16.

16. Yves Benhamou, "Pantouflage des juges: Un danger pour l'impartialité de l'État?," *Recueil Dalloz,* 2001.

the discretion of the government. This proposed reform was far from innocuous, for it would have moved the *commission de déontologie* out of the administrative hierarchy, and would have instituted publication of its opinions on crossovers of civil servants at the highest level.[17] A new battle ensued just a year later when the Parliament was examining the Sapin II legislation. Despite the opposition of the government and its secretariat general, a small group of Socialist Party MPs secured language to place the *commission de déontologie* under the auspices of the HATVP. Without success again, however, because this time the *Conseil constitutionnel* revoked the measure, even though no recourse had been brought before the council. This gave rise to a polemical debate on the ascendancy of the *grands corps* and in particular the *Conseil d'État* on this institution.[18] The many resistances coming from within the state *grands corps* have eventually been overcome in August 2019 when a statutory law was enacted that merged the *commission de déontologie* with the HATVP. Yet this was only made possible as a counterpart for the unprecedented incentivization of *pantouflage* by the Macron executive which went as far as granting seniority rights to civil servants during their working period in the private sector.[19]

This structural reluctance to political oversight and publicity is not a characteristic of state *grands corps* alone. The working groups of the two chambers of Parliament have also opted for the flexibility afforded by an ethics code, and for pragmatic ethics officers who see their role as an advisory rather than supervisory function. Ironically, the National Assembly even chose as its first ethics officer Noëlle Lenoir, a genuine expert in matters of circulation between the public and private sectors. Lenoir, who served as ethics officer from 2012 to 2014, had previously been a parliamentary administrator, member of the *Conseil d'État*, member of the *Conseil constitutionnel*, cabinet head of staff, mayor, partner in a law firm, minister, arbitration officer at the International Chamber of Commerce, and so on. During her term, she actually continued to practice as a corporate lawyer heading the Competition Law–Public Law team at the Kramer Levin firm.[20] In the absence of power to make decisions, much less impose sanctions,

---

17. "La commission de déontologie des fonctionnaires sauve (encore une fois) ses prérogatives," *Acteurs publics*, June 10, 2016.

18. See the commentary by Thomas Perroud, "Le Conseil constitutionnel contre la transparence," December 15, 2016, http://blog.juspoliticum.com/.

19. On these policies, see Antoine Vauchez, "L'Etat public-privé", AOC, September 13, 2018: https://aoc.media/analyse/2018/09/13/letat-public-prive/.

20. "L'ex-déontologue de l'Assemblée nationale désormais avocate d'un laboratoire pharmaceutique," *Libération*, November 3, 2015.

the parliamentary ethics officers have little room for action. Noëlle Lenoir said so herself, underscoring that "the ethics officer reviews, discusses, advises and perhaps files a report with the bureau of the Assembly as the case may be, but has no power of decision."[21] Her successor announced that he would above all aim for "*integration* with the parliamentary community,"[22] with an emphasis on "closed doors guarantees" and his role as a mere "traffic officer" orienting—if not counseling—MPs as they engage in parallel activities in the private sector At the Senate, the ethics committee proved equally weak. Since its creation, it has issued eight opinions on subjects of an individual or general nature regarding the exercise of the parliamentary mandate.[23] All these cases have been found to be in compliance with current legislation, while the underlying discussion and considerations have not been made public.[24]

Last but not least, the doctrine professed by these oversight bodies is in most cases quite lenient. Once again, the example of the *commission de déontologie* is edifying. As a former president of the commission noted a few years ago, the commission "takes care not to give an excessive scope to the list of incompatibilities associated with the exercise of (directorial) functions." Accordingly the CDFP felt it could not oppose the departure of a former secretary general of the office of the President of the Republic who left to join a corporate law firm, nor the departure of a former deputy secretary general of the same office who moved to a bank.[25] In fact, negative assessments of the transition of top civil servants to the private sector are extremely rare—three or four a year in the central government administration. The blanket of secrecy covering the "reservations" imposed by the ethics commission to former civil servants' activities prevents the formation of any coherent "jurisprudence," as revealed in our interview with a former tax inspector: "This commission had truly asymmetrical opinions, for I know of two people who appeared before me, without limitations of any sort, whereas they had done a lot of work on corporate filings" (interview no. 10, man, ENI graduate, tax law).

21. Hélène Bekmezian, "Le premier bilan de la déontologue de l'Assemblée," *Le Monde*, November 18, 2013.

22. Ferdinand Mélin-Soucramanien, Rapport annuel du déontologue de l'Assemblée nationale (Paris: Assemblée nationale, 2015), 34.

23. Senate website, presentation of the committee, 2015, http://www.senat.fr/role/comite_deontologie.html.

24. See Noëlle Lenoir, *Rapport public annuel du déontologue de l'Assemblée nationale* (Paris: Assemblée nationale, 2013).

25. Cf. Service central de la prévention de la corruption, *Rapport annuel* (Paris: La Documentation française, 2000), 48–49.

BOX 3. / The very lenient state doctrine on crossovers: The case of Sarkozy's closest economic adviser

The easy-going tradition regarding civil servants who cross over to the private sector came into the spotlight with the case of François Pérol, former deputy secretary general at the Élysée (office of the president) in charge of economic and financial affairs who in 2009 was appointed to head a new banking network *Banque populaire–Caisses d'épargne* whose emergence he had himself dealt with directly in the course of his public function under President Nicolas Sarkozy. While the press and the judiciary pointed out the issues raised by the crossover itself, there was less mention of the high level of tolerance manifested by the state itself, and its ethics commission in particular. The content of the letter addressed by the president of the *commission de déontologie*, himself a member of the *Conseil d'État*, to the secretary general of the Élysée, and published by the press, provides convincing evidence of this. The letter in effect validates the appointment, arguing that "the members of cabinet offices, unlike civil servants in government departments, do not have, in most cases, administrative authority, whether delegated or held by virtue of their position."[26] This reasoning shows a juridical formalism that runs counter to all that political science has shown to be the role of advisers in the office of the president. The letter pursues with a list of the flexible and tolerant attitudes manifested in preceding years:

> In 2007, pertaining to the application of the provisions under discussion, the *commission de déontologie* accepted the *pantouflage* of an adviser to the Élysée secretariat general who had come from the financial sector and returned to finance two years later (decision no. 07.A0629 of 22 July 2007); likewise, a member of the *Inspection des finances*, successively advisor to the prime minister, then director of the cabinet of the minister of the economy, was allowed to become director of strategy at a major bank (decision no. 07.A0627 of 19 July 2007); and yet again, a deputy director who had served in the cabinets of several successive housing ministers was authorized to take a position as director of social housing in a property development company (decision no. 07.A0999 of 5 December 2007). Public reports (of the *commission de déontologie*) from earlier years contain similar examples. The report for 2004 indicates that the commission authorized the departure of the Élysée palace former deputy secretary general, the former director of the cabinet of the prime minister, and the former director of the cabinet of a finance minister, for positions in an investment bank where they exercised executive functions in the capacity of managing associates (decisions of 24 May 1995, 30 November 1995 and 11 January 1996).[27]

While the letter of the president of the *commission de déontologie* attests to the role of "facilitator" that the commission assumed for its work and to its chronic underestimation of ethical

---

26. Letter of February 24, 2009, from Olivier Fouquet, president of the Commission de déontologie, to Claude Guéant, secretary general of the presidency: see "Pérol, la commission n'a pas statué," *Le Figaro*, February 24, 2009.

27. Ibid.

risks, the president later adopted a line of defense that demonstrates a form of intolerance to disclosure of these issues that he deemed to be internal affairs of government administration. When two Socialist Party MPs, Arnaud Montebourg and Michel Sapin submitted a question to the members of the commission regarding the conformity of Perol's crossover, the president of the commission was, in his own words, "flabbergasted," and added: "only in Soviet countries would you see something like this."[28]

There are many other examples of relative insensitivity to situations of conflict of interest, and reticence regarding any form of public scrutiny. In conclusion, nothing has arisen to invalidate the severe assessment given a few years ago by Christian Vigouroux, former alternate president of the CDFP, and eminent member of the *Conseil d'État*: "the commission is not interested . . . in the top civil servants' crossovers and wastes a lot of time on minor cases that are anecdotal. . . . The commission is, in point of fact, merely a commission to manage transitions between civil service and the private sector."[29]

Gaps and Holes in Parliamentary Oversight

As for classical parliamentary oversight, this also appears to be toothless, particularly when it comes to the ongoing development of regulatory agencies within the state, agencies that provide one of the main revolving doors for circulation and exchange between public service and the private sector. As the scope of action of these agencies has been continually extended, by successive acts of law to liberalize insurance markets, banking, rail transport, broadcasting, publishing, and so forth, a crucial question is raised—who controls this "State within the State"?[30] Since 2000 one parliamentary report after another has voiced concern over the chaotic expansion of this zone of independent regulation that continues to be only vaguely defined.[31] "Unidentified juridical object," these agencies are so hard to identify that as of this writing, there is no exhaustive list of all these entities in France. In the absence of a unified legal and political framework,[32] their

---

28. Patrick Roger, "Affaire Pérol: La commission de déontologie a été 'tout près de démissionner collectivement,'" *Le Monde*, March 12, 2009.

29. Nicolas Tenzer and Christian Vigouroux, "Les règles du 'pantouflage' sont-elles respectées?," *Acteurs publics*, June 28, 2010.

30. Mézard, *Un État dans l'État*.

31. Patrice Gélard, *Rapport sur les autorités administratives indépendantes: Rapport du Sénat* (Paris: Sénat, 2006).

32. A recent piece of legislation (January 20, 2017) has attempted to clarify the situation by defining a list of twenty-six "autorités administratives indépendantes" (regulatory agencies) for which a

structures, hiring policies, jurisprudence (in particular in relation to conflicts of interest), and policy orientations are very poorly known. Furthermore, there is no body charged with systematic monitoring of this space in which public policy is produced. The selection of qualified members appointed to the collegial boards of these agencies, recruitment of collaborators (rapporteurs, deputy rapporteurs) who play a central role in these organizations, the overlapping activity of agency members within or outside of the state apparatus—all these factors are entirely under the radar of Parliament. Although senator Jacques Mézard drew up a report in 2015 that provided initial insight into the staffing of these agencies, and pointed out large areas of opacity, this report said nothing about evaluation of the agencies' policy orientations as such. In short, faced with steady expansion of this regulatory pole, MPs are very poorly equipped and they themselves confess to having "no consolidated and cross-cutting vision of the resources furnished to these independent administrations, either in terms of budgetary allocations or earmarked fiscal receipts." And occasional hearings with the presidents of these agencies will not suffice to constitute parliamentary oversight. In point of fact, as the Parliament can neither summon the agencies to appear before the chamber nor demand replies to questions raised by MPs, the Parliament is very hard put to exercise control over this new offshoot of the executive branch. Parliament may not even always receive the agencies' annual reports, and when it does often the MPs have to make do with documents that resemble tools of media communication rather than actual accounts.

The ramping up of the powers invested in these regulatory agencies encroaches not only on the executive branch, which finds itself despoiled of many of its prerogatives. It is detrimental to the Parliament body as well, which is deprived of tools that allow it to ensure its constitutional role of oversight and evaluation of public policy. In short, the agencies are sheltered from the hierarchical power of the executive branch, and are also safely out of the range of parliamentary supervision. This leads to a bitter assessment: "The State, far from being a vigilant comptroller, is merely an observer."[33] Consequently, regulatory agencies "can, within the scope of their area of competence, conduct policy for which they are not called accountable before the parliamentary assemblies under the same terms as the members of the government."[34] The same reasoning could be applied to the various ways public missions are outsourced to the private sector; to begin with, public-private partnerships, over which Parliament, and also

---

number of obligations in terms of transparency, accountability, and deontology are specified. Yet the list of regulatory agencies has remained so far incomplete.

33. Mézard, *Un État dans l'État*, 27.

34. Ibid.

to some extent government ministries, have lost control, if only because of the highly technical nature of these assignments. More often than not the state has deprived itself of the requisite technical competence, by the very act of carving up and farming out these tasks. On the whole, the rise of the regulatory state has brought conventional forms of political responsibility to a stalemate: Parliament can no longer hold the executive branch accountable for the activity of these agencies, and the executive itself has neither the tools for oversight nor the expertise that would enable it to continuously monitor this new regulatory pole.

The new politics of influence that emerged alongside the field of public-private collusion has therefore developed in a blind spot, out of the view of professional regulations, administrative control, or Parliament oversight. The traditional tools of democratic inquiry and oversight are today foiled by the opaque and often informal nature of this border space and its dynamics that lie below the radar of government institutions. The steady enlargement over the past two decades of this "black hole" at the core of France's field of power leads us to wonder what it is costing us in terms of political and democratic life.

Outsourcing Public Interest: Political and Democratic Costs

Here one must start by pointing out a fundamental paradox. The reshaping of the state and its economic policy according to the neoliberal model—breaking up public monopolies, public-private partnerships, outsourcing, development of independent regulatory agencies—that was justified by the need to correct the short-sighted tunnel vision of public authorities, has created a new form of "rent" at the intersection of the public and private spheres.[35] It is as if, to avoid at all costs the purported inefficiency and immobility of public entities, public regulation has been handed over to another form of rent-seeking, even more opaque and unaccountable. By initiating the regulatory turn that thrust public institutions (government administrations, agencies, European institutions, local authorities) into the very heart of markets, these institutions have become the prime target of competition between big companies. For these companies, access to regulators (whether national or European, administrative or political), now determines their capacity to do business and develop over the long term in the marketplace. As they have become increasingly dependent on resources

---

35. On this, see Colin Crouch, *The Strange Non-Death of Neoliberalism* (Cambridge: Polity, 2011).

dispensed by governments and administrations, these major players in the economy have focused their strategy on enhancing their capacity to steer political and administrative powers to their advantage. In other words, the public institutions' zeal in setting up free competitive markets has made them the target of multiple strategies to gain and wield influence, and has spurred large companies to link the accumulation of economic power with the acquisition of political and bureaucratic clout. There is worse to come. Each successive piece of legislation reinforcing the trends to outsourcing, the development of independent regulatory agencies, the breaking up of public monopolies, and encouraging closer public-private partnerships has dug a deeper trench, raising the market value of political and administrative resources and assets. Far from clarifying the respective roles of private enterprise and the state, as the advocates of the neoliberal transformation would have had us believe, these policies have vastly muddied the waters; the intermediate zone where the market meets the state (and the EU) has never had more importance. Far from loosening the ties between economic power and political power, the neoliberal transformation of the state has given birth to a new system of collusive relationships characterized by a configuration of closely imbricated and mutually dependent large companies, corporate lawyers, and public regulators.[36]

One could choose to minimize the import of this change, and see here only limited mutations of public action, essentially restricted to spaces of economic regulation while most of the state is purported to remain steadily loyal to its tradition of autonomy.[37] Or on the contrary, one can emphasize the steep slope of this curve, and point out the steady expansion of this politics of influence over the past two decades—underscoring the deleterious effects of this field's gravitational force on the public and democratic spirit of our political and administrative institutions. These effects are of course visible in the new forms of corruption (from influence peddling to direct bribes) that have sprouted up in the soil of these dangerous liaisons on both sides of the public-private divide.[38] But the corrosive effects of this black hole are much more insidious. To grasp

---

36. This evolution parallels the emergence of a "private technocratic capitalism" that has made considerable gains in the wake of privatization trends; this phenomenon is marked by the enhanced role of business leaders drawn from the pool of political and administrative talent (between 40 percent and 49 percent of French top corporate executives in the 1990s) and the simultaneous sidelining of leaders who do not come from the elite managerial corps. Dudouet and Grémont, "Les grands patrons et l'État en France, 1981–2007."

37. See recently Pierre Birnbaum, *Où va l'État? Essai sur les nouvelles élites du pouvoir* (Paris: Seuil, 2018).

38. Guillaume Sacriste, "Sur les logiques sociales du champ du pouvoir européen: L'exemple de l'affaire Dalli," *Politique européenne* 44 (2014): 52–96.

the scope of these effects, one must take a look through the lenses of democratic theory, to see that this border between public and private is not simply a sectoral or professional segmentation.

As a key political thinker of social differentiation, Michael Walzer puts us on the right track: the emergence of a democratic space was made possible by drawing borders, always uncertain and constantly contested, that ensured the relative autonomy of the public sphere. The protection of the public sphere from the "tyranny" of adjoining sectors governed by other types of authority—religious, military, economic, or other—or, to put it another way, this policy of containment that holds these authorities at bay, sufficiently distant from the spaces where the public interest is deliberated, is a social and institutional condition needed to ensure equal exercise and enjoyment of political liberties, of conscience, expression, demonstration, and so on. Absent this separation that distinguishes the rationales and interests of the public and private spheres, the egalitarian aspirations that are part and parcel of citizenship in a democracy are countered by the anti-egalitarian pressures that are inherent to the functioning of the market economy. What is at stake here are forms of negative conversion, or in Walzer's terms, tyrannical conversion, because "those who could succeed in a specific sphere may be excluded from this success by the success of powerful entities who convert assets drawn from another sphere." In sociological terms, this vision of the democratic space can be read as the preservation of a low political convertibility of social capital accumulated in one or another of the sectors mentioned here. To put it differently, the norms of equality and liberty, conditions that are inherent to the definition of the public interest, can exist only if the dividing line between public and private remains unblurred. In this sense, as Walzer says, "the interference between the spheres," that is in this case the domination of market logic over the functioning of the public sphere, constitutes one of the pathological situations of democratic societies.[39] If one follows the theory of normative social differentiation as developed by Michael Walzer, "society enjoys both freedom and equality when success in one institutional setting isn't convertible into success in another, that is, when the separations hold,"[40] and thus the protection of the borders of each sphere against the mechanisms of tyrannical conversion is not simply a matter of sector or professional stakes, or even a matter of state, but well and truly an issue of democracy.

In this sense, the blurring of the public-private dividing line described above is accountable not only under the ordinary categories of law (conflict of interest,

39. Walzer, "Liberalism and the Art of Separation."
40. Ibid., 321.

misuse of corporate assets, unlawful advantage, etc.) and of professional ethics, as applied for professions such as doctors, architects, and so on. Blurring this distinction calls into question the very conditions in which the public interest is defined.[41] In other words, the marking of social space established by the public-private distinction pertains not only to the applicable legal regime or to the type of economic profitability in place. It also delimits the legitimate space and jurisdiction of the public will, set out by procedures of deliberation, decision-making, and conflict resolution that are necessarily different on the two sides of the dividing line. And because the integrity of the two spheres, public and private, is valuable in and of itself, the line that separates them is a particularly precious object. To express this in the terms of the theory of "the Commons," here there is a "common good" that cannot be legitimately seized by anyone.[42] In this instance, it is a symbolic good, differing from the material goods (air, pasture land, etc.) most often invoked by the theory of Commons, when it suggests ways to establish a regime of shared property. But it would be a mistake to fail to see the very real effects that would be felt by all if this symbolic good was seized or captured by the development of a field of public-private intermediation.

In recognizing the collective and fully political value attached to the preservation of the dividing line between public and private, it becomes possible to determine the costs incurred when this field of intermediation becomes increasingly autonomous. The first of these costs is related to the seizure of this space by a group of intermediaries and major market players, who in this way acquire an unprecedented political capacity to define the public interest at stake when public services are organized as competitive markets. The notion of "capture" developed in American economics literature since the late 1960s expresses one of the corollaries of the autonomization of the politics of influence. If defined broadly, the notion allows us to underscore how doctrinal, professional, and methodological pressures can be exercised to bring a policy or institution under the control of a group of actors and institutions, and inversely the eviction and silencing of citizen's voices and causes in this framework.

Along with the emergence of this field of public-private intermediation, a sort of fence has emerged around a relatively small number of protagonists who manage to move from one side of the public-private dividing line to the

---

41. For a constitutional discussion in a similar vein about the threat of privatized and businesslike government, see Jon Mitchaels, Constitutional Coup. Privatization's Threat to the American Republic (Cambridge: Harvard University Press, 2017).

42. Pierre Dardot and Christian Laval, *Common: On Revolution in the 21st Century* (London: Bloomsbury, 2019).

other, as evidenced by the impressive array of clubs, talks, and other meetings and conferences in the public-private domain. Taking advantage of looser statutory constraints on the part of the state in the spaces of economic regulation, in particular in the areas entrusted to regulatory agencies, and of the flexible conditions granted to the exercise of the profession of corporate lawyer, the crossovers and, by extension, the corporate law firms are now in a position of brokers. Having acquired the know-how specific to this hybrid space, they are well placed to profit from the successive waves that have shaped the neoliberal state and its relationship to the marketplace. The *Cour des comptes* itself has expressed concern with respect to some particularly visible phenomena, such as "former public servants who participate in missions involving their former administrations,"[43] and what the *Cour* calls "subscriptions," pointing at *repeat players* who get past the rules of public procurement by positioning themselves as the systematic advisers of a given state administration. As a result, 40 percent of the total amounts billed to the state for private consultancy services between 2011 and 2013 was paid to just ten consulting firms.[44]

This social and professional fence also has a cost in terms of the ways public institutions (agencies, administrations, even jurisdictions) use their regulatory capacity to impose sanctions. The public-private revolving door, and the increasing confusion regarding the arenas where public economic policies are produced, evaluated, and overseen, have the effect of undermining the ethical yardsticks designed to gauge conflict of interest as well as corruption. The blurring of the public-private dividing line makes it more difficult to exercise criticism "from the outside," and hinders consideration of interests and causes that are not those of stakeholders. It also undermines the effectiveness of internal evaluation and of oversight systems. In a context in which law firms and public-private professionals emerge as border guards, the public interests and values at stake tend to be underestimated, a euphemistic vision of the risk of conflict of interests holds sway, and the costs of publicity, disclosure, and public regulation are overestimated. As a result, the increasing autonomy of the field of influence politics diminishes our collective capacity to regulate the pressure exercised by the main market players and the professionals who represent them on public regulation.

The related risks are not just the influence of a small group of intermediaries, or weaker control mechanisms. The development of bureaucratic expertise and the politicoadministrative networks of large law firms give major market

43. Cour des comptes, *Le Recours par l'État aux conseils extérieurs*, 9.
44. Ibid.

players—large companies and economic interest groups—an unprecedented political capacity that cuts to the very core of the state. Harnessing these law firms, the new middlemen between the state and the marketplace, large companies have boosted their skills and capacity to undo or at least mitigate the constraining effects of national and EU legislation, or to play on their contradictions. Using their political and administrative influence, corporate lawyers work to reinforce the capacity of major companies to steer rulemaking to their advantage and to disarm penal and administrative control mechanisms and sanctions, or to minimize their effects.[45] This is readily seen in fiscal matters, where tax lawyers make it possible for "dominant categories to domesticate fiscal constraints" via "measured application" of the relevant legislation.[46] It is also seen in regulation of competition:[47] crossovers from the civil service are asked to do in the private realm "exactly the opposite of what they were paid to do in the public sector,"—that is, "remove the company from the scope of any eventual inquiry"[48] and the application of constraining legal measures. In so doing, they undermine the effectiveness of public action, and all the more that, as policy to farm out and "agencify" its action has taken effect, the state has deprived itself of the technical expertise that would enable it to pursue its action in critical areas such as public-private partnerships, competition policy, and financial and stock market operations. This has created a vicious circle, in which the relative lack of state expertise in these domains reinforces the conviction, within the state structure, of incompetence and even illegitimacy, further justifying the need for ever greater recourse to the expertise and services of private operators. This is spelled out in the above-mentioned report of the *Cour des comptes*, which states that the state has lost some of the "core competencies of the trade [*sic*]":

> even if consultancy services remain limited in volume and in value in State expenditure, they are concentrated on certain themes of strategic importance for conducting public policy (assistance to decision-making, project support, investments, modernization of the State, etc.) and can gradually create a dependence on key outsourced competencies, entraining a risk for the State of loss of internal expertise and capacity

---

45. Generally speaking, on the growth of political power held by large corporations, we refer readers to Crouch, *The Strange Non-Death of Neoliberalism*.

46. Spire, "La domestication de l'impôt par les classes dominantes."

47. Angela Wigger and Andreas Nölke, "Enhanced Roles of Private Actors in EU Business Regulation and the Erosion of Rhenish Capitalism: The Case of Antitrust Enforcement," *Journal of Common Market Studies* 45, no. 2 (2007): 487.

48. Service central de la prévention de la corruption, *Rapport annuel*, 1990, 43.

to conduct its strategic projects. The capital of experience amassed by certain firms that are strongly implanted in different administrations gives them a far-reaching transversal vision of interministerial activity that no one State administration possesses.[49]

BOX 4. / How the state lost control: Christine Lagarde and the Tapie-Adidas arbitration case

The trial that opened in December 2016 before the *Cour de justice de la République* (France's special court to try ministerial misconduct) in which the defendant was former minister of the economy Christine Lagarde, was destined to delight lovers of riddles and enigmas. How could it be that in an affair with several hundreds of millions of euros in public money at stake, the state had twice removed itself from the procedure? The first time, the state (under the lead of its economic ministry) chose to abandon action before the courts and turned to a trio of arbitrators to settle its dispute with Bernard Tapie. The second time, the state chose to forgo its right to recourse in response to the extremely heavy sanction inflicted by this arbitration tribunal.

To help us unravel this enigma, the work accomplished by the pretrial inquiry commission of the *Cour de justice de la République* provides highly valuable documentation. Beyond the strictly judicial question of the penal accountability of the different protagonists in this affair, who were charged with "negligence" or "conspiracy to commit fraud," the pretrial inquiry offers a singular viewpoint for observing the functioning of the economic and financial arm of the state. One aspect is immediately apparent: business lawyers were omnipresent in the halls of government administrations and the antechambers of ministerial cabinet offices. They are found at each of the cardinal points of the decision process, posted like a backup to political and administrative instances. There was the minister of the economy herself Christine Lagarde—who came from a prominent career in the Baker McKenzie law firm—and on this occasion was advised by August & Debouzy, one of the most influential law firms in Paris. There was also a nebula of public bodies involved in the case—the public refinancing office (*Établissement public de financement et de restructuration*, EPFR) entrusted with defending the interests of the state within the liquidation consortium (*Consortium de réalisation*, CDR) tasked with clearing the assets and debts mishandled by the Crédit Lyonnais bank, plus the state holding agency (*Agence des participations de l'État*, APE)—all of which had engaged their own lawyers. In fact, much of the debate that roiled the state, on the subject of the utility of arbitration, or the risks of appealing the arbitration decision, took place through and among lawyers. The impact of their involvement can also be measured by the essential role they played at key junctures in the case. These crucial junctures came when the state was in talks with the liquidators or with Bernard Tapie, and the lawyer Gilles August was all alone in conducting "in the name of the minister" the negotiations that led to the arbitration compromise. Another key stage came when the option of recourse to seek annulment of the arbitration decision was being debated, and Christine Lagarde and her head of cabinet

---

49. Cour des comptes, *Le Recours par l'État aux conseils extérieurs*, 35–36.

preferred to call upon outside corporate lawyers rather than turn to the legal affairs division of the ministry, or consult the *Conseil d'État* informally. It looks very much like the law firms constituted in the case a sort of exoskeleton of the state, an auxiliary bureaucracy, that bypassed and deactivated the internal spaces of evaluation and oversight.

This astonishing penetration of corporate lawyers into the affairs of the state had a cost, of course. A budgetary cost—to suggest a first-order estimate, let us consider the fees incurred for the arbitration process alone, evaluated at approximately one million euros, each arbitrator receiving remuneration of 300,000 euros . . . or the words of the former minister of the economy at her trial, who spoke of the "hemorrhage of legal fees," "up to 32 million euros a year"![50] But perhaps more significant there was a political cost, from the point of view of the action of the state. In deciding not to develop the in-house expertise needed for large-scale financial transactions (divestiture of share capital, capital increases, etc.), the state created the conditions for its own marked dependency on outside private counsel (legal and financial). Indeed, the *Cour des comptes* had diagnosed this state of dependency in its 2014 report mentioned above. The pretrial inquiry shows how the political and professional corporate mindset made its way into the heart of the state: how a preference for the justice of business lawyers came to prevail, opting for the private justice of arbitration that is deemed to be quicker and better suited to the needs of the business world. Inversely, how the risks, difficulties, and costs of retaining the affair within the purview of the state and its judicial system were overestimated—as it was feared that the intervention of public judiciary deemed too critical or exterior to market actors could drive away future investors. Last, how the decision in favor of a confidential arbitration procedure took shape allowing avoidance of the scrutiny of public exposure and parliamentary oversight.

Deprived of the necessary expertise to carry out its own assessment of the public interest at stake, the state created its own disability as it were, being persuaded that it was not founded to act and defend its own rights. In sum we have here an archetypal case of the collapse of self-confidence on the part of the state, as described by the British sociologist Colin Crouch in relation to the effects of the neoliberal shift. Beyond the finding of individual responsibility, which was ultimately handed down in condemnation of Christine Lagarde, the negligence is above all a systemic negligence, tied to the net of private counseling and revolving doors that now underpins the economic and financial pole of the state.

Placed beyond the reach of parliamentary oversight and administrative hierarchy, wedged in between the pole of agencies and the corporate bar, the developing field of public-private intermediation thereby fosters a form of outsourcing of the public interest, benefiting first and foremost the professionals of influence and major private corporate groups. Because they impinge upon the principles of equal citizenship, on the possibility of public ethics, and in fine on the conditions ensuring the functioning of the democratic state, the collapse of

---

50. Quoted in *La Croix*, December 12, 2016.

the wall separating public from private (and the monopolization of the profits drawn from this intermediate space) constitute a definite risk for democracy, and oblige us to reflect on the framework of a new separation policy. From this point of view, the issue of the line between the public and the private spheres is not merely an internal administrative problem at the level of career management, let alone a matter of efficiency of public institutions, as successive governments have held it. The dividing line, in a democratic regime, is a common good, as defined in the theory of Commons,[51] underscoring that it cannot be appropriated and must remain common property—because this line determines the conditions under which public decisions are constructed and controlled. This is not a purely theoretical distinction. Depending on the administrative or democratic nature attributed to this line, different forms of protection and degrees of vigilance ensue. Either we collectively settle for the current system of self-regulation under the auspices of the state *grands corps*, a system that has now become problematic as the latter are the ones most immediately affected by the dividing line between public and private. Or we consider that the degree of permeability, or impermeability, at the summit of the state—the degree that we deem to be compatible with the proper functioning of our democracy and public action—is a determination that must necessarily be made by bodies that are open and public, with a regime of collective deliberation that extends well beyond the circle of stakeholders alone.

The Difficult "Art of Separation"

Let us say it outright: we do not envision a complete impermeability, that in fact has never existed, nor do we long for an unlikely return to an earlier state of affairs. Social and political criticism has too long been inclined to go no further than an evocation of a golden age of the state that is more myth than reality, and which confines us to an attitude of indignant lamentation. The continual reference to this idealized past is not unrelated to the feeling of impotence that disturbs us as we face these transformations that escape us and over which we seem to have no control. To think about this new situation, surely one should start by "forgetting nostalgia"[52] that too often induces a form of intellectual laziness when discussing the unprecedented challenges raised by the neoliberal evolution of democratic states. One should not be too quick to forget that these "Hegelian"

---

51. Dardot and Laval, *Common*.
52. Albert Ogien and Sandra Laugier, *Le Principe démocratie* (Paris: La Découverte, 2015).

top civil servants leading the nation in the name of a higher ideal of the public interest, and keeping their distance from the world of business—an image sometimes called up with nostalgia today—formed a "State nobility" firmly ensconced in a deeply stratified class structure.[53] Last and most important, there is a kind of irreversibility in this history. It is not possible to upend, by the magic of a political crisis or emotional response to a scandal, a collusive system that has been consolidated by nearly three decades of neoliberal legislation, and is supported by a social and institutional groundwork of multiple public policies, professional groups, and legal mechanisms, both French and European.

Blind Spots in the Transparency Paradigm

It is true that there are new tools for fighting the adverse effects of this blurring of the lines; over the last fifteen years, policies in favor of transparency in public life and prevention of conflicts of interest have emerged as the principal toolkit used by advocates of reform as well as moral entrepreneurs in Europe.[54] Transnational expertise in fighting corruption has developed over the years, driven by the recommendations of the Organisation for Economic Co-operation and Development (OECD) and the Council of Europe, the media campaigns of Transparency International and other NGOs, and the mobilization of EU institutions. Intended to foster the emergence of a virtuous lobbying force that would be useful to public decision makers, this new policy of public ethics is framed in the neomanagerial lexicon of accountability. Its main objective is to ensure that public decisions are "traceable," and that the "legislative footprint" is transparent, by making public the schedules of ministers and top civil servants, by publishing the content of their talks and discussions, by facilitating access to administrative documents, by listing the identity of lobbyists and special interest groups, and so forth. The EU has become the prime laboratory for these new techniques of public ethics. In the wake of the collective resignation of the European Commission in 2000 on charges of conflicts of interests, and following publication of the White Paper on European Governance, the EU Commission and Parliament launched the European Transparency Initiative (2005) and created what has since become the flagship measure of this new arsenal—namely, the Transparency Register, a register that includes a large variety of EU public affairs specialists from lobbyists to NGOs, think tanks, and lawyers. The stakes are high,

---

53. Bourdieu, *The State Nobility*.
54. On this point see "L'Europe en transparence: La mise en politiques d'un mot d'ordre," special issue, *Politique européenne* 3 (2018).

because the consulting and lobbying industry without a doubt has an in-built preference for informal and opaque settings in which their activities are more difficult to identify.

These new instruments of democratic governance also raise some problems, however. Inspired by the theory of public choice that disaggregates *all* players (whether public or private) into separate interest bearers fighting for influence in the norm-making process,[55] these new mechanisms are most often blind to the distinction between public and private actors. This was pointed out in the 2003 OECD report on "conflict of interest" in public service that was in many ways a seminal publication: "The strategy devised to manage conflict of interest relies not only on rigorous oversight of private interests," but also on the equally dangerous risk of competing public interests that may interfere in the decision-making process. In other words, the conflict of interests is not just between private and public interests but equally among different public interests. As a result, each public entity (state-owned companies, regulatory agencies, government departments, etc.) is a lobbyist that should be overseen in the same way as private entities in the economy.[56] The recent Sapin II legislation (2017) in France, enacted to promote transparency and fight corruption, partly adopted this perspective. The definition it gave of the notion of conflict of interest (the first official definition in French law) stems directly from this paradigm as it includes "any situation of interference between a public interest and [other] public and private interests, that might influence the independent, impartial and objective exercise of a function." While the Transparency Register created to list all potential "lobbyists" does not encompass parties and government administrations, it does cross a symbolic threshold by adopting a broad conception of the notion of "interest representatives," extending beyond private interest groups to include publicly owned companies or public bodies engaged in industrial or commercial activity. Better yet, as it pursues its search for a full transparency over normative footprints, whatever the interests at stake, this legislation approves a redefinition of the political playing field, less focused on the classical actors of representative democracy than on stakeholders, whoever they may be—interest groups, private operators in the economy, NGOs, religious denominations and entities, government administration, and so on. In the end—and this is only an apparent

---

55. Sylvain Laurens, "Des élites politiques et économiques encore loin d'une réelle transparence," Médiapart (blog), March 29, 2016, https://blogs.mediapart.fr/les-invites-de-mediapart/blog/290316/loi-sapin-ii-des-elites-politiques-et-economiques-encore-loin-d-une-reelle-transparenc.

56. Organization for Economic Co-operation and Development, *Managing Conflict of Interest in the Public Service*, 2003, http://www.oecd.org.

paradox—these new measures for fighting corruption do nothing to prevent the blurring of the public-private line. On the contrary, they make it even more difficult to distinguish between public and private.

As a result, we are still short of a new microphysics of the public-private border, which would do away with the black hole that obscures the dividing line. A separation policy will certainly make use of the classic set of tools that traditionally serve to protect professionals from outside pressures: these are rules for managing conflicts of interest (incompatible functions, recusal procedures, mandatory resignation, regimes of immunity and protection of position, waiting periods, etc.), and the array of penal statutes, from influence peddling to unlawful advantage, that sanction violation of these rules.[57] They constitute a key institutional toolbox to protect the integrity of the public sphere. But this barrier is most often weakened by policies that aim to "let the public sector breathe [sic]": legislation to modernize the public service (February 2, 2007) sought to incite all civil servants to be mobile in their careers, by reducing from five to three years the waiting period to be respected before former civil servants can take a job (or work as a consultant) in sectors which were under their supervision in the public service. This toolbox is also often criticized, and preference given to the flexible law of ethics codes and prevention policies. Mistakenly. Because they touch upon the conditions that allow civil servants to gainfully exploit in the private sector their experience in the public sector, these tools are particularly well suited to address the growing fuzziness of the dividing line. In other words, they provide the most effective way to juridically and symbolically delimit the public sphere. Because it is out of the question to impose a general and absolute interdiction banning civil servants or politicians from crossing over to the private sector—something that would be neither feasible, nor desirable—the whole system of incompatible positions and waiting periods must be overhauled, to target the most exposed sectors (banking, taxes, etc.) and the most vulnerable public positions.[58] Why not consider the idea, outlined with reference to central banks by the American political scientist Christopher Adolph, that "noncompetition clauses" be required for appointments to executive positions in regulatory agencies and the highest jurisdictions (*Conseil d'État, Conseil constitutionnel, Cour de cassation*), along the lines of the clauses companies include in their contracts with

---

57. Working out the details is far from simple, as shown by a ruling of the *Conseil constitutionnel* in January 2013 that annulled a legislative provision that would have prohibited members of Parliament from becoming lawyers in the course of their term of office.

58. Other ideas can be found in Joël Moret-Bailly, Hélène Ruiz Fabri, and Laurence Scialom, "Les Conflits d'intérêts: Nouvelle frontière de la démocratie," Terra Nova, 2017, http://tnova.fr/rapports/les-conflits-d-interets-nouvelle-frontiere-de-la-democratie.

newly hired employees, to protect their legitimate corporate interests?[59] These clauses could specify the sectoral fields that would be off limits, and the waiting period to be respected before taking employment in the private sector.

As necessary as these instruments are to symbolically and juridically trace the borders of the public sphere, they also have their limits. Their first drawback is the structural weakness of penal action intended to sanction violation of these rules.[60] While the legislation on transparency in public life (enacted October 11, 2013) did indeed stipulate stiffer punishment of unlawful advantage, it is generally agreed that these charges are rarely effectively pressed.[61] For instance, charges were dropped in 2009 in the case of François Pérol, who pivoted to the large French banking federation *Banque populaire–Caisses d'épargne* (see box 3), just a few months after having himself directly overseen the creation of this federation in his role as Sarkozy's main economic adviser; and the former ministry of economy Christine Lagarde, who was actually proved guilty of "negligence" in the handling of the Tapie-Adidas arbitration case and yet suffered no penalty— just two examples among many others. Moreover, these mechanisms aimed at preventing conflicts of interest, constructed first and foremost for legal and judiciary purposes, focus on corrupt practices or on individual circumstances. They thus underestimate the systemic dimension, and the more diffuse corruption of the "public spirit" that is taking hold in political and administrative institutions, with the emergence of a field of public-private brokerage. In addition, as the conflict of interest paradigm merely focuses on the *prevention* of conflict of interests, it fails to address the broader need for an active *protection* that would positively ensure that all parties are equally equipped in the process of defining the public interest. In other words, when it comes to securing the autonomy of public decision-making, there are not only negative obligations, but also positive ones.

It is not within the scope of this book to prescribe in detail the content of this new policy of separation, but it is easy to see—on the basis of our inquiry—the forces that could serve to leverage a new stewardship of the public sphere. These would be: reinforced vigilance and oversight of the various hubs in this field of intermediation (consulting firms, regulatory agencies, *grands corps*); a policy of knowledge and intelligence that would make it possible to map out the structuring dynamics in this border space (crossovers, outsourcing, consulting, and also

---

59. For the proposal developed for central banks, see Christopher Adolph, *Bankers, Bureaucrats and Central Bank Politics: The Myth of Neutrality* (Cambridge: Cambridge University Press, 2013), 311.

60. On the general issues of differential treatment of illegal practices see Lascoumes and Nagels, *Sociologie des élites délinquantes.*

61. See Teitgen-Colly, "Déontologie et pantouflage de la haute fonction publique."

the policy orientations of regulatory agencies, etc.); a precaution principle with regard to laws that further neoliberalize the state, such as those that have progressively undermined the public-private dividing line.

A New Stewardship of the Public Sphere

The transparency policy put into place by public institutions in Paris and Brussels is not in itself sufficient. It can even create a halo that renders our understanding of the phenomenon even hazier, buried underneath an avalanche of data. Paradoxically, the policy may add another veil of opacity if one does not undertake the necessary work of aggregation and analysis. As of this writing, the state has not yet embarked on this task: it does not possess today "a global vision of the networks of influence that it has itself nourished,"[62] to quote the lucid remarks of a report drawn up by the corruption prevention office (*Service de la prévention de la corruption*), nearly twenty-five years ago. In its 2015 report on public sector outsourcing, the *Cour des comptes* recognized that there is "no common reference shared by all government administrations pertaining to the departure of public employees to the private sector, and notably to consulting activity."[63] Likewise, no statistical treatment or summary analysis is made of the statements of interests and assets that are collected by the High Authority for transparency in public life, and which could constitute a valuable resource of knowledge about public managers, ministers, and members of Parliament. To complete the picture, the extremely fragmented institutional framework and the limited resources of the public entities in charge of inducing more ethical behavior in public life, restrict these bodies to a partial view of the situation. In short, the state is afflicted with short-sightedness, and continues to be astonishingly ill equipped to see what is going in its backyard. Is it not surprising that to date there exists no interministerial observatory capable of mustering an overall view of this borderline space, and of the flows of dossiers, funds, and people that stream through the revolving door by virtue of the private careers of crossovers, the outsourcing of the state. Furthermore, the recent abundance of figures has not yet produced the type of data activism that has proliferated around EU institutions ever since transparency policies have emerged—for example, the Integrity Watch launched by Transparency International in 2015, and the work of Spinwatch and LobbyControl that describe themselves as lobby surveillance groups that cross

---

62. Service central de la prévention de la corruption, *Rapport annuel, 2000*, 50.
63. Cour des comptes, *Le Recours par l'État aux conseils extérieurs*.

academic research with advocacy.[64] These groups, which are often linked to militant organizations and to activist media, collate, organize, and contextualize data generated by numerous transparency mechanisms. For certain groups, the purpose is to establish a critical analysis of public data (structural bias, incomplete scope, unwanted side effects, etc.); others aim to complete the necessary task of compiling and analyzing data available online. Working from publicly available schedules of the top tier of political and administrative figures at the EU Commission, from statements of assets held by members of Parliament, and from the EU Transparency Register, these groups have developed search engines and tracking mechanisms that reveal the interaction between elected officials, civil servants, and lobbyists and interest groups.[65]

Perhaps we must also collectively change our thinking about the stewards of public ethics. Today three corps of magistrates, the *Cour des comptes*, the *Cour de cassation*, and the *Conseil d'État* dominate and confer a strongly bureaucratic coloring to the scene. Let us take a look. The *Haute Autorité pour la transparence de la vie publique* is currently presided over by Jean-Louis Nadal, former prosecutor general at the Court of Cassation. The membership of this body includes, in addition to six qualified members who are elected, two magistrates from the Council of State, two judges and two representatives from the Court of Accounts. In the same way, the *commission de déontologie* is headed by a member of the *Conseil d'État*, and relies on the work of a rapporteur general and a deputy rapporteur general, both from the *Conseil d'État*, assisted by a team of some twenty rapporteurs drawn for the most part from the younger portions of the *grands corps*. Generally speaking, all the thinking on public ethics seems to have been delegated to this trio of magistracies—judiciary, administrative, and audit of public accounts. This is illustrated in an emblematic fashion by the commission constituted by Nicolas Sarkozy in 2010 to make proposals in the field of "prevention of conflict of interest in public life," which was organized around the triumvirate of the vice president of the *Conseil d'État*, the chief presiding judge of the *Cour de cassation*, and the president of the *Cour des comptes*. This is not an insignificant circumstance, for these commissions devoted to thinking about the ethics of the state form what the political scientist Philippe Bezes calls the "reflexive fraction of the state"[66]—that is, the space in which the state is examined and diagnosed, calibrated, evaluated, and supervised. Nourished by a broad body of documentation, from annual reports to judicial rulings, in this space is discussed

---

64. See Cécile Robert, "Les dispositifs de transparence entre instruments de gouvernement et 'machines à scandales,'" *Politique européenne* 61, no. 3 (2018): 174–210.

65. Ibid.

66. Bezes, *Réinventer l'État*.

the border between what is in the public purview and what falls into the private domain, and what, in this age of competition, is subject to public regulation and what is decreed to be a question of economic freedom. Here the ethical norms are defined that are used to judge the state and its political and administrative personnel. Last, this is the triage center where social demands for ethical conduct are deemed acceptable, or inversely extravagant, and where the toolkit of options is assembled, from which politicians draw their ideas for reform. In this sense the triumvirate that oversees stewardship of public ethics in France has a strong political meaning: it signifies the role of stewardship granted to these three *grands corps* with respect to definition of the public interest, and reveals the unwritten administrative constitution that underpins the Fifth Republic today. But it also underscores, by the negative, the marginal role assigned to nonstate entities, NGOs, citizens' groups, and so on, in the oversight of public integrity.

For a long time, this state of affairs was accepted. The omnipresence of these state *grands corps* even seemed to be the best way to ensure the independence of the state vis à vis the individual interests of parties in civil society. Today, this arrangement is no longer satisfactory. First and foremost because it is now well established that these very top portions of the state have often been the vector— not the shield—for the penetration of managerial imperatives, reaching into the heart of the state and actively abetting the blurring of the public-private line. And also because these stewards of the state are today the prime purveyors of private consultants and corporate lawyers, transmogrifying the marches of state into a flourishing marketplace of public affairs. Can the elite of the *Conseil d'État* be at once the guardians of the public spirit, the judges of government administration, the main breeding ground for regulatory agencies, and prime players in the corporate bar? Judge and plaintiff, guardians of the temple and go-betweens, the members of the *Conseil d'État* no longer have the legitimacy they once had to profess to be impartial spokespersons proclaiming the public interest.[67] The art of separation does not easily tolerate this confusion of roles.

Controlling Intermediaries between the State and the Marketplace

If it is true that the politics of influence described here has its professionals, they should be the prime focus of reform efforts. Maybe the first step should be to

---

67. Indeed voices are heard today in favor of eliminating the counseling role of the *Conseil d'État* that has been traditionally conceived around a double role, counsel to the government and judge of state practices; see Dominique Rousseau, *Radicaliser la démocratie: Propositions pour une refondation* (Paris: Grasset, 2015).

scrutinize the off-radar position acquired by the legal profession, and to point out that this profession is reticent to accept that its new role at the intersection of the state and the marketplace warrants new guarantees and new controls. Over time, a powerful system has been erected to protect the independence of lawyers, relying on a three-pronged array: monopoly privileges to represent and assist parties before judiciary and disciplinary tribunals, self-regulation in deontological and disciplinary matters, and rules of professional confidentiality.[68] Yet it is important to recall that this singular status of this profession, liberal and monopolistic, finds its theoretical grounds in the mission to protect citizens and uphold the rights of defendants. Codes of ethical conduct and the discourse of the representatives of the legal profession alike exalt the mission of lawyers, raised to the level of "auxiliaries of justice" (article 3 of the 1971 legislation), and their function as spokespersons for the public, a role that goes beyond that of a mundane merchant of law or an ordinary vendor of services. As stated by the Code of Conduct for European Lawyers the "independence [of the lawyer] is as necessary to trust in the process of justice as the impartiality of the judge." In other words, a sort of proxy has been given to the profession to take charge of managing a public interest—namely, the proper functioning of the justice system and of the state of law.[69]

These guarantees and privileges, designed to ensure the independence of lawyers with respect to the political and judiciary branches of power, take on entirely new dimensions in a context where the profession has become a multifaceted profession. At the crossroads of business, politics, and government, lawyers can exercise multiple activities, often far from the functions of judiciary assistance and defense. In this context, the outlines of the profession have been nearly totally redrawn, and if its privileges are conserved in toto, it may be to the detriment of another public interest—namely, our collective capacity to maintain a dividing line between the public and the private. It is not necessary to dwell on the central role played by lawyers (Swiss ones, in particular) in the international system of money laundering and fiscal fraud revealed by the Panama Papers, to point out the limitations of self-regulation for a profession that today plays a crucial role at the crossroads where the state meets the marketplace.

Maintaining professional secrecy and confidentiality for all lawyers' activities is hardly compatible with the art of separation. A line would have to be drawn

---

68. The conditions prevailing at the inception of this system show that the aim was to escape, insofar as possible, the oversight of judges over the profession: Jean-Louis Halpérin, "L'indépendance de l'avocat en France au XIXe et au XXe siècle," in *L'indépendance de l'avocat*, ed. Louis Assier Andrieu (Paris: Dalloz, 2015), 65–76.

69. Wickers, *La Grande transformation des avocats*, 30.

between legal defense and assistance, on the one hand, and consulting services and lobbying on the other.[70] This is undoubtedly not easy to achieve, but bar associations in other countries have opened the way. Some limit lawyer-client privilege to the traditional roles of the legal profession, legal advice and litigation. The Flemish bar in Belgium, for example, issued a statement in 2010 indicating that "it is not accurate to say that because lawyers are in all areas and at all times 'interest representatives,' the fact of representing interests as a lobbyist falls within the limits of normal and essential law practice. . . . It is completely incorrect to claim that the name of a client is ipso facto a professional secret belonging to the lawyer. . . . Lobbying cannot be considered to be among the basic tasks of lawyers. This activity is not protected by rules of lawyer-client confidentiality."[71] And the Flemish bar suggests that "firewalls" or systems of "separation of activities" could be instituted. The French bar is far from such an audacious stance. Anticipating the introduction of mandatory registration with the EU Transparency Register for all lobbyists, the National Council of Bar Associations (*Conseil national des barreaux*) did however take an initial step in 2016. The CNB accepted a first incursion into the domain of professional secrecy when a clause was included in its rules of procedure indicating that "members who represent third parties' interests before European or national public administrations, must, as the case may be, and after having informed their clients, mention the identity of these parties in the registers opened by these institutions and administrations, and must report the fees pertaining to these missions."[72] But the road to enforcement of these rules is a long one, judging by the strong reticence manifested by the profession, as mentioned above, which is reluctant to take up its part in the public money-laundering alert system set up the Tracfin unit.

One question remains: are lawyers well placed to identify and judge, all alone, behaviors that are contrary to their mission in the public interest that has historically been their charge? Doubt is permitted. Not because one should doubt the good will of the representatives of the profession who participate in disciplinary and ethical conduct bodies, but because they are also mandated by their peers to ensure the economic attractiveness of the bar, subject to ever sharper competition from other professionals in the field of consulting and influence. From this point of view, the control over the conditions of access to the profession itself

---

70. In this sense, see the reasoning of the European Court of Human Rights in the ruling *Michaud v. France* of December 6, 2012.

71. Orde van Vlaamse Balies, "Lobbying, avocats et secret professionnel," October 10, 2010, quoted in Coraline Schornstein. "Les Avocats-lobbyistes: Émergence, légitimité, incertitudes." Master's thesis, Université Paris 2, 2015.

72. Ibid.

(i.e., the dispensatory conditions of access given to top civil servants and politicians, incompatibility rules, bans on multiple functions, etc.) are an essential stake of interprofessional competition. For instance, the goal to forge a broad cross-disciplinary advisory profession is backed by a broad segment of the bar elites when they call for a merger of the bar with in-house legal counsels, and when they seek to have the many bans on multiple functions lifted. Likewise, the sweeping interpretation of the decree pertaining to bridges between the public sector and private sector that is pushed by certain bar associations, in particular the Paris bar, when it comes to integrating members of Parliament and ministers into the categories of civil servants targeted by the decree. Because they are caught between objectives that are contradictory in their terms—fostering an economically dynamic profession, for one, and defending its ethics, for the other—the representatives of the bar do not appear to be in the best position to assume alone the responsibility for ethical matters linked to the development of the business bar. And yet citizens and civic groups, of consumers, human rights advocates, opponents of corruption, and so on, have no voice today in deontological and disciplinary affairs. They have no capacity for direct recourse before the ethics commissions of bar associations and are not represented on any of the disciplinary bodies, which all function along the lines of professional chumminess.

There is no lack of ideas, however, for ways to eliminate the blind spots in self-regulation. Via the office of the public prosecutor, the state has a key role in the oversight of the professional activity of lawyers: it can file complaints with the bar's disciplinary council and can appeal its decisions in disciplinary matters, and even in cases to grant dispensatory access to the profession to this or that politician or top civil servant. But for lack of time or motivation, the office of the prosecutor has kept a low profile. It does use its capacity to pursue disciplinary action, but most often this action accompanies penal charges that are brought elsewhere.[73] As for oversight of decisions to allow dispensatory access to the bar for politicians, for a long time the office of the prosecutor was silent. It was not until 2011 that it decided to examine a deliberation of the council of the order of the Paris bar, and contested the decision to admit ex–transport minister Dominique Bussereau to the bar—not ineffectively, as ultimately Bussereau withdrew his candidacy.[74] But beyond the reappearance of the prosecutor's office in oversight of the profession, litigants and citizens are still missing from the

73. Chaserant and Harnay, "La déontologie professionnelle en pratique: Enquête sur l'activité disciplinaire de la profession d'avocat."

74. Olivier Toscer, "Le parquet recale Dominique Bussereau," *Nouvel Observateur*, May 11, 2011.

scene. A first breach could be pierced by opening disciplinary commissions to litigants, or by granting human rights bodies and anti-corruption organizations the right to issue alerts or the right to file complaints. Unless it becomes necessary to adopt a radical reform along the lines of the Legal Services Act enacted in the United Kingdom in 2007 that instituted a Legal Ombudsman, breaking with the centuries-old tradition of self-regulation of the bar. Conceived as an "independent body representing the interests of the public and consumers in a responsible, coherent, flexible and transparent way"[75] appointed outside the profession by a public body whose members are in majority not lawyers, this Legal Ombudsman can undertake legal action on the basis of complaints filed by clients of legal services providers. The ombudsman has broad powers of inquiry into questions of professional misconduct and ethics, and can also award financial compensation to victims.

In sum, the traditional path of self-regulation chosen by lawyers and top civil servants alike has its limitations. We do not impugn the competence or the integrity of the *grands corps* or the representatives of the legal profession when we write that they are not the best placed to assume, alone, the role of border guard at a dividing line that is highly sensitive and which concerns their professions first and foremost. Indeed, it is a common trait of social and political elites, as underscored by French sociologist Pierre Lascoumes, that they are structurally insensitive to the possibility of conflict of interest, and have a strong tendency to deny that conflicts exist, either because said conflicts are justified by the considerable responsibility assumed and personal sacrifices made by the elites in the collective interest, or because they are deemed to be necessary, in the name of pragmatism and the efficacy of public action. The elites protest that they are in absolute good faith, witness the financial sacrifices they have made in pursuing public careers that are much less well paid than in the private sector. But this line of argument neglects the process of symbolic accreditation that the exercise of public functions (cabinet offices, directorial positions in regulatory agencies, etc.) continues to play as it builds reputation and expertise that are then convertible in the private sector at a high price, particularly in the corporate bar. These tendencies to minimize, tolerate, and euphemize[76] are an incitation for more comprehensive oversight of this dividing line. The separation of the public

---

75. Mary Seneviratne, "The Legal Ombudsman: Past, Present, Future," *Nottingham Law Journal* 24 (2015): 1–19; this article assesses the first five years of operation of the ombudsman's office and the 24,000 complaints received.

76. Pierre Lascoumes, "Condemning Corruption and Tolerating Conflicts of Interest: French 'arrangements' Regarding Breaches of Integrity," in *Corruption and Conflicts of Interest*, ed. Jean-Bernard Auby, Emmanuel Breen, and Thomas Perroud (London: Edward Elgar, 2014), 67–84.

and private spheres is a common good that cannot be allowed to be monetized or appropriated by a few, and management of the border and establishment of its rules cannot be left to the *grands corps* nor to stakeholders alone. This is the very spirit of article 15 of the Declaration of the Rights of Man and of Citizens, which proclaims that it is "society" as a whole that "has the right to hold all public servants accountable for their administration."

CONCLUSION / On the "Public-ness" of the State

In the course of this inquiry, the center of gravity of our research has progressively shifted: what started as a survey limited to a novel form of the revolving door phenomenon became a plunge into the depths of the corporate bar, an exploration of the new forms of state action, and in the end an analysis of the realignment of the borders separating public and private. Lawyers, as tracers of the neoliberal reconfiguration of the state, served as our guides through the meandering byways of a field of public-private brokerage that has unceasingly grown and expanded over the past two decades. In the end, one thing is evident: far from having fulfilled the trumpeted promise of clarifying the respective roles of the state and the marketplace, the neoliberal turn has given birth to a space of mingling and exchange that has no precedent. An extraterritorial zone has grown up at the margins of business, politics, and government. In this new framework, confusion of roles and mixing of genres are not individual deviations from the norm or symptoms of occasional administrative anomalies. On the contrary, they constitute the new normal when it comes to the functioning of the state in its relationships with the market economy. This book, in the end, tells the story of a "black hole" that has appeared at the very heart of our democracies: its birth in a blind spot hidden from the view of professional regulations and political oversight, the expansion of its gravitational pull at the core of the state, and the ensuing political and democratic costs that we face today.

We are seemingly powerless to confront this new cycle of the state that has consolidated since the 1980s. Battered and brainwashed by two decades of injunctions vaunting the virtues of synergy and of public-private partnerships, we have underestimated the cumulative effects of these reforms on the "public spirit" that animates our political and administrative institutions. Not without consequences. After two decades of incessant reminders that private management is the superior mode, the self-confidence of the state, or in other words, its capacity for autonomous action in reaction to the market, has been gradually eroded.[1] Worse still, our

---

1. Crouch, *The Strange Non-Death of Neoliberalism.*

collective capacity to distinguish the public from the private and to theorize the specific nature of the public sphere with regard to the realm of private action is degraded. Tricked by the constant and misleading use of the "public" vocabulary of the state, we have collectively failed to see that the presumed correspondence between the public interest and the interest of the state, long the essential reference point of our democracies, had broken down. For if the lexicon of the public sphere remains omnipresent and central in administrative law, defining its agents and stipulating their missions—there are still "public" establishments, "public service" missions, and so on—these words now have a hollow ring. As a consequence of the blurring of lines, the fiction of the state that parades "the spectacle of public respect for public truth" in its relation to the marketplace appears to be a dupery and a sham.[2]

Can we however afford to give up this special relationship between the state and the public interest, as the proponents of good governance who proclaim a principle of nondifferentation between public and private persons, would have us do? Must we repudiate the normative ideal of the state as a repository of the universal values associated with the notion of the public in favor of public-private synergy by which market dynamics would conveniently correct the failings of the public sector? Surely not, for what is at stake are the very conditions in which the public interest is articulated and the functioning of a democratic space elaborated, beyond the reach of the unequal workings of the marketplace. But after two decades of neoliberal ascension, the work to rebuild the intellectual ties between the public realm and the state and to muster the collective political forces capable of championing the autonomy of the public sphere is still extraordinarily embryonic.

We are still inclined to cling to old relics and nourish the obsessive memory of a golden age of the state, and we are slow to awaken from our long dogmatic slumber. We do not presume to undertake in a few lines here a task that will require collective work over the long term. We simply suggest a few markers that point in this direction. The first step is a renunciation: we must renounce the more or less explicit delegation of the public interest to the state *grands corps*. The aptitude of these elites to be the "ethical prophets" of public interest, those who convey "the official truth in which the totality of society is supposed to recognize itself,"[3] thus implicitly casting the imprint of the collective ethics, this capacity is today in tatters. This "State nobility" is no longer legitimate in this role, having frequently introduced the imperatives of new public management

2. Pierre Bourdieu, *On the State: Lectures at the Collège de France* (Cambridge: Polity, 2015), 28
3. Ibid.

into the central workings of the state, and opened new possibilities of cross-over to the private sector. The scope of circulation and the degree of separation between the public and private spheres condoned by society cannot be left to the decision of administrative commissions or ethics committees dominated by these elites alone. As noted by Walzer, the art of separation of social spheres is difficult and controversial. In this respect, drawing the respective borders of the public and the private spheres, and enforcement of this separation, is "a popular, not an esoteric, art."[4] A new political vision must emerge that holds all citizens collectively accountable for this separation and makes them the guardians of this dividing line; only public deliberation can decide what level of autonomy is seen to be compatible with the proper functioning of democracy.

This new democratic stewardship of the state calls for mobilization of all those—anti-corruption NGOs, citizens' collectives, public service unions, and other divisions of civil service—who have over the years pinpointed the risks for politics and democracy that stem from the confusion of roles. Faced with the new collusive system described in this book, a system which has sprung up at the periphery where business, politics, and government meet, it is important to envision a new coalition of forces that can roll back the process of blurring and nondifferentiation that is at work before our very eyes. We pass over the mechanisms designed to protect whistleblowers, but we can mention the breach tentatively opened by creation of the High Authority for transparency in public life under the legislation enacted October 11, 2013. This legislation allows authorized anti-corruption NGOs to file complaints with the authority "when they have knowledge of a situation or facts that could constitute a failure to comply with the various obligations set by law"—for example, improper conduct, conflict of interest, failure to make mandatory filings, noncompliance with the rules of departure to the private sector, and so forth. There has been little success to date, seeing that only four groups have been recognized (Anticor, Transparency International, Pour la démocratie directe, and Sherpa), and that as of the end of 2016 just one case had been referred to the authority, regarding a completely innocuous matter of an incomplete statement by a member of Parliament who failed to mention his role as president of a nonprofit entity.

It remains that the Gordian knot is indeed a political affair. All the institutional apparatus of modern democracy (transparency, access to data, participatory mechanisms, etc.) will not suffice to change matters. What is needed is an awakening of consciousness and recognition of the political accountability of

---

4. Walzer, "Liberalism and the Art of Separation," 328.

the various majorities that have succeeded each other over the past thirty years. Far from the enchanted vision of a virtuous circle by which recourse to the private domain would allow the public sphere to keep its promises—a notion long espoused by advocates of the "third way"—the proliferation of reforms since the late 1980s has not been neutral in terms of definition of the public interest. One of the unseen effects of decades of multiplication of independent regulatory agencies, private counsel to public bodies, public-private partnerships, and competition between public establishments, has been precisely the incessant expansion of this gray area at the heart of our democracies. We must undertake an inventory, if we hope to halt this expansion that puts the public spirit of the state at risk. This inventory will enable us to measure the cumulative political effects of the neoliberal remaking of the state. On this basis, a new principle of precaution can be founded, to in the future make proposed legislation subordinate to impact studies to assess the consequences in terms of further development of the politics of influence at the margins of the state. And from this inventory can start over the never-ending work of reinventing the *raison d'être* of the "public" in democracies.

France is blocked by the self-serving tendencies of its elite. And I'll tell you a little secret: I know it, I was part of it.

Emmanuel Macron, Rally in Pau, April 2017

As the French edition of this book was barely making its way into bookshops and libraries, a major political breakdown suddenly hit France. Thirty-nine-year-old Emmanuel Macron, who was virtually unknown to the general public up to three years earlier, and had never before run a single campaign large or small nor been democratically elected to any political position, unexpectedly won the presidential election on his first try. As a victor over France's National Front leader Marine Le Pen, he immediately became the object of liberal admiration throughout a world that saw Macron's France as an island of resistance in a global context of the rise of populisms. As he claimed to govern France "neither at the left, neither at the right," Macron's political positioning that combined promarket, socially liberal, and pro-European ideas profoundly broke away from France's past political coordinates. Within only a few months, his political movement *En Marche!* had literally "Uberized" the French political system. It brought the two governing parties that had ruled the country ever since the establishment of the Fifth Republic (the Socialist Party [PS] and the neo-Gaullist party [UMP]) to near collapse, and forced an entire political class into retirement.[1]

The book suddenly took on a different light. As the profile of the Macronist governing elite was progressively delineated, and the reform agenda was disclosed, it became clear that Macron's success could hardly be reduced to "the

---

Note to epigraph: Quoted in Michel Rose, "Macron Banking Whizz-Kid Is Anti-Establishment Presidential Favorite," Reuters, April 14, 2017.

1. For a rich collection of inquiries into the meteoric rise of Macron: see Bernard Dollez, Julien Frétel, and Remi Lefebvre, eds., *L'entreprise Macron* (Grenoble: Presses Universitaires de Grenoble, 2019).

fruit of a brutal form of history, of a breaking-and-entering,"[2] as he himself actually put it. While he and others tend to produce a narrative that points at the ways in which the disruptive and charismatic leader skillfully managed to take advantage of an unprecedented political context (the demise of the Hollande presidency and the corruption of the conservative candidate), what this book shows is that his access to power is in tune with larger and deep-seated transformations of French politics and government that had been taking place for decades. Even though (or maybe precisely *because*) it was written before Macron's ascent to power, this book allows us to consider Macron's "structural banality"—in sharp contrast with the many lazy discourses about his extraordinary gifts or radically unique nature. Beyond the heroic illusion that has contaminated much of the interpretative work on the "Macron phenomenon," this book allows us to reposition Macron's rise in a deeper sociological and ideological context and account for the part of France's field of power in which it has been able to prosper.

If one agrees that social fields are always personified by idiosyncratic "heroes" and "great men" who embody the very logic of a given field more and better than the others, then Macron is definitely a representative agent of the field of public-private brokerage that is described in this book. Not only because of his being typical in terms of social properties and educational trajectory, but also because of the professional and political strategies he has built over the years, the type of capital he was able to accumulate, and the specific worldview and political platform that consolidated as he was progressively rising to power. Interestingly enough, Macron encountered the field's gravitational effect early on in his career, almost immediately after passing all the steps of the *cursus honorum* of French state nobility leading from Sciences Po to the *École nationale d'administration* and ultimately to the most selective state *grand corps* (*Inspection des finances*).[3] His trajectory was indeed profoundly marked by his being called, at the age of thirty, to act as *rapporteur* to the important wise men committee set up by then president Sarkozy "for the liberation of French growth" (2007–2008). The so-called Attali Commission, named after its president (a former *Élysée* secretary general turned banker), gathered a mixed bag of highly prominent personalities coming from the public and the private sectors (CEOs of large private as well as state-owned firms, economists, business lawyers, presidents of regulatory

---

2. Quoted in Lauren Collins, "Can Emmanuel Macron Stem the Populist Tide?," *New Yorker*, June 24, 2019.

3. For a detailed account of Macron's trajectory, see Collins, "Can Emmanuel Macron Stem the Populist Tide?"

agencies, etc.) who would eventually converge in promoting "market competition" as the new public policy holy grail.[4]

The fact that Macron's career debut as high civil servant implied crossing through this public-private hub has indeed proved critical both in terms of setting his policy preferences and structuring the range of professional opportunities that he would later encounter. Right after the Attali Commission his career started featuring an intense series of moves in-between the public and the private sectors. After spending four years in the financial sector as a senior banker at Rothschild Bank (2008–2012),[5] he was called by François Hollande who made him his top economic adviser during his 2012 presidential campaign. This position then led him to become deputy secretary general of the *Élysée* (the second top bureaucratic position in the president's staff) after Hollande eventually won the election. From there, it only took two years before Macron moved again, this time to the private sector where he was hosted for a couple of months in the offices of the law firm whose managing partner was a fellow member of the *Inspection des finances*.[6] But a government crisis was soon to open up a new unexpected opportunity as he was called to replace the resigning minister of economy from the left of the Socialist Party.

While the pace and breadth of Macron's accumulation of titles and experiences did set him on an exceptionally fast track, the public-private pattern of his trajectory as well as his constant positioning at the intersection of politics, government, and business, is in no way exceptional in the context of the neoliberal turn of the French state described in this book. Interestingly enough, as he progressively built an entourage of his own that would eventually follow him to the presidency subsequent to his successful 2017 bid, Macron drew heavily from these emerging public-private professionals, selecting a governing elite very homologous to his own social and professional profile. Prime minister Edouard Philippe is quite emblematic in this regard: despite being drawn from the conservative ranks, he is by many standards a "structural clone" of the president. Just like him, he successfully climbed all the steps of state nobility's *cursus honorum* (Sciences Po-ENA-*grands corps*). Just like him, he then started moving back and forth between top bureaucratic positions (notably at the *Conseil*

---

4. Commission Attali pour la libération de la croissance économique, *Increase Competition for a Better Purchasing Power*, October 2007.

5. There, he led the nine-billion-dollar acquisition of Pfizer's baby-food division by Nestlé, a dossier that had been brought to him by the chairman of the Nestlé Group he had met in the Attali Commission.

6. Antoine Gosset-Grainville, a former economic adviser of Pascal Lamy during his time at the European Commission and later deputy chief of staff of prime minister François Fillon (2007–2012).

d'État) and the realm of public affairs in the private sector—as a partner at the Debevoise & Plimpton law firm (2004–2007) or lobbyist in chief for Areva (the French publicly owned nuclear company: 2007–2010).[7] Generally speaking, Macron's marching wing, the little group that now populates both his and the prime minister's offices, is emblematic of the neoliberal state nobility described in this book—one that is deeply engaged in a continuous crossover between public positions (whereby they promote a probusiness and procompetition agenda) and private positions (whereby they "commercialize" their public assets and state knowledge).[8] Strikingly, Macron and his close group of advisers have immediately adopted for themselves the "bilingual" jargon that is spoken in the remit of this public-private field. As they express themselves in this mixture of corporate slang and old bureaucratic motto, they dream a dream of a France that would be striving to become "a start-up nation [*sic*]."

But there is more to Macron than his being the field's representative agent: through his insurgency in politics, he has progressively turned into its "structural hero" skillfully interpreting its growing impatience with the functioning of representative politics. Truly enough, in the years that immediately preceded Macron's meteoric rise to power, it was not difficult to feel the growing frustration of this new public-private elite vis-à-vis the traditional governing parties and their politics of compromise and electoral clienteles. The fate of the Attali Commission had served as a clear signal in this regard, dashing the hopes of directly feeding the regulatory reform agenda (an all-out promotion of the market competition paradigm) into politics. The commission's final report had heavily insisted on the fact that the list of reforms proposed were not a menu for politicians to pick and choose but a package whose efficiency depended on its complete and integral implementation. But yet again, filtered through the hot waters of representative politics and the complex interplay of party factions, the agenda hardly made its way into Sarkozy's and Hollande's policies—despite their paying lip service to its value and importance.

This failure to adopt what had been presented as a self-evident nonpartisan reform agenda was met with increasing incredulity in the different quarters of this field of public-private intermediation. It should be said that, as the field

---

7. Interestingly enough, newspapers suggest that his unexpected nomination as Macron's prime minister took him by surprise as he was envisaging a move back again to private legal practice in a context where his political mentor and former prime minister Alain Juppé had announced his retirement from politics.

8. For a sociology of Macron's government elite see Valentin Behr and Sebastien Michon, "Le gouvernement Macron et les nouveaux technos: Noblesse d'État et circulations public-privé," *Revue française d'administration publique* (2019): forthcoming.

had progressively expanded and consolidated along the coral reefs of the state, its agents had grown in both political authority and self-confidence. Law firms, regulatory agencies, parts of the *Conseil d'État*, were accumulating experience and authoritativeness in their claim to identify common sense reforms of market government. As they produced surveys, policy memos, annual reports, in which the private-public reform agenda was been promoted, these so-called regulators were gaining media visibility and political leverage vis-à-vis central government as well as in the public debate. The traditional self-censorship vis-à-vis representative politics that had long dominated among these unelected actors with experience both in public service and private companies, was increasingly felt as a undue limitation to the necessary reforms of the French State and economy. Frustrated in its reform agenda, a whole field of actors was moving into politics and yet we were collectively unable to see it, as the traditional routine of party politics and its game of alternance between socialists and conservatives continued, apparently unchanged.

As this slow-moving landslide was producing cumulative political effects, it increasingly encountered the hurdles of representative politics blocking the full recognition of the governing role of this *nouveau monde*. Access to government remained dependent upon going through the long trials of partisan politics, and the lengthy *cursus honorum* of local campaigns and party positions: an obstacle course that had been patiently followed by Sarkozy and Hollande whose ascent to power had taken more than two decades. For an elite who had accumulated an unprecedented variety of government, bureaucratic, and business positions, the trials of lengthy political careers in party politics was considered too costly and too uncertain. As Macron himself confessed as early as 2010, at the time of his entering at Rothschild Bank: "today, I am not ready to make the concessions that are required in parties, that is to excuse myself to be a white educated male and to have succeeded in exams (to access the *grands corps*) that were open to all."[9] Even as he became minister of the economy, he would not hide his reluctance to engage in the traditional career of professional politicians: "a lot of people tell you—or present things to you: to be part of the political life, one has to become MP first; but this is the *cursus honorum* of ancient times."[10]

His impatience was that of a whole field of public-private intermediation for which he would later coin the term "*nouveau monde*." His bold move directly

---

9. See https://www.emilemagazine.fr/article/2017/3/23/il-y-a-7-ans-emmanuel-macron, accessed August 2019.

10. "Pour Emmanuel Macron, devenir député est un 'cursus d'un ancien temps,'" *Le Monde*, September 30, 2015.

into the presidential race is indeed hard to understand without seeing that the tree hides the forest: what was somehow pushing behind was an entire field of actors and institutions which had grown increasingly confident of its credentials to rule and increasingly frustrated with the impediments of representative politics. Interestingly enough, while Macron's insurgency into the presidential race was met with irony and sarcasm among the ranks of the governing parties who took time to identify him as a "serious" candidate, it received almost immediately an enthusiastic echo among the business and the administrative elites—as can be traced by his many prominent supporters (starting with Attali himself) as well as by the money he was able to raise in a limited amount of time.[11] In a few months, as he was professing his nonpartisan and promarket beliefs, exactly in the terms of the Attali Commission's report,[12] and engaged in a stringent criticism of the French political elite, he had become the point of convergence and spokesman of a whole field, whether center-right or center-left leaning. His capacity to revamp the rather unglamorous set of ideas delineated in the Attali report into a *Revolution*, as Macron entitled his campaign book (2016), turned him into an object of liberal admiration. An unlikely candidate for charisma given his career in finance and bureaucracy, Macron was indeed becoming the field's "structural hero" opening an unexpected breach into politics and government, and providing full political recognition to the field's increasing claim to govern.

As a result, it would be misleading to equate Macronism with the mere promotion of business interests; neither should it be understood as just a late avatar of Reaganism or Thatcherism. Precisely because it is deeply grounded in the coral reefs of the French regulatory state, and because it originates *within* the state's *grand corps*, Macronism proposes less a retreat of the state than a redefinition of its elites and missions from the interventionist tradition to a promarket "regulatory state."[13] By many standards, his programmatic platform reads like a patchwork of the many reformatory mottos that have fermented ever since the first decade of the twenty-first century in the different (public and private) poles of the regulatory state, from the Attali Commission to the set of law firms,

11. "Ce que révèle la liste des donateurs de Macron," Journal du dimanche, December 1, 2018.

12. "The moment has come. . . . This is not a report, nor a study, but an instruction manual for urgent foundational reforms. It is neither partisan nor bipartisan: it is non partisan. This is not an inventory in which the government could pick and choose, and even less a competition for original ideas bound to remain marginal. This is a coherent block where each piece is articulated with the others, in which each element is key to the success of the whole," in Commission Attali pour la libération de la croissance économique, *Increase Competition for a Better Purchasing Power*, 1.

13. See in particular two bills (the so-called *Avenir professionnel* Bill of August 2018, "*Transformation de la fonction publique*" Bill of May 2019) that have facilitated, even incentivized the *pantouflage* and *retro-pantouflage* of top civil servants.

regulatory agencies, and ministerial cabinets described in this book. Macron's first legislative fiat, the so-called Macron Act that he promoted when he was still minister of economy, is a mixed bag of reforms aimed at liberalizing the economic activity (legal professions, coach transport) while reinforcing the powers of the regulatory state (in particular the *Autorité de la concurrence*).[14] The ideas put forward were far from novel as most of them had long been peddled in the reports of the competition agency. Yet, they had remained dispersed and restricted to a variety of semipublic circles and only partially fed into the programs of the successive governing parties. In this regard, Macronism can be read like the entering into politics of this public-private world whose reformatory common sense has been turned into a full-fledged programmatic platform, and branded as a new political offer.

---

14. The package was actually welcomed as a "*refreshing breeze*" by the president of the *Autorité de la concurrence*, himself a former member of the Attali Commission: "Projet de loi Macron: L'autorité de la concurrence dans les starting-blocks," *Lettre des juristes d'affaires*, July 9, 2015.

The idea for this research initially came from a few newspaper articles in the French national press that mentioned what appeared at the time as a very rare and surprising phenomenon—the passage of a prominent political figure to the Paris corporate bar. The first case was mentioned in 2007 by *Le Canard enchaîné*, an important investigative journal, which revealed that the majority leader in the *Assemblée nationale*, Jean-Francois Copé, was leading a parallel career as a part-time corporate lawyer. As the media started identifying more and more cross-overs, it became clear that there was more at stake here than just a few anecdotal cases.

The research started with the simple objective to identify the scope and breadth of what looked like an important yet imprecise phenomenon. While the media focus had remained almost exclusively centered on the political profession, first empirical evidence seemed to indicate that this was just the tip of the iceberg. Our initial ambition was to collect all cases of crossing over from the public sector to the corporate bar along a period of twenty-five years.

Our first contacts in the legal profession did not prove very encouraging as the Paris bar authorities denied access to its data on the revolving door phenomenon between political elites and the legal profession. However, the research has benefited from the very changes it was trying to account for: while lawyers have historically made a point of maintaining discretion and low profiles, the rise of the Paris corporate bar has changed things dramatically. The emerging world of Paris law firms has developed a rich public façade with sophisticated websites, new professional magazines, numerous public events, rankings, and prizes, thereby producing an unprecedented amount of data on the inner life of this milieu: beyond the traditional *Annuaire du barreau de Paris*, and more international yearbooks (the *Legal 500* and *Chambers*), there is now a rich material of online CVs, press releases, presentation brochures, anniversary books. As law firms increasingly resort to communication professionals and consultancy firms, they feed new professional journals and specialized websites (*Legalnews, Le Monde du droit, La Lettre des juristes d'affaires, Option Droit & Affaires*, etc.) with invaluable data on lawyers' career moves inside and in-between law firms.

This material certainly has its own biases as it heavily depends on the information that law firms and the specialized press themselves consider worthy to communicate. As a result, some less important or more routine career moves from public to private remain less documented—as is the case for example for tax inspectors moving to tax law firms or local government employees recruited by local law firms. This has required a variety of research techniques to cross-reference and enrich our knowledge of the phenomenon with *Who's Who*, the website *biographies.com*, the ENA yearbook (*Annuaire de l'ENA*), biographical and historical dictionaries for various *grands corps* (*Conseil d'État, Cour des comptes, Inspection des finances*) and a website specialized on the French public sector: Acteurs publics.

This made a rich material for a biographical database of 217 profiles of top civil servants and politicians that have become lawyers in the 1990–2015 period, with a special focus on Paris and the Hauts-de-Seine bars where all the leading law firms are concentrated. With a view to build a collective biography of this population, we have collected information on: gender, birthdate, education, career moves in the public sector as well as in the legal profession, social capital (assessed through participation in expert committees, affiliation to clubs and think tanks, teaching positions in universities, op-eds and books).

As the biographical database revealed the breadth and depth of the public-private blurring, the inquiry moved to identify more closely the world of practices and the types of expertise that were emerging alongside this continuous movement of crossover in-between the public and the private. For lack of opportunity to study lawyers at work in a more ethnographical manner, we have had recourse to two research strategies.

First, we have built another database, not of people this time but of cases, with a sample of legal deals in which the public sector (local and national government, state-owned firms, etc.) has had recourse to law firms. This work was processed together with Charlotte Ducouret, at the time a master's student in political science, in Paris 1 Panthéon-Sorbonne. Drawing from the specialized website http://www.lemondedudroit.fr which references important legal deals (for a critical assessment of this source, see chapter 1), two hundred cases were selected.

To this, we have added 25 in-depth interviews which were conducted with some of the key actors we had identified while exploring the specialized press: most of them are crossovers whom we have asked to account for their transitioning into the legal profession (motivations and difficulties) as well as the connections they have maintained with the public sector. Among the interviewees, we met 6 women and 19 men, 13 ENA graduates, 2 ENI (*École Nationale des*

Impôts, the French National Tax School) and 1 *Polytechnique* graduate (engineer school). Another series of interviews was carried out with nonlawyers that were familiar with our phenomenon: the head of ministry's legal service, a former secretary general of the *Conseil d'État*, the human resources director of a regulatory agency, two senior executives from the Paris bar, and two senior consultants. We also did interviews with "ordinary" corporate lawyers to hear about the experiences of insiders who worked with these crossovers.

Interviews (2012–2014)

Interview 1, woman, ENA, *Conseil d'État*

Interview 2, woman, regulatory agency

Interview 3, woman, specialized journalist

Interview 4, man, specialized consultant

Interview 5, woman, ENA, lawyer, financial law

Interview 6, man, lawyer, corporate law

Interview 7, man, lawyer, public law of business, environmental law

Interview 8, man, ENA, lawyer, tax law

Interview 9, man, *Conseil d'État*, lawyer, public law of business

Interview 10, man, ENI (*École nationale des impôts*), lawyer, tax law

Interview 11, man, ENI (*École nationale des impôts*), lawyer, tax law

Interview 12, man, ENA, *Conseil d'État*, lawyer, arbitration and public law of business

Interview 13, man, ENA, lawyer, financial law

Interview 14, man, ENA, *Conseil d'État*, lawyer, public law of business

Interview 15, man, ENA, lawyer, public-private partnerships

Interview 16, man, *Polytechnique*, lawyer, corporate law

Interview 17, man, ENA, lawyer, competition law

Interview 18, man, ENA, lawyer, public law of business

Interview 19, man, ENA, lawyer, EU competition law

Interview 20, woman, lawyer, national bar council (*Conseil national des barreaux*)

Interview 21, woman, magistrate, lawyer, financial law

Interview 22, woman, lawyer, criminal law

Interview 23, man, ENA, *Conseil d'État*

Interview 24, man, ENA, *Cour des comptes*, lawyer, public law of business

Interview 25, man, ENA, former minister, lawyer, public law of business/lobbying

As the reader engages in this exploration of France's field of power, he or she is bound to come across a whole set of idiosyncratic notions from the political and bureaucratic lexicon. Rather than providing a word-by-word translation or identifying at all costs functional equivalents for these many historically rooted institutions and professions, we have decided to keep the French wording while listing all of these into a little glossary that provides the definitional and con- textual elements needed to make sense of these often "untranslatable" terms. These institutions and groups cover essentially five clusters of words mentioned in the body of the text (noted in italics): state elites, the ministry of economy and finance, regulatory agencies, ethics of public officials, and supreme courts.

State Elites

École nationale d'administration: the ENA was created in 1945 to professional- ize the training provided to French top civil servants and democratize the access to the state *grands corps*. It is based on a highly selective national *concours* which selects each year 50 to 100 students (to whom must be added career civil servants who come for vocational training). After two years of seminars and internships, the ENA ranks the *énarques* (former graduates) according to their results: the top-ranked students (between 12 and 15 students) usually join the three state *grands corps* (*Inspection des finances, Conseil d'État,* or *Cour des comptes*). The other students will join the French treasury, the diplomatic service, lower ranks of administrative justice, ministries' bureaucracy, and so on. Generally speaking, ENA graduates monopolize the state's top managerial positions such as min- istries' bureaucratic departments (*directions d'administration centrale*). Beyond administration, the ENA has also become the main breeding ground for top positions in politics (three presidents, half of the prime ministers and a count- less number of ministers, etc.) as well as in business.

Grands corps: While there is no formal list of the *grands corps*, they are usually divided into two categories: the *grands corps techniques* (mostly engineers) and the *grands corps administratifs* (hereafter state *grands corps*), which are recruited through the *École nationale d'administration* and composed of the *Inspection des finances*, the *Cour des comptes*, and the *Conseil d'État*. While the *grands corps* hold most of the top executive positions of the state, it is important to add that most CEOs of large French companies are former members of the *grands corps*.

Cabinets ministériels: Ministers are allowed to constitute a *cabinet*, a small staff of five to twenty members (depending on the importance of the ministry) headed by a *directeur de cabinet* (cabinet's chief of staff), an experienced civil servant drawn from the state *grands corps* who plays a key role in all interministerial negotiations needed when it comes to drafting new decrees or bill projects. Positions in *cabinets ministériels* are also often a springboard for top positions in the public or private sector.

In addition to his or her own *cabinet*, prime ministers are also helped by a specific administrative unit, the *secrétariat général du gouvernement*, a body of nearly a hundred top civil servants, traditionally headed by a member of the *Conseil d'État*, in charge of securing the coordination of the work of government. Similar yet sector-specific coordinating units include the *Secrétariat général pour les affaires européennes*, and the *Secrétariat général de la défense nationale*. The president of the Republic is also backed by a *cabinet* and an administrative unit, the *secrétariat général de l'Élysée* (after the name of the *Élysée Palace* where French presidents have their official residence).

Ministry of Economy and Finance

It is hard to overstate the importance of the Ministry of the Economy and Finance. Often referred to as "*Bercy*," after the district in Paris where the huge building of the ministry is located, it is arguably the most important and influential ministry in French government. It brings together all key economic and financial functions of the state from budget drafting to tax and financial regulation (and control thereof), state holdings, external trade, as well as the financing of French sovereign debt and public investment funds. Given its size, there are often various junior ministers attached to the ministry. Among its key departments, one should mention:

The **Direction du Trésor** (Treasury Office) considered as the most prestigious department, populated by members of the *Inspection des finances* (state *grand corps*). They are in charge of macroeconomic forecast, financing of French public debts, and national funds (*Agence France Trésor*) as well as international and European negotiations in economic and financial matters. In 2004, a new unit was created, the *Agence des participations de l'État* (APE), in order to manage the state's holdings (about seventy firms including large companies such as Gaz de France, Engie, France Telecom, Renault, Aéroport de Paris, Banque publique d'investissement, Air France, SNCF, etc.).

The **Direction générale de la concurrence, de la consommation et de la répression des fraudes** (DGCCRF—General Directorate for Competition Policy, Consumer Affairs, and Fraud Control) is in charge of regulating market competition together with the competition regulatory agency (*Autorité de la concurrence*), protecting consumers' safety, and ensuring compliance with competition rules "favoring the development of open and transparent markets."

The **Direction générale des Finances publiques** is in charge of drafting tax bills but also of collecting taxes (VAT, corporate tax, income tax) and controlling the biggest firms. While the top managers of the DGFIP come from the ENA, tax inspectors are mostly recruited through a special *concours* leading to the *École nationale des finances publiques* (formerly *École nationale des impôts* [ENI]).

Regulatory Agencies

From the late 1980s onward, the liberalization of a number of former state monopolies in the fields of transport, media, and energy sectors has led to the creation of a dense web of regulatory agencies in charge of regulating these new markets. These new bodies, formally independent from the bureaucratic circuit of command, are composed of a president and a board of five to twenty members nominated by political authorities (but most of them are chosen within the state *grands corps*).

The **Autorité des marchés financiers**, was created in 2003 (as a continuation of the former *Commission des operations boursières*) is one of the most important regulatory agencies in terms of size (circa 450 employees) and jurisdiction. It regulates participants and products in France's financial markets. Where necessary, it can conduct investigations and issue sanctions.

The **Autorité de la concurrence** created in 2008 as France's national competition regulator—replacing and strengthening the powers of the old *Conseil de la concurrence*. Its role is to fight against anticompetitive practices (cartels, abuse of dominant position, etc.) and control the proper competitive function of the markets in tight coordination with the European Commission Competition Directorate General. It has about two hundred employees. The *Autorité de la concurrence* is complemented by sector-specific agencies: the *Autorité de régulation des activités ferroviaires* (ARAF) founded in 2010 is the regulatory agency in charge of ensuring and "encouraging competition in rail transport"; the *Commission de régulation de l'énergie* (CRE) created in 2000 which regulates the electricity and gas markets, and so on.

Ethics of Public Officials

Pantouflage: the term was initially coined for former graduates of the *École Polytechnique* (France's *grande école* recruiting state engineers) who left public service immediately after obtaining their degree and needed to pay to the state a so-called *pantoufle* (slipper) to compensate for the education costs. It now applies to all public agents and politicians who join the private sector after assuming a public office. It is important to note that the word *pantouflage* bears a different meaning than *revolving doors* as it does not imply moves back and forth but rather a *departure* from the public sector. Indeed, when it was noticed that some of these individuals were actually coming back to the public sector, a new word was coined: *retro-pantouflage*.

Up until 2019, the *pantouflages* were controlled by a consultative *commission de déontologie* (ethics committee) composed of members of the state *grands corps* which would give an Opinion (not public) and, in some cases, express Reservations that the outgoing civil servant was supposed to follow in his or her activities in the private sector. A new statute law was adopted in August 2019 which merges the *commission de déontologie* into the *Haute Autorité pour la transparence de la vie publique* (High Authority for transparency in public life), thereby further reinforcing the ever-growing competences of this public body initially created in 2013 to receive and control the declarations of assets (*déclaration de patrimoine*) and of interests of close to fifteen thousand "public managers" (*responsables publics*) whether politicians or civil servants, when taking their official duties. In 2017, the High Authority had also been given the task to compile and manage a public register of lobbysts (*Répertoire des représentants d'intérêts*).

French Judicial System

The French judicial branch is two-fold: it is composed of administrative courts (headed by the *Conseil d'État*) that have jurisdiction over claims against administrators or public bodies on the one side; and of civil and criminal courts (headed by the *Cour de cassation*) on the other. To this traditional dualist structure, one should add the *Conseil constitutionnel* which has the monopoly of constitutional review, and the *Cour des comptes* which is a specialized administrative court charged with conducting financial and legislative audits of most public institutions.

The **Conseil d'État** (located in the *Palais-Royal* palace) decides on claims against national-level administrative decisions (e.g., orders, rules, regulations, and decisions of the executive branch) and appeals from lower administrative courts. Initially created by Napoleon in 1799, it acts *both* as a legal adviser to the government and as a supreme court for administrative justice. It recruits first of all among the top ranking ENA graduates (but also in part through political nomination): its members constitute a state *grand corps* and are called to top managing positions in the state from ministers' and president's chief of staff positions to ministerial legal departments, regulatory agencies, and so forth.

The **Cour de cassation** is the supreme court of appeal for civil and criminal litigation. It is exclusively composed of end-of-career *magistrats*. French *magistrats* are most often recruited for lifetime civil service positions through a national *concours* immediately after law school and trained at the *École nationale de la magistrature* in Bordeaux.

The **Conseil constitutionnel** is the supreme constitutional court. Housed in the Palais-Royal palace (just like the *Conseil d'État*), its main activity is to rule on the conformity of statutes with the Constitution of the Fifth Republic (October 1958) and constitutional principles and rules, notably those from the 1789 French *Déclaration des droits de l'homme et du citoyen* and the Preamble of the Constitution of the Fourth Republic (1946). The president of the Republic as well as sixty MPs or senators can request a constitutional review immediately after the vote of a new statute law (a priori constitutional review). A constitutional amendment introduced in July 2008 has created a new procedure, the so-called *Question prioritaire de constitutionnalité*, which allows for citizens as well legal persons that are part to a lawsuit to ask the *Conseil* to review whether the law applied in the case is constitutional (a posteriori constitutional review).

Lawyers and Bar Associations: French *avocats* are historically organized around principles of independence and self-government of the 164 local bar associations (*barreau*). Every two years, each one of these bar associations elects its *Conseil de l'ordre* (Council of Order) that has regulatory as well as disciplinary powers, and a *batônnier* who acts as president.

In December 1990, an important statute law integrated the *conseillers juridiques* into the *avocats* profession. While historically French *conseillers juridiques* were not allowed to go and plead before courts, they were often structured in large law firms and practiced in particular tax law. Conversely, *avocats* had a quasi monopoly on defense but remained mostly structured around small structures centered on litigation.

Today, the profession counts circa 67,000 members. The Paris Bar association (*barreau de Paris*) represents no less than 42 percent of French lawyers (28,000 lawyers) and the Hauts-de-Seine Bar which is also considered in this book as its jurisdiction covers the district of La Défense where most large French companies have their headquarters, has circa 2,200 members.

For the sake of clarity, the general bibliography has been divided into two parts. The first one (Printed Sources) collects all written material that we have used as part of the empirical corpus: articles from the general press and specialized media, lawyers' as well as doctrinalists' articles or op-eds, annual reports from public institutions such as the *Conseil d'État* or regulatory agencies (see appendix 1 on methodology). The second part (Bibliography) brings together the scholarly body of literature that has been used in the course of this research.

PRINTED SOURCES

"Comment réussir la privatisation." *Le Monde*, September 29, 1986.

"Ubiquistes avocats." *Le Monde*, November 25, 1986.

"Le parquet fait enquêter sur les 600,000 francs versés à DSK par la MNEF quand il était avocat d'affaires." *Libération*, December 9, 1988.

"Création d'un 'grand syndicat' du barreau d'affaires." *Les Échos*, February 24, 1992.

"Les fins de mois de Copé." *Le Canard enchaîné*, September 26, 2007.

"Les avocats et le lobbying: Un gisement d'opportunités." *Le Monde du droit*, February 1, 2008.

"Les Entretiens de l'AMF." *Lettre des juristes d'affaires*, October 6, 2008.

"La fidèle: Loraine Donnedieu de Vabres." *Lettre des juristes d'affaires*, December 15, 2008.

"L'art de plaider devant les autorités de régulation." *Lettre des juristes d'affaires*, December 15, 2008.

"Pérol, la commission n'a pas statué." *Le Figaro*, February 24, 2009.

"Les avocats mobilisés sur la Question prioritaire de constitutionnalité." *Lettre des juristes d'affaires*, June 7, 2010.

"Question prioritaire de constitutionnalité et droit des affaires." *Les Petites Affiches*, September 2011.

"Georges Tron: Pour moi ça a été la double peine." *Le Parisien*, September 17, 2012.

"L'irrésistible ascension du barreau des Hauts-de-Seine." *La Gazette du palais*, September 18, 2012.

"Gilles August et associés, un cabinet très politique." *Le Monde*, December 21, 2012.

"Femmes au barreau en 2013." *Bulletin de l'ordre des avocats de Paris*, March 2013.

"Un businessman nommé Villepin." *Le Monde*, January 11, 2013.

"Réception de M. Bruno Lasserre, président de l'Autorité de la concurrence, et de Virginie Beaumeunier, rapporteure générale de l'Autorité de la concurrence." *Bulletin de l'ordre des avocats de Paris*, December 10, 2013.

"Décideurs 100 des cabinets d'avocats." *Décideurs*, July 16, 2014.

"Déontologie, esprit d'entreprise: Faut-il choisir?" *Les Petites Affiches*, March 11, 2015.

"Projet de loi Macron: L'autorité de la concurrence dans les starting-blocks." *Lettre des juristes d'affaires*, July 9, 2015.

"L'ex-déontologue de l'Assemblée nationale désormais avocate d'un laboratoire pharmaceutique." *Libération*, November 3, 2015.

"La commission de déontologie des fonctionnaires sauve (encore une fois) ses prérogatives." *Acteurs publics*, June 10, 2016.

"Ce que révèle la liste des donateurs de Macron." *Journal du dimanche*, December 1, 2018.

Agence des participations de l'État. *Rapport de l'État actionnaire*. Paris: La Documentation française, 2009.

Babonneau, Marine. "Lutte contre le blanchiment: Les avocats toujours mauvais élèves." *Dalloz Actualité*, April 20, 2015.

Basini, Bruna. "Mon conseiller fiscal est un transfuge." *L'Expansion*, October 12, 2000.

Bekmezian, Hélène. "Le premier bilan de la déontologue de l'Assemblée." *Le Monde*, November 18, 2013.

Benhamou, Yves. "Pantouflage des juges: Un danger pour l'impartialité de l'État?" *Recueil Dalloz*, 2001.

Bézard, Bruno, and Éric Preiss. "L'agence des participations de l'État." *Revue française d'administration publique* 124 (2007): 601–14.

Boy, Laurence. "Réflexion sur le 'droit de la régulation.'" *Recueil Dalloz*, 2001, 3031.

Cassin, Fabrice. "Entretien: Que sont-ils devenus?" *La Gazette de l'Institut de droit public des affaires* 16 (2016).

Club des Partenariats public-privé. "Lettre des 7e rencontres internationales des PPP." 2013.

Commission Attali pour la libération de la croissance économique. *Increase Competition for a Better Purchasing Power*. Paris: La Documentation française, 2007.

Commission de déontologie de la fonction publique. *Rapport d'activité 2000*. Paris: La Documentation française, 2001.

Conseil d'État. *Les autorités administratives indépendantes: Rapport annuel*. Paris: La Documentation française, 2001.

Conseil d'État. *Collectivités publiques et concurrence: Rapport public*. Paris: La Documentation française, 2002.

Conseil d'État. *Colloque sur Les Aides d'État, École nationale d'administration*, March 14, 2008. http://www.conseil-etat.fr/.

Cour des comptes. *Le Recours par l'État aux conseils extérieurs: Rapport à la commission des finances de l'État*. Paris: La Documentation française, 2014.

Dal, Georges-Albert. *Le Secret profession de l'avocat dans la jurisprudence européenne*. Brussels: Larcier, 2011.

Debouzy, Olivier. "Les avocats et le rôle du droit dans la société française." In "Lawyers: The New Challenges." Special issue, *ENA Mensuel: La revue des anciens élèves de l'ENA* 329 (2003).

Debouzy, Olivier. "Lobbying: The French Way." *Notes de l'Ifri* 54 (2003): 5–23.

Deruy, Laurent. "Adapter le droit administratif français pour le rendre plus attractif." *Semaine juridique*, April 16, 2007, 2095.

Deves, Claude. "Droit public des affaires et collectivités locales." *Les Petites Affiches* 75 (April 15, 1999): 35.

Dosière, René, and Christian Vanneste. *Rapport d'information sur les autorités administratives indépendantes: Rapport de l'Assemblée nationale no. 2925.* Paris: Assemblée nationale, 2010.

Fabra, Paul. "Vademecum de la privatisation." *Le Monde*, April 8, 1986.

Follorou, Jacques. "Les mésaventures d'Hervé de Charrette, avocat novice." *Le Monde*, September 11, 2007.

Foucard, Frédéric. "Le recrutement de personnalités chez les professionnels du droit." *Droit et patrimoine*, May 1993.

Frison-Roche, Marie-Anne. "Droit et économie de la régulation." In *Les Risques de regulation*, edited by Marie-Anne Frison-Roche. Paris: Dalloz, 2001.

Frison-Roche, Marie-Anne, ed. *Les régulations économiques: Légitimité et efficacité.* Paris: Presses de Sciences Po, 2004.

Garrouste, Frédérique. "Anne Maréchal conjugue le droit public à la Bourse chez DLA Piper." *L'Agefi Hebdo*, July 7, 2011.

Gélard, Patrice. *Rapport sur les autorités administratives indépendantes: Rapport du Sénat.* Paris: Sénat, 2006.

Goanec, Mathilde. "Quand les avocats d'affaires écrivent les lois." *Le Monde Diplomatique*, January 2013.

Goldsmith, Jean-Claude. *L'avocat d'affaires.* Paris: Béranger, 1964.

Haute Autorité pour la transparence de la vie publique. *Renouer la confiance: Rapport annuel.* Paris: La Documentation française, 2015.

Jeantet, Fernand-Charles. "Le rôle de l'avocat, conseil des sociétés." *La Vie judiciaire*, December 28–January 2, 1965, 1.

Jouyet, Jean-Pierre. "Le pouvoir de sanction de l'Autorité des marchés financiers." In *Études à la mémoire de Fernand-Charles Jeantet.* Paris: LGDJ, 2010.

Lefort, Isabelle. "Il faut un cursus deux fois supérieur à celui d'un homme pour réussir . . . Entretien avec Anne Maréchal." *La Tribune*, June 10, 2011.

Lenoir, Noëlle. *Rapport public annuel du déontologue de l'Assemblée nationale.* Paris: Assemblée nationale, 2013.

Martin, Raymond. "Le droit en branches." *Recueil Dalloz*, 2002.

Mathieu, Mathilde. "Dans les coulisses du Conseil constitutionnel, cible des lobbies." Médiapart (blog), October 12, 2015.

Mathieu, Mathilde, and Michael Hajdenberg. "Parlementaires-avocats: Le gouvernement est passé outre les réserves du Conseil d'État." Médiapart (blog), April 17, 2012.

Maynial, Patrice. *Le Droit du côté de la vie: Réflexions sur la fonction juridique de l'État; Rapport au Premier ministre.* Paris: La Documentation française, 1996.

Mélin-Soucramanien, Ferdinand. *Rapport annuel du déontologue de l'Assemblée nationale.* Paris: Assemblée nationale, 2015.

Mézard, Jacques. *Un État dans l'État: Canaliser la prolifération des autorités administratives indépendantes pour mieux les contrôler; Rapport du Sénat.* Paris: Sénat, 2015.

Mission d'appui aux partenariats public-privé. *Rapport d'activité 2012*. Paris: La Documentation française, 2013.

Neuer, Laurence. "Think tank ou la fabrique d'idées 'prêt-à-réformer.'" *La Semaine juridique* 44–45 (October 28, 2013): 1996–99.

Nicinski, Sophie. *Droit public des affaires*. Paris: Lextenso, 2009.

Orde van Vlaamse Balies. "Lobbying, avocats et secret professionnel." October 10, 2010.

Organization for Economic Co-operation and Development. *Managing Conflict of Interest in the Public Service*, 2003. http://www.oecd.org.

Perrin, Christophe, and Laurence Gaune, eds. *Parcours d'avocat(e)s: Témoignages de Rémi Barousse, Jean-Michel Darrois, Éric Dupont-Moretti, Gisèle Halimi et al.* Paris: Le Cavalier bleu, 2010.

Perroud, Thomas. "Le Conseil constitutionnel contre la transparence." December 15, 2016. http://blog.juspoliticum.com/.

Portier, Philippe. "Des avocats revendiquent (enfin?) leur rôle de lobbyistes." *Option Droit & Affaires*, June 8, 2011.

Repiquet, Yves. "Un avocat à la tête de l'État." *Bulletin: Ordre des avocats du barreau de Paris* 15 (May 15, 2007): 1.

Reynier, Hubert. "Le cas de l'autorité de régulation des marchés financiers." *Revue française d'administration publique* 109 (2008): 93–97.

Ribadeau Dumas, Benoît. "Les carrières dans et hors le Conseil d'État." *Pouvoirs* 123 (2007): 73–88.

Roger, Patrick. "Affaire Pérol: La commission de déontologie a été 'tout près de démissionner collectivement.'" *Le Monde*, March 12, 2009.

Rose, Michel. "Macron: Banking Whizz-Kid Is Anti-Establishment Presidential Favorite." Reuters, April 14, 2017.

Sauvé, Jean-Marc. "Corriger, équilibrer, orienter: Une vision renouvelée de la régulation économique." École nationale d'administration, September 24, 2013. http://www.conseil-etat.fr/.

Sauvé, Jean-Marc. "Pouvoirs publics et concurrence." Entretiens du Conseil d'État en droit public économique, May 2010. http://www.conseil-etat.fr/.

Sauvé, Jean-Marc. "La valorisation économique des propriétés des personnes publiques." Entretiens du Conseil d'État en droit public économique, July 6, 2011. http://www.conseil-etat.fr/.

Service central de la prévention de la corruption. *Rapport annuel*. Paris: La Documentation française, 2000.

Silicani, Jean-Ludovic. *La Rémunération au mérite des directeurs d'administration centrale: Mobiliser les directeurs pour conduire le changement*. Paris: La Documentation française, 2004.

Tenzer, Nicolas, and Christian Vigouroux. "Les règles du 'pantouflage' sont-elles respectées?" *Acteurs publics*, June 28, 2010.

Tinayre, Alain, and Denis de Ricci, eds. *Au service de la justice: La profession juridique de demain*. Paris: Dalloz, 1967.

Toscer, Olivier. "Le parquet recale Dominique Bussereau." *Nouvel Observateur*, May 11, 2011.

Touboul, Charles. "Juger l'action économique, c'est encore agir sur l'économie." *Revue française de droit administratif* 1 (2016): 83.

Tracfin. *Rapport annuel d'activité 2011*. Paris: Ministère de l'économie et des finances, 2012.

Tracfin. "Tracfin 2014: 1 avocat pour 1 soupçon." http://www.cercle-du-barreau.org/.

Wickers, Thierry. *La Grande transformation des avocats*. Paris: Dalloz, 2014.

BIBLIOGRAPHY

Adolph, Christopher. *Bankers, Bureaucrats and Central Bank Politics: The Myth of Neutrality*. Cambridge: Cambridge University Press, 2013.

Amar, Michel. "Les très hauts salaires du secteur privé." Insee Première no. 1288, April 2010.

Assier Andrieu, Louis. *Les avocats: Identités, culture et devenir*. Paris: Lextenso, 2011.

Avril, Lola. "Le costume sous la robe: Les avocats en professionnels multi-carte de l'État régulateur (1957–2019)." PhD diss., Université Paris 1 Sorbonne, 2019.

Badie, Bertrand, and Pierre Birnbaum. *The Sociology of the State*. Translated by Arthur Goldhammer. Chicago: University of Chicago Press, 1983.

Bancaud, Alain, and Yves Dezalay. "Des 'grands prêtres' du droit au marché du droit des affaires." *Politiques et management public* 12, no. 2 (1994): 203–20.

Baradji, Eva, Dorothée Olivier, and Erwan Pouliquen. "L'encadrement supérieur et dirigeant dans les trois versants de la fonction publique." *Point Stat DGAFP*, February 2015.

Barbou des Places, Ségolène. "La *summa divisio* en droit communautaire." In *L'Identité en droit public*, edited by Xavier Bioy. Paris: LGDJ, 2010.

Barley, Stephen. "Building an Institutional Field to Corral a Government: A Case to Set an Agenda for Organization Studies." *Organization Studies* 31, no. 6 (2010): 777–805.

Beaud, Olivier. "La distinction entre droit public et droit privé: Un dualisme qui résiste aux critiques." In *The Public Law/Private Law Divide: Une entente assez cordiale?*, edited by Mark Freedland and Jean-Bernard Auby. Oxford: Hart, 2006.

Beaud, Olivier. *Le Sang contaminé: Essai critique sur la criminalisation de la responsabilité des gouvernants*. Paris: Presses Universitaires de France, 1999.

Behr, Valentin, and Sebastien Michon. "Le gouvernement Macron et les nouveaux technos: Noblesse d'État et circulations public-privé." *Revue française d'administration publique* (2019) forthcoming.

Bessy, Christian. *L'organisation des activités des avocats*. Paris: LGDJ, 2015.

Bezes, Philippe. "The Reform of the State: The French Bureaucracy in the Age of New Public Management." In *Developments in French Politics 4*, edited by Alistair Cole, Patrick Le Galès, and Jonah Levy, 172–90. London: Palgrave Macmillan, 2008.

Bezes, Philippe. *Réinventer l'État: Les réformes de l'administration française, 1962–2008*. Paris: Presses Universitaires de France, 2009.

Bezes Philippe, and Patrick Le Lidec. "French Top Civil Servants within Changing Configurations: From Monopolization to Contested Places and Roles." In *From the Active to the Enabling State: The Changing Role of Top Officials in European Nations*, edited by Edward C. Page and Vincent Wright, 121–63. Basingstoke: Palgrave Macmillan, 2007.

Biland, Émilie. "Quand les managers mettent la robe: Les grandes écoles de commerce sur le marché de la formation juridique." *Droit et société* 83, no. 1 (2013): 49–65.

Birnbaum, Pierre. *Où va l'État? Essai sur les nouvelles élites du pouvoir.* Paris: Seuil, 2018.

Birnbaum, Pierre. *Les sommets de l'État: Essai sur l'élite du pouvoir en France.* Paris: Seuil, 1994. First published 1977 by Seuil.

Boigeol, Anne. "Les magistrats 'hors les murs.'" *Droit et société* 44–45 (2000): 225–47.

Boigeol, Anne, and Yves Dezalay. "De l'agent d'affaires au barreau: Les conseils juridiques et la construction d'un espace professionnel." *Genèses* 27 (1997): 49–68.

Boigeol, Anne, and Laurent Willemez. "Fighting for Monopoly: Unification, Differentiation and Representation of the French Bar." In *Organization and Resistance: Legal Professions Confront a Changing World,* edited by Bill Felstiner, 41–65. Oxford: Hart, 2006.

Boltanski, Luc, and Pierre Bourdieu. "La production de l'idéologie dominante." *Actes de la recherche en sciences sociales* 2 (1976): 3–73.

Bosvieux-Onyekwelu, Charles. "Profit, temps d'emploi et plus-value morale: Le travail *pro bono* dans les multinationales du droit en France." *Socio-économie du travail* 60, no. 4 (2019).

Bourdieu, Pierre. *On the State: Lectures at the Collège de France.* Cambridge: Polity, 2015.

Bourdieu, Pierre. *The State Nobility: Elite Schools in the Field of Power.* Stanford, CA: Stanford University Press, 1996.

Bourdieu, Pierre, and Loïc Wacquant. *An Invitation to Reflexive Sociology.* Chicago: University of Chicago Press, 1992.

Boussebaa, Mehdi, and James Faulconbridge. "The Work of Global Professional Service Firms." In *Perspectives on Contemporary Professional Work: Challenges and Experiences,* edited by A. Wilkinson, D. Hislop, and C. Coupland, 105–22. Cheltenham: Edward Elgar, 2016.

Brown, Wendy. *Undoing the Demos: Neoliberalism's Stealth Revolution.* Cambridge, MA: MIT Press, 2015.

Bui Xuan, Olivia. *Les Femmes au Conseil d'État.* Paris: L'Harmattan, 2001.

Bui Xuan, Olivia. "La moralisation de la vie publique." *Droit administratif* 2014, 10–16.

Caillosse, Jacques. "Le discours de la réforme administrative." In *Le rapport public annuel du Conseil d'État: Entre science du droit et discours institutionnel,* edited by Pascal Mbongo and Olivier Renaudie, 125–44. Paris: Cujas, 2010.

Caillosse, Jacques. "Droit public—droit privé: Sens et portée d'un partage académique." *Actualité juridique: Droit administratif,* 1996, 955–64.

Caillosse, Jacques. "Personnes publiques et concurrence: Quels enjeux théoriques?" *Actualité juridique: Droit administratif* 14 (2016).

Charle, Christophe. "Le pantouflage en France (vers 1880–vers 1980)." *Annales: Histoire, Sciences Sociales* 42, no. 5 (1987): 1115-37.

Chaserant, Camille, and Sophie Harnay. "La déontologie professionnelle en pratique: Enquête sur l'activité disciplinaire de la profession d'avocat." *Revue française de socio-économie* 16 (2016): 119–39.

Chevallier, Jacques. "Le Conseil d'État, au cœur de l'État." *Pouvoirs* 123 (2007): 5–17.

Chevallier, Jacques. "L'élite politico-administrative: Une interpénétration discutée." *Pouvoirs* 80 (1997): 89–100.

Clamour, Guylain. *Intérêt général et concurrence: Essai sur la pérennité du droit public en économie de marché*. Paris: Dalloz, 2006.

Coen, David. "The Evolution of the Large Firm as a Political Actor in the EU." *Journal of European Public Policy* 4, no. 1 (1997): 91–108.

Cœurdray, Murielle. "La conversion d'un savoir judiciaire en un capital symbolique au service de multinationales françaises." *Droit et société* 72 (2009): 411–32.

Colliot-Teitgen, Catherine. "Déontologie et pantouflage de la haute fonction publique: L'exemple du Conseil d'État." *Mélanges en l'honneur de Gérard Marcou*. Paris: IRJS, 2017.

Colera, Christophe. *Les services juridiques des administrations*. Paris: L'Harmattan, 2009.

Collins, Lauren. "Can Emmanuel Macron Stem the Populist Tide?" *New Yorker*, June 24, 2019.

Courty, Guillaume, and Hélène Michel. "Interest Groups and Lobbyists in the European Political Space." In *The Field of Eurocracy: Mapping EU Actors and Professionals*, edited by Didier Georgakakis and Jay Rowell, 166–87. Basingstoke: Palgrave, 2013.

Crouch, Colin. *The Strange Non-Death of Neoliberalism*. Cambridge: Polity, 2011.

Dardot, Pierre, and Christian Laval. *Common: On Revolution in the 21st Century*. London: Bloomsbury, 2019.

de Carratier Dubois, Laurent. "Le Conseil d'État, l'économie et le service public: Concessions et services publics industriels et commerciaux (années 1880–1950)." *Revue d'histoire moderne et contemporaine* 52, no. 3 (2005): 51–74.

Decroly, Jean-Michel, Mathieu Van Criekingen, Moritz Lennert, Pierre Cornut, and Christian Vandermotten. "Local Geographies of Global Players: International Law Firms in Brussels." *Journal of Contemporary European Studies* 13, no. 2 (2005): 173–86.

Deffontaines, Gery. "Les consultants dans les partenariats public-privé: Entre expertise au service du client public et intermédiation pour protéger le 'marché.'" *Politiques et management public* 29, no. 1 (2012): 113–33.

Demazière, Didier, and Patrick Le Lidec. *Les mondes du travail politique*. Rennes: Presses Universitaires de Rennes, 2014.

Dezalay, Sara. "Lawyers in Africa: Brokers of the State, Intermediaries of Globalization; A Case-Study of the 'Africa' Bar in Paris." *Indiana Journal of Global Legal Studies* 25, no. 2 (2018): 639–69.

Dezalay, Yves. *Marchands de droit: La restructuration de l'ordre juridique international par les multinationales du droit*. Paris: Fayard, 1992.

Dezalay, Yves, and Bryant Garth. "Merchants of Law as Moral Entrepreneurs: Constructing International Justice out of the Competition for Transnational Business Disputes." *Law and Society Review* 29, no. 1 (1995): 27–64.

Dezalay, Yves, and Bryant Garth. "State Politics and Legal Markets." *Comparative Sociology* 10, no. 1 (2011): 38–66.

Dogan, Mattei, ed. *Elite Configurations at the Apex of Power*. Leiden: Brill, 2003.

Dogan, Mattei. "The Mandarins among the French Elites." In *Elite Configurations at the Apex of Power*, edited by Mattei Dogan. Leiden: Brill, 2003.

Dollez, Bernard, Julien Frétel, and Remi Lefebvre, eds. *L'entreprise Macron*. Grenoble: Presses Universitaires de Grenoble, 2019.

Dubois, Françoise, Maurice Enguéléguélé, and Marc Loiselle. "La contestation du droit administratif dans le champ intellectuel et politique." In *Le Droit administratif en mutation*. Paris: Presses Universitaires de France, 1993.

Dudouet, François-Xavier, and Éric Grémont. "Les grands patrons et l'État en France, 1981–2007." *Sociétés contemporaines* 68, no. 4 (2007): 105–31.

Duval, Julien. "Les enjeux symboliques des échanges économiques." *Revue française de socio-économie* 10, no. 2 (2012): 13–28.

Dreyfus, Françoise. "Les autorités administratives indépendantes: De l'intérêt général à celui des grands corps." In *Perspectives du droit public: Mélanges offerts à Jean-Claude Hélin*, 219–27. Paris: Litec, 2004.

Eymeri, Jean-Michel. *La fabrique des énarques*. Paris: Economica, 2001.

Eymeri-Douzans, Jean-Michel. "Les bons endroits, les bons amis, les bons moments." In *L'État, le droit, le politique: Mélanges en l'honneur de Jean-Claude Colliard*. Paris: Dalloz, 2014.

Ferguson, James. "The Uses of Neoliberalism." *Antipode* 41, no. 1 (2009): 166–84.

Flood, John. "Megalawyering in the Global Order." *International Journal of the Legal Profession* 3 (1996): 169–213.

Galbraith, John. *The Economics of Innocent Fraud*. Boston: Houghton Mifflin, 2004.

Gerber, David. *Law and Competition in Twentieth Century Europe: Protecting Prometheus*. Oxford: Oxford University Press, 1998.

Gervais, Julie. "The Rise of Managerialism as a Result of Bureaucratic Strategies and Power Games." In *Administrative Reforms and Democratic Governance*, edited by Jon Pierre and Jean-Michel Eymeri-Douzans, 80–93. Abingdon: Routledge, 2011.

Gervais, Julie. "Les sommets très privés de l'État: Le 'Club des acteurs de la modernisation' et l'hybridation des élites." *Actes de la recherche en sciences sociales* 194 (2012): 4–21.

Granfield, Robert, and Lynn Mather, eds. *Private Lawyers and the Public Interest: The Evolving Role of Pro Bono in the Legal Profession*. Oxford: Oxford University Press, 2009.

Granger, Marie-Pierre. "From the Margins of the European Legal Field: The Governments' Agents and Their Influence on the Development of European Union Law." In *Lawyering Europe: European Law as a Transnational Social Field*, edited by Antoine Vauchez and Bruno de Witte, 55–74. Oxford: Hart, 2013.

Halpérin, Jean-Louis. "L'indépendance de l'avocat en France au XIXe et au XXe siècle." In *L'indépendance de l'avocat*, edited by Louis Assier Andrieu, 65–76. Paris: Dalloz, 2015.

Hecquard-Theron, Maryvonne. "La notion d'État en droit communautaire." *Revue trimestrielle de droit européen* 26, no. 4 (1990): 693–711.

Heinz, John, and Edward Laumann. *Chicago Lawyers: The Social Structure of the Bar*. Rev. ed. Evanston, IL: Northwestern University Press, 1994.

Heinz, John, and Edward Laumann. *Urban Lawyers: The New Social Structure of the Bar*. Chicago: University of Chicago Press, 2005.

Hennette-Vauchez, Stéphanie. "Les droits et libertés que la constitution garantit: *Quiproquo* sur la Question prioritaire de constitutionnalité?" *Revue des droits de l'homme* 10 (2016).

Henry, Odile, and Frédéric Pierru. "Les consultants et la réforme des services publics." *Actes de la recherche en sciences sociales* 193, no. 3 (2012): 4–15.

Jabko, Nicolas. *Playing the Market: A Political Strategy for Uniting Europe, 1985–2005.* Ithaca, NY: Cornell University Press, 2006.

Jamin, Christophe. "Services juridiques: La fin des professions?" *Pouvoirs* 140 (2012): 33–47.

Karpik, Lucien. *French Lawyers: A Study in Collective Action, 1274–1994.* Oxford: Oxford University Press, 2000.

Karpik, Lucien. *Valuing the Unique: The Economics of Singularities.* Princeton, NJ: Princeton University Press, 2010.

Kelemen, Daniel. *Eurolegalism: The Transformation of Law and Regulation in the European Union.* Cambridge, MA: Harvard University Press, 2011.

Kessler, Marie-Christine. "L'évasion des membres du Conseil d'État vers le secteur privé." In *Le Droit administratif en question*, 122–38. Paris: Presses Universitaires de France, 1993.

King, Desmond, and Patrick Le Galès. "Conclusion: The Making of a Transnational, Capitalist Policy Member State." In *Reconfiguring European States in Crisis*, edited by Desmond King and Patrick Le Galès, 451–68. Oxford: Oxford University Press, 2017.

Lace, Susanne. "Mergers, Mergers Everywhere: Constructing the Global Law Firm in Germany." In *Legal Professions: Work, Structure and Organisation*, edited by Jerry Van Hoy, 51–75. Greenwich: JIA Press, 2001.

Lahusen, Christian. "Law and Lawyers in the Brussels World of Commercial Consultants." In *Lawyering Europe: European Law as a Transnational Social Field*, edited by Antoine Vauchez and Bruno de Witte, 177–96. Oxford: Hart, 2013.

Lascoumes, Pierre. "Condemning Corruption and Tolerating Conflicts of Interest: French 'arrangements' Regarding Breaches of Integrity." In *Corruption and Conflicts of Interest*, edited by Jean-Bernard Auby, Emmanuel Breen, and Thomas Perroud, 67–84. London: Edward Elgar, 2014.

Lascoumes, Pierre, and Dominique Lorrain. "Trous noirs du pouvoir: Les intermédiaires de l'action publique." *Sociologie du travail* 49 (2007): 1–9.

Lascoumes, Pierre, and Carla Nagels. *Sociologie des élites délinquantes: De la criminalité en col blanc à la corruption politique.* Paris: Armand Colin, 2014.

Latour, Bruno. *The Making of Law: An Ethnography of the Conseil d'État.* Cambridge: Polity, 2009.

Laurens, Sylvain. *Bureaucrats and Business Lobbyists in Brussels: Capitalism Brokers.* Abingdon: Routledge, 2017.

Laurens, Sylvain. "Des élites politiques et économiques encore loin d'une réelle transparence." Médiapart (blog), March 29, 2016. https://blogs.mediapart.fr/les-invites-de-mediapart/blog/290316/loi-sapin-ii-des-elites-politiques-et-economiques-encore-loin-d-une-reelle-transparenc.

Lazega, Emmanuel. *The Collegial Phenomenon: The Social Mechanisms of Cooperation among Peers in a Corporate Law Partnership.* Oxford: Oxford University Press, 2001.

Le Beguec, Gilles. *La République des avocats.* Paris: Armand Colin, 2003.

Le Galès, Patrick, and Desmond King. "Introduction: A Reconfigured State? European Policy States in a Globalizing World." In *Reconfiguring European States in Crisis*, edited by Desmond King and Patrick Le Galès, 1–42. Oxford: Oxford University Press, 2017.

Lemercier, Claire. *Un si discret pouvoir: Aux origines de la chambre de commerce de Paris (1803–1853)*. Paris: La Découverte, 2003.

Lemoine, Benjamin. *L'ordre de la dette: Enquête sur les infortunes de l'État et la prospérité du marché*. Paris: La Découverte, 2016.

Lemoine, Benjamin. "The Politics of Public Debt Financialisation: (Re-)Inventing the Market for French Sovereign Bonds and Shaping the Public Debt Problem (1966–2012)." In *The Political Economy of Public Finance: Taxation, State Spending and Debt since the 1970s*, edited by Marc Buggeln, Martin Daunton, and Alexander Nützenadel, 240–61. Cambridge: Cambridge University Press, 2017.

Levy, Jonah. *The State after Statism: New State Activities in the Age of Liberalization*. Cambridge, MA: Harvard University Press, 2006.

Levi-Faur, David. "The Odyssey of the Regulatory State. Episode 1: The Rescue of the Welfare State." Jerusalem Papers in Regulation and Governance, working paper no. 39, 2011.

Majone, Giandomenico. "The Rise of the Regulatory State in Europe." *West European Politics* 17 (1994): 77–101.

Malatesta, Maria. *Professional Men, Professional Women: The European Professions from the 19th Century until Today*. Thousand Oaks: Sage, 2011.

Mbongo, Pascal, and Olivier Renaudie, eds. *Le rapport public annuel du Conseil d'État: Entre science du droit et discours institutionnel*. Paris: Cujas, 2010.

McConnell, Grant. *Private Power and American Democracy*. New York: Alfred Knopf, 1966.

Medvetz, Tom. *Think Tanks in America*. Chicago: University of Chicago Press, 2012.

Mény, Yves. *La corruption de la République*. Paris: Fayard, 1992.

Michaels, Jon. *Constitutional Coup: Privatization's Threat to the American Republic*. Cambridge, MA: Harvard University Press, 2017.

Miller, Mark. *The High Priests of American Politics: The Role of Lawyers in American Political Institutions*. Knoxville: University of Tennessee Press, 1995.

Mills, Charles Wright. *The Power Elite*. With a new afterword by Alan Wolfe. Oxford: Oxford University Press, 2000.

Mitchell, Timothy. "The Limits of the State: Beyond Statist Approaches and Their Critics." *American Political Science Review* 85, no. 1 (1991): 7–96.

Moret-Bailly, Joël, Hélène Ruiz Fabri, and Laurence Scialom. "Les Conflits d'intérêts: Nouvelle frontière de la démocratie." Paris: Terra Nova (website), 2017.

Morgan, Glenn, and Sigrid Quack. "Institutional Legacies and Firm Dynamics: The Growth and Internationalization of British and German Law Firms." *Organization Studies* 26, no. 12 (2005): 1765–85.

Mudge, Stephanie, and Antoine Vauchez. "Building Europe on a Weak Field: Law, Economics, Scholarly Avatars in Transnational Politics." *American Journal of Sociology* 118, no. 2 (2012): 449–92.

Nelson, Robert, and John Heinz. "Lawyers and the Structure of Influence in Washington." *Law and Society Review* 22, no. 2 (1988): 237–300.

Novak, William. "The Public Utility Idea and the Origins of Modern Business Regulation." In *Corporations and American Democracy*, edited by Naomi R. Lamoreaux and William J. Novak, 139–76. Cambridge, MA: Harvard University Press, 2017.

Ogien, Albert, and Sandra Laugier. *Le Principe démocratie*. Paris: La Découverte, 2015.

Osiel, Mark. "Lawyers as Monopolists, Aristocrats, and Entrepreneurs." *Harvard Law Review* 103, no. 8 (1990): 2009–66.

Parsons, Talcott. "A Sociologist Looks at the Legal Profession." In *Essays in Sociological Theory*. Rev. ed., 370–85. New York: Free Press, 1964.

Patel, Kiran, and Heike Schweitzer, eds. *The Historical Foundations of EU Competition Law*. Oxford: Oxford University Press, 2013.

Pierru, Frédéric. "Les mandarins à l'assaut de l'usine à soins: Bureaucratisation néolibérale de l'hôpital et mobilisation de l'élite hospitalo-universitaire en France." In *La bureaucratisation néolibérale*, edited by Béatrice Hibou. Paris: La Découverte, 2013.

Pinçon, Michel, and Monique Pinçon-Charlot. *Le Président des riches*. Paris: Zone, 2010.

Pistor, Katharina. *The Code of Capital: How the Law Creates Wealth and Inequality*. Princeton, NJ: Princeton University Press, 2019.

Powell, Michael. *From Patrician to Professional Elite: The Transformation of the New York City Bar Association*. New York: Sage, 1988.

Powell, Michael. "La nouvelle presse juridique et les métiers du droit." *Actes de la recherche en sciences sociales* 101–2 (1994): 63–76.

Ritleng, Dominique. "L'influence du droit de l'Union européenne sur les catégories organiques du droit administratif." In *Traité de droit administratif européen*. 2nd ed. Brussels: Bruylant, 2014.

Robert, Cécile. "Les dispositifs de transparence entre instruments de gouvernement et 'machines à scandales.'" *Politique européenne* 61, no. 3 (2018): 174–210.

Rouban, Luc. "L'accès des femmes aux postes dirigeants de l'État." *Revue française d'administration publique* 145 (2013): 89–108.

Rouban, Luc. "Le Conseil d'État, 1958–2008: Sociologie d'un grand corps." *Cahiers du Cevipof* 49 (2008).

Rouban, Luc. "Les énarques en cabinet (1984–1996)." *Cahiers du Cevipof* 17 (1997).

Rouban, Luc. "L'État à l'épreuve du libéralisme: Les entourages du pouvoir exécutif de 1974 à 2012." *Revue française d'administration publique* 142 (2012): 467–90.

Rouban, Luc. "L'inspection générale des finances 1958–2008: Pantouflage et renouveau des stratégies élitaires." *Sociologies pratiques* 21 (2010): 19–34.

Rousseau, Dominique. *Radicaliser la démocratie: Propositions pour une refondation*. Paris: Grasset, 2015.

Roussellier, Nicolas. *La force de gouverner: Le pouvoir exécutif en France, XIXe–XXIe siècles*. Paris: Gallimard, 2015.

Sacriste, Guillaume. "L'Europe est-elle un État comme les autres? Retour sur la distinction public/privé au sein de la commission juridique du Parlement européen des années 1960." *Cultures et Conflits* 85–86 (2012): 35–60.

Sacriste, Guillaume. "Sur les logiques sociales du champ du pouvoir européen: L'exemple de l'affaire Dalli." *Politique européenne* 44 (2014): 52–96.

Sawicki, Frédéric. "Classer les hommes politiques." In *La profession politique, XIXe–XXe siècles*, edited by Michel Offerlé, 135–70. Paris: Belin, 1999.

Schmidt, Patrick. *Lawyers and Regulation: The Politics of the Administrative Process*. Cambridge: Cambridge University Press, 2005.

Schornstein, Coraline. "Les Avocats-lobbyistes: Émergence, légitimité, incertitudes." Master's thesis, Université Paris 2, 2015.

Seneviratne, Mary. "The Legal Ombudsman: Past, Present, Future." *Nottingham Law Journal* 24 (2015): 1–19.

Shamir, Ronen. *Managing Legal Uncertainty: Elite Lawyers in the New Deal.* Durham, NC: Duke University Press, 1995.

Spire, Alexis. "La domestication de l'impôt par les classes dominantes." *Actes de la recherche en sciences sociales* 190 (2011): 58–71.

Spire, Alexis, and Katia Weidenfeld. *L'impunité fiscale: Quand l'État brade sa souveraineté.* Paris: La Découverte, 2015.

Suleiman, Ezra. *Politics, Power, and Bureaucracy in France: The Administrative Elite.* Princeton, NJ: Princeton University Press, 1974.

Teitgen-Colly, Catherine. "Déontologie et pantouflage dans la haute fonction publique: L'exemple du Conseil d'État." In *Mélanges en l'honneur de Professeur Gérard Marcou.* Paris: IRJS, 2017.

Topalov, Christian. *Laboratoires du nouveau siècle: La nébuleuse réformatrice et ses réseaux en France 1880–1914.* Paris: EHESS, 1994.

Trubek, David, and Yves Dezalay. "Global Restructuring and the Law: Studies of the Internationalization of Legal Fields and the Creation of Transnational Arenas." *Case Western Reserve Law Review* 44, no. 2 (1994).

Truchet, Didier. "La distinction du droit public et du droit privé dans le droit économique." In *The Public Law/Private Law Divide: Une entente assez cordiale?*, edited by Mark Freedland and Jean-Bernard Auby, 49–59. Oxford: Hart, 2006.

Truchet, Didier. *La Fonction de l'intérêt général dans la jurisprudence du Conseil d'État.* Paris: LGDJ, 1977.

Vanneuville, Rachel. "Les enjeux politico-juridiques des discours sur l'inflation normative." *Parlement(s)* 11 (2009): 80–91.

Vauchez, Antoine. *Brokering Europe: Euro-Lawyers and the Making of a Transnational Polity.* Cambridge: Cambridge University Press, 2015.

Vauchez, Antoine. "Une élite d'intermédiaires: Genèse d'un capital juridique européen (1950–1970)." *Actes de la recherche en sciences sociales* 166–67 (2007): 54–65.

Vauchez, Antoine. "L'État public-privé." AOC, September 13, 2018. https://aoc.media/analyse/2018/09/13/letat-public-prive/.

Vauchez, Antoine. "The Force of a Weak Field: Law and Lawyers in the Government of the European Union." *International Political Sociology* 2, no. 2 (2008): 128–44.

Vauchez, Antoine. "Quand les juristes faisaient la loi: Le 'moment Carbonnier' (1963–1977), son histoire et son mythe." *Parlement(s)* 11 (2009): 105–15.

Vauchez, Antoine, and Laurent Willemez. *La justice face à ses réformateurs (1980–2006): Entreprises de modernisation et logiques de résistances.* Paris: Presses Universitaires de France, 2007.

Vogel, Steven. *Freer Markets, More Rules: Regulatory Reform in Advanced Industrial Countries.* Ithaca, NY: Cornell University Press, 1996.

Walzer, Michael. "Liberalism and the Art of Separation." *Political Theory* 12, no. 3 (1984): 315–30.

Wigger, Angela, and Andreas Nölke. "Enhanced Roles of Private Actors in EU Business Regulation and the Erosion of Rhenish Capitalism: The Case of Antitrust Enforcement." *Journal of Common Market Studies* 45, no. 2 (2007): 487–513.

Willemez, Laurent. "La 'République des avocats': 1848; Le mythe, le modèle et son endossement." In *La profession politique, XIXe–XXe siècles*, edited by Michel Offerlé, 201–29. Paris: Belin, 1999.

INDEX

administrative elites
confusion of roles between political elites
and, 66
recruitment of, 36–40, 56–58
Adolph, Christopher, 141
Agence des participations de l'État (APE),
44–45, 168–69
*Agence nationale de prévention et de détection de
la corruption*, 123
American law firms, entry into Paris bar, 22–23
annual conferences/conventions, as hubs of
public-private sociability, 97–102
anti-corruption NGOs, 106, 153
Areva, 45, 49, 88, 96
Association des avocats lobbyistes (AAL), 32
Attali Commission, 156–57, 158, 160
August, Gilles, 37–38, 136
August & Debouzy, 37–38, 95, 136
Aurillac, Michel, 64
Autorité de la concurrence, 41, 50, 51–52, 87, 169
Autorité de régulation des activités ferroviaires
(ARAF), 50, 87, 169–70
Autorité des marchés financiers, 50, 51n97,
52, 169
avocats, 22, 59–61, 171–72
avocats d'affaires, 17, 18. See also corporate
lawyers

Banque populaire–Caisses d'épargne, 142
bar exam and training exemptions, 59–63
barreau classique (classical bar), 15, 17n7
barreau d'affaires (corporate bar), 17, 23–24
Bézard, Bruno, 124
Bezes, Philippe, 144
Blue Book Report, 20
Boltanski, Luc, 101
Bourdieu, Pierre, 11, 101
bridge decree (1991), 59–63
British law firms, entry into Paris bar, 22
Bruno Kern et associés (BKA), 87, 93
Burguburu, Jean-Marie, 24–25

business law, 17–18, 30. See also *droit public
des affaires*
business lawyers. *See* corporate lawyers
Bussereau, Dominique, 148

cabinets ministériels, 168
capitalism, private technocratic, 131n36
"capture," 133
Castelain, Jean, 25, 32
Cazeneuve, Bernard, 1
de Charette, Hervé, 67
Charzat, Michel, 44
classical bar (*barreau classique*), 15, 17n7
Clément, Pascal, 33
Clifford Chance, 34, 35–36, 82
Club des Juristes network, 98
Club des Partenariats Public-Privé (PPP),
99–100
clubs, as hubs of public-private sociability,
97–102
colloquia, as hubs of public-private sociability,
97–102
De Combles De Nayves, Dominique, 89
*Commission de déontologie de la fonction
publique* (CDFP), 123–24, 125, 126, 144,
170
Commission de régulation de l'énergie (CRE),
50, 87, 170
Commission des infractions fiscales, 53
Commons, theory of, 133, 138
competition circuit, 87–88
competition law, 3–4, 52, 87, 97, 105, 110
competitive neutrality, 41
competitive policy, public turn of, 25
compliance
and multidisciplinary legal expertise of
corporate layers, 27–31
and reputation of corporate lawyers, 36
conferences/conventions, as hubs of public-
private sociability, 97–102
confidentiality, 119–22, 146–47

185

CPSIA information can be obtained
at www.ICGtesting.com
Printed in the USA
LVHW041045250322
714381LV00015B/668